# AFRICA RISING

## HOW 900 MILLION AFRICAN CONSUMERS OFFER MORE THAN YOU THINK

**VIJAY MAHAJAN**

with Robert E. Gunther

Vice President, Publisher: Tim Moore
Associate Publisher and Director of Marketing: Amy Neidlinger
Wharton Editor: Yoram (Jerry) Wind
Acquisitions Editor: Martha Cooley
Editorial Assistant: Pamela Boland
Development Editor: Russ Hall
Operations Manager: Gina Kanouse
Digital Marketing Manager: Julie Phifer
Publicity Manager: Laura Czaja
Assistant Marketing Manager: Megan Colvin
Front Cover Design: MVB Design
Managing Editor: Kristy Hart
Project Editor: Betsy Harris
Copy Editor: Keith Cline
Proofreader: Kathy Ruiz
Senior Indexer: Cheryl Lenser
Senior Compositor: Jake McFarland
Manufacturing Buyer: Dan Uhrig

Wharton School Publishing offers excellent discounts on this book when ordered in quantity for bulk purchases or special sales. For more information, please contact U.S. Corporate and Government Sales, 1-800-382-3419, corpsales@pearsontechgroup.com. For sales outside the U.S., please contact International Sales at international@pearson.com.

Printed in the United States of America

Third Printing: November 2008

ISBN-10 0-13-233942-0
ISBN-13 978-0-13-233942-1

Pearson Education LTD.
Pearson Education Australia PTY, Limited.
Pearson Education Singapore, Pte. Ltd.
Pearson Education North Asia, Ltd.
Pearson Education Canada, Ltd.
Pearson Educatión de Mexico, S.A. de C.V.
Pearson Education—Japan
Pearson Education Malaysia, Pte. Ltd.

Library of Congress Cataloging-in-Publication Data

Mahajan, Vijay.

Africa rising : how 900 million African consumers offer more than you think / Vijay Mahajan.

p. cm.

ISBN 0-13-233942-0 (hbk. : alk. paper) 1. Africa—Commerce. 2. Africa—Economic conditions. 3. Investments, Foreign—Africa. 4. International business enterprises—Africa. I. Title.

HF3876.5.M34 2009

382.096—dc22

2008012190

This book is dedicated to my children, Ramin and Geeti, who share my love, passion, and respect for African consumers, entrepreneurs, NGOs, institutions, and governments who are making a difference in Africa.

# Contents

# Part II Realizing the Opportunity

# About the Author

**Vijay Mahajan** is former dean of the Indian School of Business and the John P. Harbin Centennial Chair in Business at the McCombs School of Business, University of Texas at Austin. He is the author or editor of ten books, including his recent book on emerging markets, *The 86% Solution: How to Succeed in the Biggest Market Opportunity of the 21st Century*, which received the 2007 Book of Year Award (Berry-AMA) from the American Marketing Association. He is one of the world's most widely cited researchers in business and economics and has been invited to make presentations to more than 100 universities and research institutions around the world. He has consulted with Fortune 500 companies and delivered executive development programs worldwide. Among his numerous lifetime achievement awards is the American Marketing Association's Charles Coolidge Parlin Award for visionary leadership in scientific marketing. The AMA also instituted the Vijay Mahajan Award in 2000 for career contributions to marketing strategy. Mahajan received his Bachelor's degree in chemical engineering from the Indian Institute of Technology at Kanpur, and his M.S. in chemical engineering and Ph.D. in management from the University of Texas at Austin. In 2006, he received the Distinguished Alumnus Award from the Indian Institute of Technology (Kanpur) for his contributions to management research.

# Preface: Consumer Safari

I have to admit that until a few years ago, I was guilty of overlooking Africa. My book on emerging markets, *The 86% Solution,* included only a few African examples. As a professor of marketing at the University of Texas, I have extensive experience working with companies in Latin America. I have traveled and lectured extensively in Asia and the Middle East. Like most scholars in the developed world, however, I saw Africa more as a charity case than a market opportunity. I was wrong, and this book is here to set the record straight.

It is particularly surprising to me that I failed to recognize the story in Africa because I remember when India was discussed in the same way. As Ramachandra Guha recently wrote in a book review in the *Financial Times,* "Western writers of the 1960s warned their readers that India was a losing proposition, the laboratory, as it were, of failed experiments in democracy and nation-building."[1] He could be writing about Africa today. In fact, one of the reasons I started writing about opportunities in emerging markets was because of a conversation I had with a colleague for a panel considering how we could stop the developing world from "begging." As the son of an entrepreneur, I found this shocking and insulting. I knew that entrepreneurship is alive and well in India. But when I told colleagues a decade or two ago that India would be an important global market, they were incredulous. They are incredulous no longer.

I have experienced the transformations in India firsthand. I was born in Jammu City in the state of Jammu and Kashmir a few months after Mahatma Gandhi was assassinated and India became a republic. I became part of a generation that Salman Rushdie called "Midnight's Children," referring to those who lived through the transformational time after the independence of India at midnight on August 15, 1947. In 2002, I had the opportunity to return to India as dean of the Indian School of Business in Hyderabad. I saw how a country that had been written off as a charity case was now seen as a powerful emerging market.

Now I see the same view of Africa. Despite all the attention it has received for its social, medical, humanitarian, and political challenges, it is still undervalued as a consumer market. I set out to rectify my own lack of knowledge about the continent and to understand the market opportunity it presents—in all its rich complexity and wealth. I traveled thousands of miles across Africa and met with or interviewed leaders of major African companies, smaller entrepreneurs, and Asian and Western firms with long experience on the continent. I have had the opportunity to meet some truly extraordinary and creative business leaders. I feel blessed for the opportunity to do this in the autumn of my life. I learned important lessons from these many teachers, which I share in this book.

As I was finishing this book, President George Bush announced in February 2008 the launch of five funds through the U.S. Overseas Private Investment Corporation, totaling $875 million, for investment in Africa. On the eve of his trip to Benin, Tanzania, Rwanda, Ghana, and Liberia, he stated a conclusion that I had reached in my own journeys through Africa in the preceding years. "This new era is rooted in a powerful truth: Africa's most valuable resource is not its oil, it's not its diamonds, it is the talent and creativity of its people." The true wealth of Africa is its more than 900 million consumers, and its countless entrepreneurs and business leaders who are already demonstrating the wealth of the continent by building successful enterprises. If you look beyond the headlines, these individuals are propelling the rise of Africa. They are building businesses, economies, and societies. They are the hidden natural resource that may present greater opportunities than oil or minerals in the long run.

I am not a political scholar. I am not an economist. I am a marketing professor, so my focus is on the market opportunity. There will soon be a billion consumers on the continent of Africa, and this is one of the fastest growing markets in the world. Every day, they need to eat. They need shelter. They want education for their children. They would like to have soaps to wash their clothes. They desire cell phones, metal roofs for their homes, televisions, music, computers, movies, bicycles, cosmetics, medicines, cars, and loans to start businesses. They celebrate marriages, births, and religious holidays and commemorate death.

I have sought to learn as much as I possibly could about the African market—what it offers, how it is structured, and its potential. Others have looked at Africa through a political lens, some have engaged in economic analysis, some have examined its complex history, and others have looked at medical or social challenges. A few have even started telling the stories of specific African businesses. But my focus is on understanding the continent through the perspective of the consumer. What is the African market? What opportunities does it offer? How are companies recognizing and realizing the opportunities in Africa's rising?

Many tourists come to Africa every year to see the big game there—the elephants, lions, and rhinos. But I came for a different type of big game. I was seeking out the successful enterprises that are identifying and capitalizing on the market opportunities, and seeking lessons from those that are not so successful, too.

In Nairobi, Maserame Mouyeme of The Coca-Cola Company told me how important it is "to walk the market." Then, in Harare, I first heard the term "consumer safari" in a meeting with Unilever executives. This is what they call their initiatives to spend a day with consumers in their homes to understand how they use products. Years after I started on this journey, I now had a term to describe the quest I was on. I was on a consumer safari. The market landscape that is Africa is every bit as marvelous and surprising as its geographic landscape. It presents as big an opportunity as China and India. On the following pages, I invite you to come along on this safari. I think it will change your view of Africa, as it has changed mine, and perhaps your view of where the future global market opportunities—and future wealth—can be found.

Vijay Mahajan
University of Texas at Austin
March 2008

# Part I
## The African Opportunity

# 1  ———————————————————

# Baking Bread in Zimbabwe

*Africa has more than 900 million consumers. Despite the challenges, every day they need to eat. They need clean water. They need shelter, clothing, and medicine. They want cell phones, bicycles, computers, automobiles, and education for their children. Businesses are already seizing these opportunities to build markets across Africa.*

The headlines from Zimbabwe when I visited in July 2006 were dismal. Inflation was above 1,000 percent. Unemployment was over 70 percent.[1] Gas stations had not had official supplies of fuel for years, so people carried cans of gas in their trunks for long trips. Borrowing rates ran as high as 400 percent to 500 percent. A combination of the policies of President Robert Mugabe and Western sanctions had brought the nation to its knees.

When I arrived at the airport in Harare, it was a ghost town. Gift shops and car rentals were closed. One line snaked away from the exchange window where an ATM door was flung open, exposing its interior machinery. There used to be 20 flights a week here. Now there were three or four. Tourism revenues in Zimbabwe dropped from $340 million in 1999 to $98 million in 2005.[2] An advertisement for cellular network operator Econet Wireless at the arrival doorway in the airport seemed jarringly out of place, with its bold letters proclaiming "Inspiration is all around you." There was little inspiration here.

Outside, half a dozen taxis sat by the curb. Their engines were off. Gasoline was scarce. The drivers leaned against the rail, even after the Kenya Airways flight discharged a few passengers from Nairobi. Idle taxis at an idle airport are the clearest indication of an economy that is collapsing upon itself.

Yet even here there were market opportunities. A few days later, in downtown Harare, I met an accountant for a company that makes fiberglass roofing. Kizito Ntoro was sitting in the late morning at a table in a food court on the ground floor of the shopping mall at 105 Robert Mugabe Road. He had just purchased a hamburger from the Steers restaurant, one of about a half dozen offerings at the row of stores along the wall in front of him. But his reason for stopping for fast food would be totally foreign to a restaurant manager in the developed world. He was here because his electricity was out the night before, so he and his family had no dinner. Their lights were out. They couldn't cook. They just went to bed without eating hot food. So he stopped at the restaurant before an 11 a.m. meeting. In a country where power is unreliable, a power outage is an occasion to eat out and an opportunity for entrepreneurs to build businesses (not to mention booming sales of generators and solar cells).

Innscor, which operates the Steers restaurant chain in Zimbabwe, got its start in the restaurant business with a small chicken restaurant in Harare in 1987. When Innscor built its first Chicken Inn, there was no fast food in the country. KFC (Kentucky Fried Chicken) had tried setting up shop but closed down. Most people thought it was a foolish idea. Chicken Inn started turning a profit in six months. Now Innscor has developed a full food court with a set of restaurants that cuts across demographic segments—from the daily bread of its basic Bakers Inn to Steers to Pizza Inn and the upscale Nandos chicken restaurants (see Exhibit 1 of the insert). Innscor replicated this concept in more than a dozen countries across Africa. The company has also moved into distribution for U.S., European, and local companies in Zimbabwe and other countries, manufacturing appliances and franchising grocery stores. It forged an alliance with ExxonMobil for its On the Run convenience stores. In 2005, the company posted revenue growth of 278 percent and profit growth of 246 percent. By 2007, it was the tenth largest company in southern Africa, excluding South Africa, with a market value of $203 million. (There is an active stock market in Zimbabwe.)[3] All the news out of Zimbabwe was not bad.

Entrepreneurs have had to adapt to political and economic challenges. When Nigeria banned imports on cheese, Innscor spent nine years perfecting its own recipe to make mozzarella in Nigeria taste like European imports. In Zimbabwe, they have gone into businesses that most restaurant companies in developed countries would never have imagined, like crocodile farms. The need for foreign exchange in Zimbabwe's shaky financial system took Innscor first into the tourism business with its Shearwater Victoria Falls operation. When increasing economic uncertainty undermined tourism, Innscor moved into crocodile farms. The company whose core business is bread, chickens, and burgers was raising more than 50,000 crocodiles a year for global markets on Lake Kariba in Zimbabwe when I visited. Innscor became one of the biggest producers of crocodile meat and skins in the world and brought in much-needed foreign exchange. When the market changes, entrepreneurs adapt.

Innscor is just one of many entrepreneurial firms I have had the opportunity to study in diverse countries across Africa as I have sought to understand the African opportunity and how successful companies are capitalizing on it. These companies span industries from consumer goods to alcohol and soft drinks to metal roofing to airlines to retailers. These firms are challenging the view that Africa is a charity case. They are one of the driving forces of Africa's rise. If there are opportunities in a country such as Zimbabwe, where political mismanagement has led to a prolonged economic crisis, or Rwanda, Congo, and Southern Sudan, where new enterprises are springing from the ashes of horrific violence and genocide, imagine the opportunities to create wealth in more stable and well-managed countries in Africa. Successful companies across the continent have recognized the African opportunity that is sometimes buried in a flood of bad news that streams out of the continent.

Whatever its challenges—and there are many, from diseases such as AIDS and malaria to corruption to all-out war—Africa contains more than 900 million consumers. Every day, they need their bread. In Harare, I watched the conveyor belts of the bread factories of Innscor's Bakers Inn churn out more than 50,000 loaves of bread daily as workers in white coats inspected the line. Workers mixed massive pots of yeasty-smelling dough and monitored brown loaves rising on a Ferris wheel and running through ovens on a conveyor belt. The bakery faced challenges of finding good wheat, fluctuating diesel supplies, and government-controlled pricing. The afternoon I visited, the line had to be shut down because of a lack of diesel. But more fuel was on its way, and they would run all night to meet demand. People lined up at the shops in the morning. These loaves of bread serve the lowest end of the consumer market. Costs are unpredictable. Prices are fixed by the government. Innscor has refined its business processes, used meticulous cash management, and harnessed the power of entrepreneurship to achieve better profit margins despite higher costs and lower effective prices. The most amazing thing is that their profit margins were better than they had ever been. As one manager said at the bakery, "We are not bakers; we are entrepreneurs."

Although it was hard to imagine the situation in Zimbabwe could get worse than when I visited in July 2006, it did. By early 2008, annual inflation was estimated at more than 8,000 percent (although unofficial estimates were as high as 25,000 percent). An estimated 4 million people, one-third of the population, had fled the country by mid-2007.[4] To address widespread hunger, the government fixed prices for essentials products at a point where producers said they could no longer earn a profit. Executives were arrested for failing to implement the price controls. Entrepreneurs stepped up informal imports from neighboring South Africa. After President Robert Mugabe required all businesses to yield 51 percent of their ownership to black Zimbabweans (called "indigenization"), J. Heinz sold its interest in a Zimbabwe company in September 2007.[5]

Even so, companies were still investing billions of Zim dollars in building their brands. From banks to cellular companies to milk producers, companies were reworking their taglines and logos to redirect or reinvigorate their Zimbabwe businesses. Kingdom Bank, founded a dozen years earlier, proclaimed, "Kingdom's time has come!"[6] An April 2007 ranking by *African Business* of the top 50 companies in southern Africa (excluding South Africa) included 19 Zimbabwean firms in areas from food to retail to seeds to reinsurance. In July 2007, large South African retailers, including Massmart (owner of Makro in Zimbabwe), Edgars, OK, and Pick 'n Pay affirmed their commitment to keeping their operations open in Zimbabwe.[7] Even though squeezed by runaway inflation and government price controls, the retailers continued to express hope about the future of the country.

Most surprising, Zimbabwe is also attracting new investors. Despite worsening conditions, foreign direct investments rose from $4 million in 2003 to $103 million in 2005. With companies significantly underpriced and a belief that the country will ultimately turn around, many investors believed it was worth the risk. At the urging of investors, Imra Assets Management of South Africa, which categorized Zimbabwe as a "frontier" market, nonetheless launched a Zimbabwe-focused investment fund in March 2007. It had set a goal to raise $10 million by the end of the year, but had already brought in $11 million just a few months later. The fund is investing in a number of enterprises, including Innscor.[8] These investors believe, that with plans and patience, Zimbabwe's prospects, like the bread in Innscor's bakeries, will continue to rise.

As this book was going to press, there were historic changes underway in Zimbabwe. In elections in March 2008, Robert Mugabe's party lost control of the house of Parliament for the first time since the country's independence from white rule in 1980. His loss to Morgan Tsvangirai marked the weakening of his control of the country. Although these changes increased the threat of violence, they also signaled the most dramatic political change in the nation's recent history.

# African Wealth: The Tenth Largest Economy in the World

Africa is a continent full of surprises. The fact that people were baking and buying bread in a country that was in economic free fall is just one snapshot of the continent's hidden opportunities. Looking at the bigger picture of Africa also reveals some surprises. If Africa were a single country, according to World Bank data, it would have had $978 billion total gross national income (GNI) in 2006. This places it ahead of India as a total market. Africa would show up as the tenth largest economy in the world (see Table 1-1). In fact, this places Africa ahead of every one of the vaunted BRIC economies (Brazil, Russia, India, and China) except for China. Of course, Africa is not one country, as we consider in the next chapter, but it is richer than you think.

**TABLE 1-1    Africa Is the Tenth Largest Economy in the World**

| 1 | United States | $13.4 trillion |
|---|---|---|
| 2 | Japan | $4.9 trillion |
| 3 | Germany | $3.0 trillion |
| 4 | China | $2.6 trillion |
| 5 | United Kingdom | $2.4 trillion |
| 6 | France | $2.3 trillion |
| 7 | Italy | $1.9 trillion |
| 8 | Spain | $1.2 trillion |
| 9 | Canada | $1.2 trillion |
| **10** | **Africa** | **$978.3 billion** |
| 11 | India | $906.5 billion |
| 12 | Brazil | $892.8 billion |
| 13 | Republic of Korea | $856.6 billion |
| 14 | Russian Federation | $822.4 billion |
| 15 | Mexico | $820.3 billion |

Source: Gross National Income, 2006, World Bank, http://siteresources.worldbank.org/
DATASTATISTICS/Resources/GNI.pdf

# A Different Type of Oil and Diamonds

Is the wealth of Africa all from diamonds and oil? Perhaps, but not always the types of diamonds and oil that you might think. Although mining and oil are important industries historically, there is much more to the African opportunity than natural resources. While petroleum production has grabbed the headlines, Bidco Oil Refineries, Inc., in Kenya has created a business with more than $160 million (Ksh12.8 billion) turnover, based in large part upon a different kind of oil: *cooking oil*. Bidco began producing oil in 1991 at its Thika factory. Through very effective marketing and packaging, with products sized for any budget, it became the leading manufacturer of edible oil, fats, and soaps in east and central Africa. Bidco understands the market, from the low-income customers in Kibera who buy oil in small packages to the upper-income consumers who log on to its "Jikoni.com" website to download recipes. (The site attracted more than 11,000 registered users in mid-2006, including members of the diaspora community outside Kenya.) Bidco built over 51 percent market share in Kenya, and the company exports oil, detergents, and other products to more than a dozen African countries, including Tanzania, Uganda, Rwanda, Burundi, Ethiopia, Sudan, Eritrea, Zambia, Malawi, Madagascar, Democratic Republic of Congo, and Somalia. Not all the valuable oil in Africa comes out of the ground.

In South Africa, companies are mining a different kind of "diamond," the so-called Black Diamond, an emerging middle-class segment that is driving economic growth. Discussing this new segment, Melanie Louw, an economist for ABI, a bottler of Coca-Cola beverages in South Africa, noted that the "Black Diamond" segment has created a fundamental shift in the economy. "This has had a multiplier effect that has boosted the economy up to the point I believe that our economy has structurally changed," she said in an interview in her offices in Johannesburg in 2006. "We have lifted up to a whole new realm of economic growth." The study by the University of Cape Town's Unilever Institute that identified this Black Diamond segment called it "the most exciting market opportunity in our history." It is another sign of Africa's rise.

Although South Africa's market is farther along the curve than most of sub-Saharan Africa, the roughly 400 million people in the middle segments of the entire African market (Africa Two) are a growing opportunity everywhere in Africa, as we consider in Chapter 3, "The Power of Africa Two." Some marketers break South Africa into lifestyle segments (LSMs), on a scale of 1 to 10. They have had to recalibrate their scales over the past five years, as LSM 5 has moved up to consumption patterns that were once associated with higher segments.

In December 2007, Cape Town hosted the first "lifestyle festival" for the Black Diamond segment (followed by similar festivals in Johannesburg and Durban in 2008). The festivals celebrated what organizers call the "Afropolitan" products and brands that cater to the lifestyle of South Africa's black middle class (www.blackdiamonds-festival.co.za). This emerging South African middle class, which is growing at an estimated rate of 30 percent per year, is also driving up housing prices in the country.[9] "The past ten years have been the most exciting years we have had," said Louw. "We've seen amazing changes in consumer behavior. In terms of lifestyle, trends such as health and wellness, and even packaging preferences have changed completely. The economy structure and labor structure have changed profoundly."

Although the top 4 companies on the 2007 list of the largest Africa companies as ranked by *African Business* are in metals and mining or oil and gas (Anglo American plc, Bhp Billiton plc, Anglo American Platinum Corp. Ltd., and Sasol Ltd.), among the top 20 companies are consumer goods (SABMiller plc), telecom (MTN Group Ltd., Orascom Telcom, Itissalat Al Magrib, Telkom SA), banks (Standard Bank Group Ltd., FirstRand Ltd., Absa Group Ltd.), and real estate companies (Liberty International Plc). There is still tremendous interest in Africa's natural resources, but could cooking oil and Black Diamond consumers be the oil and diamonds that will be most significant to Africa's future rise?

## An Irish Beer Finds Its Future in Africa

Is Guinness an Irish or African brand? In the last six months of 2006, global sales of Diageo's Irish stout Guinness were down about 4 percent. They were even falling in Ireland, due to changes in consumption patterns as customers spent less time in pubs. But sales outside of Ireland were growing by 4 percent to 5 percent—especially in Africa. Chief executive Paul Walsh said in July 2007 that the company would expand sales in Africa to counter declines in its domestic market.[10] It is clear its future may not lie in the Irish pub but in the small bars in Lagos.

Thanks to a long presence in Nigeria and astute advertising, many Nigerians don't even see Guinness as an Irish brand. It has been such a long and dominant presence that it is considered domestic. When an Irish beer has become African, and when the future growth of the brand rests on expanding sales on the African continent rather than in Ireland, there is clearly something shifting in the world. Not only that, but a Nigerian immigrant was elected as the first black mayor of an Irish town in 2007. Rotimi Adebare was named head of the town of Portlaoise, an hour outside of Dublin. This is a sign of the growing reach and prominence of the African diaspora. It is getting very hard to tell where Ireland ends and Africa begins.[11]

When I met Eric Frank of Saatchi and Saatchi in a small booth at a crowded restaurant at the airport in Cape Town, he said he was glad that someone from the United States was finally paying attention to what is happening in Africa. Frank and his colleagues had developed the legendary Michael Power advertising campaign, an action hero who helped build Guinness into a "Lovemark" in Nigeria and other countries. Saatchi and Diageo had recognized the potential in Africa long ago, which helps explain why Guinness has such a strong presence across sub-Saharan Africa now. Its fortunes have risen with Africa.

Other companies are stepping up their presence in Africa. Unilever, facing increased competition and declining profits in the United States and Europe (where sales growth fell from 5 percent in 1998 to 0.7 percent in 2004), announced plans to step up its business in the developing world, including Africa, where it is already firmly established.[12] Nestlé, caught between forecasts of growth of only 1.5 percent annually in developed markets and its target of 5 percent to 6 percent organic growth, announced plans in 2006 to step up operations in West Africa and other developing markets to make up the difference.

## An Inflection Point

Although Novartis has had a long presence in Africa, I had a chance to join senior executives from Europe in July 2006 for their first major meeting in Nigeria, recognition of the rising importance of the continent and the need for an on-the-ground understanding. "It may be at this moment in time we are coming to a kind of inflection point in the development of Africa," said Kevin Kerr, who was in charge of Novartis business in the region, during a meeting in the Little Crockpot restaurant in the Sheraton Lagos.

The Coca-Cola Company, which has been in Africa since 1928, has seen its business on the continent increase steadily over the past two decades, despite the ups and downs of individual countries, as shown in the following figure. The company now sells 93 million servings of its beverages *every day* across Africa, generating about $4 to 5 billion in system revenues for the company and its bottlers in 2006.

The African business accounted for 6.5 percent of global sales by volume in 2006.

As a sign of Africa's rising development and importance, in June 2007 Coca-Cola relocated its African headquarters from Windsor, United Kingdom, to Johannesburg, South Africa. Alex Cummings, an African-born leader, was at the helm (see sidebar). Muhtar Kent, president and chief operating officer of The Coca-Cola Company, said of the move: "I believe that our business in Africa should be managed locally, by Coca-Cola associates who live and breathe the continent. Johannesburg is an ideal location for our new office since it has excellent business infrastructure, as well as good transport and communications networks with the rest of the continent."

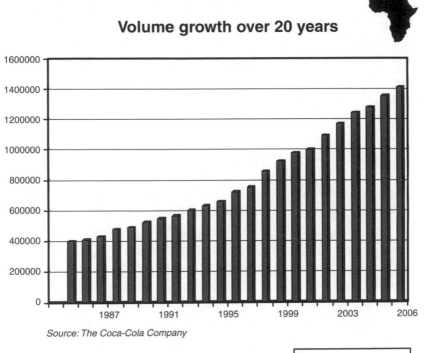

## Volume growth over 20 years

Source: The Coca-Cola Company

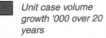

Unit case volume growth '000 over 20 years

**Coca-Cola growth in Africa**

## Alex Cummings: Bringing Coca-Cola Home to Africa

Liberian-born Alexander B. Cummings Jr., president of the Africa Group of The Coca-Cola Company, helped carry the headquarters to South Africa from London in 2007, a sign of the improvements in infrastructure and growing opportunities for business on the continent. "This move demonstrates The Coca-Cola Company's confidence in the future of Africa," said Cummings during an interview with the author in August 2007. "Furthermore, the continent's improved economic growth rate encourages us to plan for future expansion."

"On a per-unit basis, Africa is the third most profitable market in the world," he said. "The African market is quite attractive for the company and for most multinationals if they look at it with the right lens. Most people only see the negatives of Africa. You have to get beyond the perception to see the opportunities. We estimate that 350 million to 500 million people could potentially be the market for our products. That is a lot of people."

"The returns in Africa are as good as, or better than, they are in a lot of BRIC counties [Brazil, Russia, India and China] in the medium and short term. And the African market is not as competitive as BRIC countries. We have a significant opportunity to shape beverages in Africa and see the results. Beyond the business returns, there is the opportunity to impact and influence communities. For all those reasons Africa is as attractive, maybe more attractive in the medium term, than BRIC countries—but, of course, I am a bit biased."

The Coca-Cola Company is not put off by markets fragmented across more than 50 countries. "That can be a challenge, but our business model is one of producing as close to the market as possible," he said. In Liberia, a single bottling plant distributes through the country, and in countries such as Mali or Cameroon, The Coca-Cola Company has partnered with other beverage makers to enter the market. Although huge differences exist across Africa, there are common challenges across these markets. For the company, building distribution, developing the right portfolio of beverages (including juice and water), building the capacity of its people, and engaging in community development are common themes across Africa.

Cummings joined the company in 1997 in Nigeria and became the first African to lead Coca-Cola's operating unit in Africa. He earned his Bachelor's degree in finance from Northern Illinois University and a Master's degree in finance from Atlanta University. He worked for The Pillsbury Company for 15 years before joining The Coca-Cola Company. Most of the company's top leadership in Africa is from the continent. "It isn't easy finding Africans, but you can," Cummings said, "and if you look to the diaspora, you can find even more."

It is not just large companies that are finding opportunities in Africa, but also visionary entrepreneurs. We discussed the successes of companies such as Bidco in Kenya and Innscor in Zimbabwe. In South Africa, Herman Mashaba founded Black Like Me in 1984 in Garankuwa, manufacturing hair and beauty products at night and selling them during the day. He built one of the most respected brands in the industry in South Africa. The business was brought to the brink of bankruptcy in a suspicious fire that destroyed his factory in 1993, but he rebuilt it from scratch and sold a majority stake to Colgate-Palmolive two years later. Two years after that, he negotiated to buy the business back. Today it is a multimillion-rand business, with products distributed throughout Africa and the United Kingdom. He is regarded as one of South Africa's most successful entrepreneurs.

Bill Lynch, CEO of South Africa's Imperial Holdings transport group, with annual turnover of R42.5bn ($6.2 billion), was born in rural Ireland. He came to South Africa in the 1970s with nothing, and built his own multimillion-dollar fortune while growing Imperial. Lynch, named Ernst & Young World Entrepreneur in 2006, weathered economic recession and a near civil war while growing the company, but expects more growth ahead. As he told the *Financial Times* in 2006, if South Africa grows at the expected rate of 6 percent, his business should grow at 15 percent to 20 percent over the next few years.[13]

# Looking East: The New Gold Rush

Asian governments and companies are recognizing the opportunity in Africa's rise. One crisp morning in May 2006, I drove through the archway of "China Mart," a sprawling wholesale metropolis in Johannesburg. Gold was what first brought Europeans to Johannesburg during the gold rush of the 1800s. Now, in the Crown Mines section of the city, there is a new gold rush, centered around the consumer goods of China Mart. This wholesale mall contained 126 shops surrounded by a gate and heavy security sporting padded vests (as well as signs prohibiting firearms). They were not guarding gold. They were guarding stores filled with inexpensive clothing, luggage, shoes, and electronics from China, which drew retailers from South Africa and surrounding countries. In one store, Tom Fang offered flip-flops from a large box for just 2.90 rand (about 30 cents). They would retail on the shelves of stores in Zimbabwe, the Congo, or Angola for about 8 to 10 rand (just over $1). For many villagers, this will be their first pair of shoes. "They are very well made," he pointed out.

Chinese merchants and products are evident across Africa, from low-cost televisions and other appliances to generators to clothing and shoes. Astute Chinese peddlers and retailers are selling Ramadan lanterns and prayer carpets in Egypt. Egyptians shake their heads that they are buying these holy items from the Chinese, but the price is right. Jincheng motorcycles race across the roads of Nigeria. Indian and Pakistani traders in the Asian market area of Johannesburg sell leather, clothing, and other wares. The same scene is repeated at El Hamiz in Algiers, Moncef Bey in Tunisia, and many other parts of Africa I visited. Chinese stores can be found in the oldest and holiest places in Morocco, lining the Derb Ghalef and Derb Omar market areas in Casablanca. At night, hawkers are selling shoes, clothes, and toys in the street. In the Moroccan souks, you can buy inexpensive pirated goods from software to clothing. A knock-off pair of Ray-Ban sunglasses that I had seen for $120 in a formal market was on sale for just $5 by informal traders. Pirated movies were retailing for about $1.

China's trade with Africa has risen from about $10 billion in 2000 to more than $55 billion in 2006.[14] (China's trade with India, by contrast, was less than half as large, at $25 billion in 2006.) Chinese Prime Minister Wen Jibao forecast that trade with Africa would rise to $100 billion by 2010.[15] Although China has become second only to the United States as the largest importer of oil from Africa, nudging out Japan, it is far ahead of the United States in exports to Africa. Egypt expects China to replace the United States as its top trading partner by 2012.[16] In a 2007 report, "Africa's Silk Road: China and India's New Economic Frontier," World Bank economist Harry Broadman called the growing African trade and investment by China and India, particularly in sub-Saharan countries, "one of the most significant features of recent developments in the global economy."[17] With growing investments in Africa by India and China, will the West be left behind?

The African continent is looking east, as can be seen in the flight paths of Kenya Airways and other African carriers. Like neural pathways, the passenger and freight routes reflect the new thinking of Asia about Africa and vice versa. When I flew from Lagos to Nairobi on Kenya Airways in July 2006, I found out that half the passengers were continuing on to connecting flights to Asia and the Middle East. Traditional flight paths head into Europe, recognizing the continent's colonial past. But the future can be seen in the routes from Nairobi to Guangzhou, Mumbai, and Bangkok. Billboards and full-page ads from DHL in major African publications, discussing importing cell phones from China, proclaimed, "No one knows China like we do."

A Sino-African summit in 2006 brought representatives of almost every African country to Beijing, a demonstration of how important China and Africa have become to one another. China pledged $5 billion in loans and credits to Africa during the summit. And Chinese President Hu Jintao reciprocated with an eight-nation tour of Africa in January 2007 (visiting Cameroon, Sudan, Liberia, Zambia, Namibia, South Africa, Mozambique, and Seychelles). India also organized an India-Africa summit in New Delhi in April 2008. Major Indian companies such as Tata, Mahindra, Kirloskar, and Ranbaxy have set up operations in Africa and are achieving high levels of growth. In May 2008, Bharti Airtel, India's leading mobile operator, made a multibillion dollar bid for the control of South African mobile company MTN.

With so many opportunities at home, why are Indian and Chinese companies here in Africa? China and India can recognize the African opportunity because they have lived through it. In speaking with leaders of Indian companies who are active in Africa, I often heard the comment that this market seems familiar. Although some of the interest from Asia in Africa has been fueled by Africa's abundant natural resources—and there is even concern expressed about a new wave of colonialism—the Chinese, Indian, Japanese, and Korean companies in Africa also recognize the potential of the market. The demographics of Africa and challenges are not so different from those at home. They have seen the rise of their markets and expect the same in Africa.

# Entrepreneurship Is Alive and Well in Africa

At a lecture I gave to a group of entrepreneurs at the Lagos Business School in 2006, the question came up once again: What about the role of politics in business development? This is a natural question, and the political environment can have a tremendous positive or negative impact on business development. This can be seen in the serious rioting in Kenya over the presidential elections in December 2007, as I was finishing this book, which killed more than 1,200 people and displaced more than 300,000. Political rivals Mwai Kibaki and Raila Odinga ultimately negotiated an end to the conflict through a power-sharing agreement. (Despite these problems and their impact on the tourist industry, business bounced back quickly. The planned IPO of Safaricom in April 2008 sparked an "IPO fever," which attracted many first-time investors such as kiosk owners and taxi drivers.) Certainly, more stable governments, good economic policies, and pan-African initiatives such as the New Partnership for Africa's Development (NEPAD)—as well as private initiatives such as the Ibrahim Foundation's governance prize—are having a beneficial impact.

The African business environment is continuing to improve. A 2006 report from the World Bank's International Finance Corporation concluded that Africa had moved from last place to third for improvements in ease of doing business. (Although the rate of improvement was high, the highest-ranked country on the continent for ease of doing business was South Africa, ranked 29th in the world.) Countries such as Tanzania, Ghana, Nigeria, and war-ravaged Rwanda were among the most improved. At least two-thirds of African nations had achieved at least one positive reform.[18] Among the improvements are better governance, the deepening of democracy, cancellation of the debts of 14 countries, signs of reductions in tariff barriers, and positive African state interventions in Sudan, Côte d'Ivoire, and the Democratic Republic of Congo.

Haiko Alfeld, director for Africa of the World Economic Forum, noted in 2006 that the continent has "emphatically and irreversibly turned a corner." African Development Bank president Donald Kaberuka said in a summer 2007 interview in the new publication, *African Banker* (the publication of which is also a sign of the growth of banking and investment), the economic climate for Africa "is at its best in 30 years."[19]

However, entrepreneurs and successful businesses are not waiting for governments to get their acts together. These entrepreneurs have built their businesses through the twists and turns of economic, political, and military unrest. It requires great flexibility. When the Nigerian government banned imports of furniture and clothing, retailer Park n Shop quickly went into the furniture manufacturing business. It replaced an entire floor of imported furniture in its Lagos store with the products of its own domestic manufacturing. When government restrictions on gasoline all but shut down gas stations in Zimbabwe, they converted themselves to restaurants. Small entrepreneurs in Victoria Falls turned their private homes into gas stations, making runs across the border to neighboring countries for cans of petrol.

The entrepreneurial spirit is alive and well in Africa. Entrepreneurs solve problems. Take away electricity, and they sell generators and inverters. Take away a stable financial system, and they make their money on speculating on foreign currency. Take away their employment, and they set up kiosks in the street. Entrepreneurship and the development of consumer markets may be a more clean, stable, and powerful driver of long-term progress than political reform. Professor Pat Utomi of the Lagos Business School once suggested, only partly in jest, that if all the oil in Nigeria were given to the soldiers and politicians on condition that they would leave the nation alone, the nation would be better off.[20]

African countries have proven remarkably resilient. Idi Amin's repressive regime in Uganda drove out not only Indians but also many of their businesses, including Kakira Sugar Works, founded by Muljib-hai Prabhudas Madhvani. He had arrived in the country from India in 1912 and set up a trading firm in Jinja. The Madhvani Group was nationalized, and all Asians were expelled by Amin on August 5, 1972. The company's production continued to decline until 1983, when it was shut down. After Amin's overthrow, the new Ugandan govern-ment invited the Madhvani Group back into the country in 1985 in a public-private joint venture, and Madhvani Group acquired 100 per-cent ownership of Kakira Sugar Works in 2000. When it needed more power, the company began to construct a 20-megawatt power plant, which will allow it to burn sugar byproducts and sell energy back into the national grid. When this cogeneration power project is completed in 2009, electric power sales will exceed sales of sugar. It was a long, hard road, but the business has come back stronger than ever.

Africa's success in spite of politics is not so different from the story of India's rise. A few years ago, a poster at the World Economic Fo-rum in Davos summarized the nation's progress: "In ten years—three elections, three governments toppled—one direction." Although we often emphasize the way that politics affect business, remember that business affects politics, and market development has a stabilizing in-fluence on the economy. While politicians look to change regulations and charitable organizations look to make up deficiencies, entrepre-neurs create wealth. They ask: What are the opportunities?

# Trade Not Aid

Africa is receiving unprecedented attention from the West for its health, political, and humanitarian crises. Philanthropists and celebri-ties have been crisscrossing the continent drawing global attention to African challenges. The musician Bono, in a special issue of *Vanity Fair* that he co-edited in July 2007, wrote that "Africa is the proving ground for whether or not we really believe in equality." Many impor-tant African initiatives are playing a vital role in drawing attention to the plight of Africa's most vulnerable populations. But an unfortunate byproduct of these campaigns is that they also reinforce a perception that Africa is nothing but a continent of war, disease, and begging bowls. This makes it easier to overlook the business opportunities that are also there, and growing.

Although charity is important, it is not enough. Africa, like many emerging economies, has serious problems that cannot be ignored by businesses operating there. Companies such as The Coca-Cola Company, Unilever, Novartis, and many others are leading the way in addressing disease, poverty, corruption, and other challenges. Some of these activities, such as distribution of condoms to prevent AIDS, are either the result of corporate citizenship or enlightened self-interest. No company can stay in business for long anywhere without being concerned about the problems facing its employees and customers. This makes corporate social responsibility essential.

Africa's challenges, like any consumer needs, can also create business opportunities. The lack of reliable electricity in many parts of Africa has created a market for generators and solar cells. Unstable financial systems have led to systems for bartering cell phone minutes, microfinancing, and cell-phone-based banking. Health problems from AIDS to malaria have created demand for new treatments, generic drugs, testing equipment, and insurance. Concern about the environment has led to opportunities in eco-tourism. The challenges often require blended solutions of public and private cooperation, leading to successful businesses that address real societal needs while building viable long-term economic value.

Where African nations have been able to create positive and stable governments, their economies have flourished—countries such as Botswana, Mozambique, Mauritius, and even Rwanda, which is best known in the West for chaos and genocide.[21] Rwanda's leaders have announced aggressive plans to raise per-capita GDP from $230 to $900 by 2020, using information technology to transform the nation into an "African Singapore."[22] Despite the dire situation in Sudan's western province of Darfur, the country is one of the fastest-growing economies on the continent, and multibillion-dollar office towers, hotels, and other additions to the skyline of Khartoum are inviting comparisons to Dubai.[23] Next door in Somalia, while the war-torn capital of Mogadishu is a focus of international concern, Somaliland in the north is thriving and stable. Through setbacks, wars, and turmoil, the overall market development of the continent has moved in one direction—rising.

# The Need for Leadership

Celtel founder Mo Ibrahim recognized the power of entrepreneurship, as well as government leadership, in transforming Africa. He built Celtel, one of Africa's most successful start-ups and largest indigenous fortunes, at a time when few recognized the potential of the African cell phone market. Then he used his wealth to establish an annual $5 million prize, plus $200,000 for life, for retired African leaders who rule well and then stand down. This award is larger than the Nobel Peace Prize. (In many countries, retired leaders received no benefits, increasing the incentive for corruption to ensure security after leaving office.) The first prize was awarded in 2007 to Mozambique President Joaquim A. Chissano, who retired in 2004 after helping to end a 16-year civil war in his country. Ibrahim also created the Ibrahim Index of African Governance to rank the quality of governance in sub-Saharan nations (see sidebar).[24] He is demonstrating how entrepreneurial success can become a driver for political and social development.

## Mo Ibrahim: Africa Is Open for Business

Celtel founder Mohamed Ibrahim demonstrates the virtuous cycle of investment in building businesses in Africa, and the impact of expatriates in recognizing opportunities there. "All my life I have been working in the domain of mobile communications," he said in an interview with the author in August 2007.[25] "I am an African. I always felt that Africa has received very bad press – with civil wars, no rule of law, and diseases. It really has a bad image, which I think is not justified. Yes, we have all these problems, but Africa is a very big place. There are 53 countries, and maybe there are severe problems in four or five countries. And even if you go to Khartoum, you would be amazed to know that it is part of Sudan."

On the other hand, he pointed out that this negative perception is not all bad from a business standpoint. "In business, when there is a gap between reality and perception, there is good business to be made."

The Sudanese-born Dr. Ibrahim earned a Bachelor's degree in electrical engineering from the University of Alexandria in Egypt, a Master's degree from the University of Bradford, and a Ph.D. in mobile communications from the University of Birmingham in the United Kingdom. After serving as an executive with British Telecom, where he helped establish Britain's first mobile network, in 1989 Mo Ibrahim founded MSI (Mobile Systems International), a world leader in radio planning, software, and consultancy. In 1998, he launched Celtel International, which became one of Africa's leading telecom companies. Celtel was a company with global standards for customer service but also "an African company." He refused to pay bribes and created a system for good governance. He had to set up generators, use batteries, and build the communications backbone that might be taken for granted in more developed areas of the world. Banks were not interested in providing financing. He relied mainly on funding the business through successive rounds of equity. "We introduced service where telecom never existed before. We offered good quality at affordable prices." At Celtel's launch in 1998, there were just 2 million cell phone subscribers across Africa. Now there are more than 130 million. Celtel's success inspired a host of rivals. In 2005, Celtel was sold to MTC Kuwait for $3.4 billion, making it one of Africa's most successful commercial ventures. The company, now in more than 15 African countries, has invested in excess of $750 million in Africa.

Ibrahim personally continues to give back to the continent where he built his fortune. In addition to his public-sector prize for leadership and governance index, he established a $200 million venture fund to invest in African entrepreneurs. "Governance is the key," Ibrahim said. "I could buy a nice super yacht or airplane. But it is my duty. We are part of the fabric of Africa. This is money I made in Africa, and it is really their money."

But these investments in Africa are not merely charity. Ibrahim knows better than anyone the opportunities that might be hidden beneath the global perception. Africa is rising. "The environment for business in Africa is continuously improving," he said. "A large number of funds have now started working in Africa, and every week you hear about a new fund for Africa. Africa itself is trying to stop shooting itself in the foot. A civil society is developing in Africa. There is a new breed of young African people who have been educated in the best schools in the West. Many of them are coming back to do business in Africa. Things are happening. There is an energy there. You can touch it. Africa is open for business."

Patrick Awuah, a U.S.-educated Ghanaian native and former Microsoft engineer, also recognized the need to cultivate leadership. Awuah founded the Ashesi University to prepare future leaders in Africa. "I came to the conclusion that the most important reason Africa is in the shape it is in is because of a shortage of leadership," he said in a phone interview with the author. "If people like me don't become engaged, who else is going to do it?"[26] Former McKinsey consultant Fred Swaniker (also from Ghana) recognized this same need when he set up the African Leadership Academy for high school students in South Africa. "Societies are made or broken by relatively few individuals in those societies," Swaniker said in a May 2007 interview with the author, noting the positive impact Nelson Mandela and Desmond Tutu had on Africa, and the negative effect of other leaders. "We are identifying those people who can serve as change agents for Africa." With a similar impulse, Belgian NGO Echos Communication established the Harubuntu competition (from a Kirundi word meaning "there is value in this place") to recognize the "men and women who are driving Africa forward" by fostering projects that "foster hope and create wealth" (www.harubuntu.net).

# Africa's Rise: Hidden in Plain Sight

The rise of Africa is hidden in plain sight. It can be seen along the streets, and in the teeming aisles of retail stores such as Shoprite or Nakumatt. It is evident in the expanding airports and flight paths of Kenya Airways, Ethiopian Airlines, South African Airways, and many others (not to mention astute global carriers such as Virgin Nigeria).

It can be seen in the extraordinarily rapid growth of banking, cell phones, automobiles, and consumer goods. It is right there in plain sight as you walk through the streets of Africa, but you have to open your eyes to it.

This book is designed to open your eyes to the rise of Africa and the opportunities it presents. In Chapter 2, "Africa Is Richer Than You Think," we consider how Africa is richer than India, and more than a dozen African countries are richer in GNI per capita than China. The development of cell phones and banking are creating a platform for further growth. It is clear that these early developments are just the beginning. In country after country throughout Africa, I heard that the heart of the future opportunity in Africa is the middle of the market, which I call *Africa Two*. In Chapter 3, "The Power of Africa Two," we examine the opportunities presented by the more than 400 million people in Africa Two, as well as the significant and immediate opportunities of the premium segment (Africa One) and the low-income segment (Africa Three)—for companies with the right models.

With this context, we then turn our attention to some of the specific opportunities that are emerging with the rise of the African market and some of the characteristics of the market that might come as a surprise. In Chapter 4, "Harnessing the Hanouti: Opportunities in Organizing the Market," we examine how the African market is becoming increasingly organized, with transformations in retail, distribution, transportation, and other areas. Companies are building their African businesses by leading or using this process of organization. In Chapter 5, "Building Mama Habiba an Ice Factory: Opportunities in Infrastructure," we examine how the weaknesses in African infrastructure—including electricity, water, sanitation, and medicine—are actually sources of opportunities and how companies are building businesses around meeting these market needs.

Africa has one of the world's most youthful populations—and growing younger every day—creating a significant source of opportunity for products from school uniforms to diapers to education, as examined in Chapter 6, "Running with the Cheetah Generation: Opportunities in Africa's Youth Market." With the rise of Nollywood and other less-visible centers of entertainment and media across Africa, there are more opportunities for companies to get their messages out or to build businesses in media and entertainment, as considered in Chapter 7, "Hello to Nollywood: Opportunities in Media and Entertainment." In many areas, Africa is leapfrogging the West.

The African opportunity is bigger than the continent, with millions of Africans in the global diaspora sending billions of dollars into Africa, as well as bringing their experience and knowledge back home, as examined in Chapter 8, "Coming Home: Opportunities in the African Diaspora." Although the outflow of talented African professionals led to concerns about a "brain drain," this is another hidden driver of Africa's rise and growing wealth. Finally, the Conclusion looks forward to the opportunities ahead for Africa and how they can be realized.

# Inexplicable Optimism

It is perhaps no surprise that there is a sense of optimism across Africa, although this seems at first to be inexplicable if you follow the news headlines in the United States. A 2007 survey of ten sub-Saharan countries by the *New York Times* and the Pew Global Attitudes Project found that most Africans believe they are better off today than five years ago.[27] In Senegal, 56 percent felt they were better off compared to just 30 percent who felt they were worse off. In Nigeria, 53 percent felt they were better off, and in Kenya 54 percent. The respondents were also optimistic about the future. They obviously are not paying attention to the Western cable news reports on Africa. (In fact, in the same study, 71 percent of Ethiopians felt their country was not covered fairly in the international press.)

A study by McCann of optimism among 16 to 17 year olds in ten countries around the world found that many youth in developed countries such as the United Kingdom are jaded, but South African youth are among the most optimistic people in the world. A pan-African study by The Coca-Cola Company in March 2006 found this sense of optimism across African countries, although it might mean slightly different things in different regions. Across the board, optimism means self-belief and taking charge of your life.

"The paradox is that Nigeria is one of the toughest places in the world to live," Lolu Akinwunmi, CEO and managing director of Prima

Garnet Ogilvy ad agency, told me during a meeting in Lagos in 2006. "You have generators at home and have to provide your own water. You have walls that are 9 to 10 feet high with three Rottweilers and a security man. The traffic is terrible. In spite of all this, Nigerians are cheerful people. It is not unusual to see people out at night sitting in little groups over beers and pepper soup, unwinding from the stress of the day."

While those outside of Africa focus on the problems, there is a sense in many parts of Africa that nothing is impossible. Nigeria has announced plans to send a Nigerian to the moon by 2030. In 2007, Nigeria announced a plan that would make the country one of the world's top 20 economies by the year 2020, looking to Singapore as a model for transforming its economy. This is in a country that cannot provide reliable electricity to its population and where the average 2006 per capita income was just $640.

But if you doubt this could happen, consider that Chinese engineers helped Nigeria design, construct, and launch its first geostationary communications satellite, the $300 million Nigcomsat-1, in 2007. China provided financing for the project and the state-owned Chinese aerospace company, Great Wall Industry is tracking the satellite and training Nigerian engineers to staff a tracking station in Abuja. The satellite is expected to improve bandwidth for commercial customers and also support distance learning, online public access to government records, and online banking. South Africa constructed the largest telescope in the Southern Hemisphere in the little town of Southerland in 2005. Despite problems on the ground, Africa continues to look to the heavens.

As Matthew Barwell, marketing director of Africa region for Diageo, says, "The greatest export out of places like Nigeria is optimism." Some see this sense of optimism as a result of the fact that they have nowhere to go but up. Perhaps the best explanation of it was given by my driver in Lagos. Aptly named Moses, he was lost in the wilderness through most of our travels across the city, causing me to miss meetings. Yet he remained superbly self-confident about his knowledge of the route to the next location. When pressed, he admitted that in Nigeria you need to appear confident or the world will push you down. This optimism can also be seen in the platoons of unemployed who trudge through the endless traffic jams in Lagos with every product under the sun—from packs of gum and sodas, to appliances, carpets, and chairs. It is literally a department store on legs. Where there is no employment, people turn to trading. This optimism can also be seen in advertising focused on children and youth (for example, see the ad for Peak Milk in Exhibit 2). As the caption says, they believe "the future is waiting."

This is not wishful thinking. It could be a leading indicator. This optimism reflects a belief across the continent in Africa's rising opportunities. Africa is rolling up its sleeves to work on solving its own problems. This spirit can be seen in the work of community leaders such as Dr. Wangari Maathai, who became the first African woman to win the Nobel Peace Prize in 2004. She is among more than 16 recipients of Nobel Prizes from Africa (more than India or China), including 7 Peace Prize winners. After studying in the United States, Maathai returned to Kenya, where she earned her doctoral degree and founded the Green Belt Movement, which has mobilized women to plant more than 100 million trees across Kenya to prevent soil erosion and sparked a global campaign that reached its goal in November 2007 of planting a billion trees. (For more on her remarkable story, see her autobiography, *Unbowed: One Woman's Story*, and www.greenbelt-movement.com.) As she said in an interview with CNN after receiving the prize, "I really don't think that Americans will change their perception about Africans until Africans change their perceptions about themselves... what we really need is to encourage ourselves and rely on ourselves, because we have a lot of resources."[28]

Africa's optimism is shared by business leaders who have seen what they can accomplish in Africa. During a meeting at the Serena Hotel in Nairobi, James Mathenge, CEO of Magadi Soda in Kenya, said boldly, "I think the future of the world is Africa." Wearing a leather jacket and open shirt, sitting at a table by the poolside at the beautiful Serena Hotel in Nairobi, this statement was easy to believe. A tourist in a pink bathing cap floated by in the Olympic-size pool under the warm sun, as birds warbled in the foliage. This is the Africa the tourists on safari come to see as they pile into their Land Rovers every morning to head out to the bush.

The tourism business is not the African opportunity that Mathenge was looking at. His business was in the rural lands 80 miles (130 kilometers) to the south of Nairobi. Magadi Soda (now owned by Tata Group of India) makes soda ash that is used in glass, detergents, and other products. It exports around the world, especially Asia. When there were no roads and railroads to reach their sites, Magadi built them. When there were no schools and hospitals for employees, they created them. Then they opened these facilities to the surrounding community, the poor villages of the Masai tribesmen, devoting some 20 percent of after tax-revenue to community service projects. Mathenge is optimistic because he knows that with such extraordinary efforts, there is the potential for building very successful businesses in Africa. It is easy to agree with him that the future of the world is Africa.

## Rising Opportunities

- What opportunities are being created by the rise of Africa?
- What strategies will be needed to reach this potential market of more than 900 million people?
- What are the emerging market needs that can be met?
- How quickly will these markets emerge?
- What are the challenges facing the continent in its development?
- What are the opportunities in the diversity of the African continent?

# 2

# Africa Is Richer Than You Think

*Across the continent, Africa is richer than India on the basis of gross national income (GNI) per capita, and a dozen African countries have a higher GNI per capita than China. Rising investments from private equity and an active diaspora are expanding investments and opportunities. Communications, banking, and other drivers are creating the infrastructure for further development. Africa is richer than you think.*

Africa has some of the poorest nations in the world, but it is wealthier across the continent than India. The average gross national income per capita (GNIC) across all 53 African nations in 2006 was about $1,066, more than $200 above India's. As Exhibit 3 in the insert and Table 2-1 show, 12 African nations (with more than 100 million people among them) had GNICs that were greater than China's, and 20 nations (with a combined population of 269 million) had GNICs that were greater than India's. This concentration of wealth represents a huge potential market for companies worldwide. Of course, serving this market means overcoming the myriad economic, political, legal, medical, and social challenges facing the continent. However, entrepreneurial businesses across Africa have already proven that this is possible, feeding a fast-growing demand for every conceivable type of consumer good and service, from cell phones and banking to televisions and travel.

**TABLE 2-1    Africa Is Richer Than You Think**

| Country | GNI/Per Capita 2006 ($) |
| --- | --- |
| Seychelles | 8,650 |
| Equatorial Guinea | 8,250 |
| Libya | 7,380 |
| Botswana | 5,900 |
| Mauritius | 5,450 |
| South Africa | 5,390 |
| Gabon | 5,000 |
| Namibia | 3,230 |
| Algeria | 3,030 |
| Tunisia | 2,970 |
| Swaziland | 2,430 |
| Cape Verde | 2,130 |
| **China** | **2,010** |
| Angola | 1,980 |
| Morocco | 1,900 |
| Egypt | 1,350 |
| Cameroon | 1,080 |
| Djibouti | 1,060 |
| Lesotho | 1,030 |
| Congo, Rep. of | 950 |
| Côte d'Ivoire | 870 |
| **India** | **820** |
| Sudan | 810 |
| Sao Tome and Principe | 780 |
| Senegal | 750 |
| Mauritania | 740 |
| Comoros | 660 |
| Nigeria | 640 |
| Zambia | 630 |
| Kenya | 580 |
| Benin | 540 |
| Ghana | 520 |

**TABLE 2-1    Africa Is Richer Than You Think**

| Country | GNI/Per Capita 2006 ($) |
|---------|-------------------------|
| Chad | 480 |
| Burkina Faso | 460 |
| Mali | 440 |
| Guinea | 410 |
| Central African Rep. | 360 |
| Togo | 350 |
| Tanzania | 350 |
| Zimbabwe | 340 |
| Mozambique | 340 |
| Gambia, The | 310 |
| Uganda | 300 |
| Madagascar | 280 |
| Niger | 260 |
| Rwanda | 250 |
| Sierra Leone | 240 |
| Eritrea | 200 |
| Guinea Bissau | 190 |
| Ethiopia | 180 |
| Malawi | 170 |
| Liberia | 140 |
| Congo, Dem Rep. of | 130 |
| Burundi | 100 |
| Somalia | N/A |

Source: World Bank: http://siteresources.worldbank.org/DATASTATISTICS/Resources/GNIPC.pdf

# Meeting the Objections

Some might object that Africa cannot be analyzed simply based on GNI per capita. It is a continent wracked by brutal dictators, ravaging diseases, environmental crises, cultural and religious tensions, poor infrastructure, and countless other challenges. There are many objections to the idea that Africa presents a rising opportunity. First, Africa is seen as a collection of small countries, which makes it difficult to build critical mass. Second, the opportunities are seen as concentrated in South Africa and the north. Third, critics argue, the continent is filled with "sick states" that are threatening the stability of the entire continent. Consider each of these objections in turn.

## Africa Is Bigger Than You Think

Some object that Africa is a continent of small, separate countries, making it difficult to build the economies of scale needed for businesses. There are countries such as Nigeria (with 140 million people) that defy this description. The reality is that about two-thirds of African countries have populations greater than Singapore (more than 4 million), and all but 6 have populations greater than Cyprus (less than 1 million). If you can't afford to miss markets such as Singapore and Cyprus, can you afford to ignore African markets? And because some African nations share common languages, culture, or trade, small countries can sometimes be bundled together into larger regions (see Exhibit 4 in the insert). There are clusters of countries that create larger markets (see sidebar).

The Maghreb region in North Africa recognizes the region's common ties with France. With 75 million of the 100 million Africans in the region having direct or indirect ties to France, France announced an enhanced partnership with the Maghreb countries in March 2007 as a recognition of its common trade, human flows, language, and history.[1] This region represents about a ninth of Africa's population. French President Nicolas Sarkozy proposed a broader Mediterranean Union in 2008 between EU member states and 10 Mediterranean states. Regional organizations such as the five-nation East African Community (EAC) and the 14-nation Economic Community of West African States (ECOWAS) are gathering together countries to forge trade agreements and engage in other negotiations.

Companies in small countries look for opportunities outside their borders. For example, many of the business leaders I met in Tunisia, a country with about 10 million people, stressed the need to expand business into surrounding countries and Europe to grow. They are not waiting for government agreements.

Another objection is that many African countries are landlocked. This is a serious concern, but the real issue is whether the country has the infrastructure and agreements to gain access to major ports through other countries. Some states in India are landlocked but very productive. For example, the agricultural and industrial state of Punjab is landlocked but very well connected through infrastructure. Railroads enable one to go anywhere in India. The development of airlines and cell phones has helped to overcome some of the liabilities of being landlocked in Africa (see sidebar). For example, Zain, which acquired Celtel in 2005, serves 15 African countries, many of them in the interior, as shown in Exhibit 5 of the insert. Links to the coast are still vital to growth. Dr. Manu Chandaria, chairman of the Comcraft Group, which started in Kenya in the 1930s and has expanded to more than 11 countries, told me that better trains and other transportation systems are critical for growth in the interior. "Kenya is the doorway to a number of landlocked countries," he said. "Servicing these countries could be the largest business in Kenya." He notes that Kenya could use its infrastructure as a gateway in many ways, including shipping from the Mombasa Port, railroad and other transport channels, the Kenya oil pipeline, and Nairobi's airport.[2]

## Titus Naikuni: Africa and the World Meet in Nairobi

Wearing a Western silk tie and a beaded African belt, Titus Naikuni, managing director and CEO of Kenya Airways, stands at the intersection of worlds. During a meeting in his office near Nairobi's Jomo Kenyatta International Airport in July 2006, a poster above his desk proclaimed, "Africa and the world meet in Nairobi." On the opposite wall was a global map where he contemplated the next opportunities.

"The story to be told about Africa is not comprehensively understood," he said. "There are so many negative noises around us that the positive noises are lost in between."

Naikuni picked up one of the model jets that line his credenza. The aircraft showed the company's new logo with "The Pride of Africa" emblazoned along the fuselage, designed to capitalize on its African heritage and forge a pan-African strategy. Kenya Airways, building on the country's healthy tourist business and other enterprises, has made Nairobi one of Africa's de facto hubs.

Naikuni and other pioneers are not only changing the way the world thinks about Africa but also how Africa thinks about itself. "We have an obligation to open up Africa, but we have to do it profitably," he said. Kenya Airways opens two to three new destinations a year. They have pursued a local, regional, and pan-African strategy on the continent and have also connected sub-Saharan Africa to Europe, the Middle East, and Asia.

He noted that although some countries might be too small individually to support airline service, it is often possible to create clusters of related countries that define attractive markets. For example, he pointed to one group—Chad, Cameroon, Central African Republic, Gabon, Equatorial Guinea, Sao Tome and Principe, and Congo. According to his numbers, in July 2006 these countries had a combined population of 34.8 million, a desirable economic environment, and a stable political climate, common language, and culture. A flight to Cameroon could be the gateway to this entire cluster.

Between 2003 and 2006, Kenya Airways turnover increased from 27.46 billion Kenyan shillings to 52.80 (about $700 million). In a lackluster global industry, its shares in 2005–06 far outperformed British Airways, Lufthansa, and the Dow Jones Airline Index. Its profit after taxes went from 1.3 percent in 2003 to 9.2 percent in 2006, ahead of almost every rival.

Although local and regional differences remain intense, opportunities exist to build pan-African strategies, as demonstrated by cell phones and banking. For cell phones, interoperability across national borders is an advantage, as is scale. Celtel launched its One Network service that offered interoperability across 400 million people in 12

African countries by November 2007.[3] Customers can add airtime in their home currency and carry it across borders. This gives African customers something European cell phone users only dream about. The same holds true for banking, where companies such as Barclays have expanded their footprints across the continent.

### Africa Is More Than South and North

Are all the opportunities in South Africa and the various countries of North Africa? Egypt and other northern countries are a big part of the immediate African opportunity, as is South Africa at the opposite end of the continent. But the opportunities extend far beyond the northern and southern edges. Among the 12 countries richer than China, as shown in Exhibit 3, 10 are from sub-Saharan Africa, and among the 20 richer than India, 16 are from the south.

The 2006 list of the top 500 companies in Africa developed by Dr. Ayo Salami of African Business Research Ltd and reported in *African Business* magazine is neither concentrated in a single industry nor limited to one or two countries. Although South Africa and Egypt have the lion's share of top companies, some 16 different African nations are on the list. The top companies include mining, telecom, construction, banking, and consumer goods firms. The combined market value from the leading companies in each of these 16 countries equaled almost $89 billion. The African opportunity stretches across many sectors and spans the entire continent.

South Africa is not merely the leading economy in sub-Saharan Africa. It often serves the role in sub-Saharan Africa that Singapore has served in Asia (although other countries are vying for this gateway position by proclaiming themselves as future "Singapores," too). South Africa is the largest global foreign direct investor in Africa, led by Standard Bank. The country's stable economy and large market make it a gateway for companies to move to other parts of sub-Saharan Africa. To focus on South Africa as an anomaly is to miss its importance as a platform for the development of the rest of Africa. Paul Collier points out in *The Bottom Billion* that countries do better if their neighboring countries are doing well, so there is a halo effect for successful nations such as South Africa.[4]

## Sick States

Some object that the opportunities across Africa are uneven, with rapid progress in some countries and others in the dark ages. Africa is not homogeneous, but neither is China nor India—although their complexity is contained within a single nation. The nations of Africa range from basket cases and trouble spots to some of the fastest growing, most thriving economies in the world.

The situation is not so different in India. In fact, five or six states that account for about half the population of India are referred to as *bamaru*, or "sick," states. It is sometimes observed that if bamaru states were removed from India, GNI per capita would go up. A health survey by India's Ministry of Health found that child malnutrition levels in India's Uttar Pradesh (one of the bamaru states) was even higher than in sub-Saharan Africa (although this was later revised downward).[5] Every economy has its trouble spots, and the entire opportunity cannot be judged by the outliers.

## Real Challenges

This is not in any way to minimize the real challenges of doing business in Africa. Corruption is widespread, and business leaders I spoke with across Africa made a point of emphasizing that this is a serious challenge. Corruption in Nigeria alone has cost an estimated $400 billion since its independence in 1960.[6] There are other barriers to trade and investment. It takes much more time in most African countries to register companies and do business than in other places. Corrupt officials ask for a piece of the action. The situation appears to be getting better in country after country, but it is still not as simple to conduct business in Africa as it is to conduct business in the United States or Europe.

Companies also have to meet regulations in Africa for employment or partnerships with local enterprises, such as the Broad-Based Black Economic Empowerment (BBBEE) Act in South Africa. The BBBE has specific requirements for ownership, management, employment, skills development, procurement, enterprise development, and corporate social investment. Requirements for domestic production of products such as apparel and furniture, as well as restrictions on imports, can sometimes leave retailers without a supply of products for their shelves. Although noble in their goal of encouraging local entrepreneurship and building wealth, such rules create additional challenges for companies working in Africa.

It is important to recognize, however, that these same objections were raised about doing business in India or China a few decades ago. The obstacles that seemed insurmountable have somehow been surmounted. The process of business development encourages improvements in the political system. But the African market, like any developing market, is not for the faint of heart. It is for entrepreneurs and companies that recognize that where there are obstacles that might discourage others, there are opportunities for those who can persevere.

In some areas, government is encouraging the development of new enterprises. I heard from one of the leaders of the flower and vegetable export business in Ethiopia how government policies, from infrastructure support to tax considerations, are helping to grow the export industry there.

# The Magnifiers

The opportunity in Africa may, in fact, be greater than the numbers indicate. The snapshot of GNI per capita doesn't tell the whole story. The World Bank's African Development Indicators 2007 found that African economies overall were growing faster and steadier between 1995 and 2005 than the decade before. Growth rates, infusions of private equity, the informal economy, and the philanthropy and investments of a broad diaspora are all factors that magnify the potential of the more than 900 million people on the continent of Africa.

### Rapid Growth

The growth rates in Africa far outstrip those of developed markets, meaning that the future is even more promising for business there. As the World Bank concluded in its 2007 *African Development*

*Indicators*, "Many African economies appear to have turned the corner and moved to a path of faster and steadier economic growth."[7] Between 1997 and 2007, GDP growth across Africa rose from 3.5 percent to 6 percent, and inflation fell from 10.2 percent to 6.6 percent. Of the 50 countries in the entire world with the highest GDP growth rates in 2005, Angola was second (behind Azerbaijan). Other African countries with high growth rates include Equatorial Guinea, Liberia, Congo, Mozambique, Sierra Leone, and Nigeria. Combined together, more than 220 million Africans live in regions where GDP is growing at more than 6 percent.[8]

Demographics also bode well for Africa. Africa is one of the youngest markets in the world, with more than half its population under 24. Whereas Europe's population is expected to decline by 60 million people by 2050, Africa will add 900 million people, according to the Population Reference Bureau, roughly doubling its current population, although this rate of growth has raised concerns about the impact of overpopulation. In this period, the Democratic Republic of Congo, Egypt, and Uganda will join Nigeria and Ethiopia on the list of the top 15 most populous countries, according to the Population Reference Bureau.[9] With the fastest growing birthrates in the world, Africa is a continent that is growing younger every day. This creates opportunities in education, entertainment, sports, and youth-focused advertising. And it means that Africa will account for even more of the world's consumers in the future. While we are discussing the BRIC countries (Brazil, Russia, India, and China), shouldn't we also be focusing on the NEKS (pronounced "next") markets of Nigeria, Egypt, Kenya, and South Africa?

## Private Equity

Foreign direct investment (FDI) in Africa shot to about $39 billion in 2006, double the level 2004.[10] Private equity is flowing into the continent at record rates, a reflection of past successes and the positive assessment of future opportunities. There are about 200 private equity funds operating across Africa, with about $15 billion under management.[11] In 2008, South Africa for the first time was named as one of the top 25 global destinations for FDI.[12] The FDI is not just flowing into Egypt or South Africa. The top African destinations for

FDI in 2006, in descending order, were Egypt, Nigeria, Sudan, Tunisia, Morocco, Algeria, Libya, Equatorial Guinea, Chad, and Ghana.[13] In 2006, $377 million poured into Tanzania, $307 million into Uganda, and $290 million into Burundi. Investors raised more than $2 billion for sub-Saharan Africa alone in 2006 (almost as much as for Latin America and the Caribbean), according to the Emerging Markets Private Equity Association.[14] The returns are impressive.[15] Return on Equity in Nigeria, for example, is among the highest in the world, at 20 percent, and the top quartile of funds in South Africa is producing returns reported at 40 percent or more. From the success of initiatives such as Comafin in the 1990s came funds such as Zephyr Kingdom (United States), Actis (United Kingdom), Aureos Capital (United Kingdom), FMO (Holland), and Cordiant (Canada). In June 2007, the World Bank's International Finance Corporation unveiled a $320 million package to invest in mobile phones in sub-Saharan Africa, which was hailed as a sign of growing private-sector interest in the continent.

With more than $1 billion in capital under management, Emerging Capital Partners (ECP) is one of the largest private equity fund managers targeting Africa. ECP is managing a portfolio of five funds, including the $400 million AIG African Infrastructure Fund and $400 million EMP Africa Fund II, with over 40 investments in more than 30 countries throughout Africa as of 2007.

The African Development Bank Group has made total commitments of $53 billion in Africa, often using local banking partners to invest in small to midsize firms. Its investments helped to kick-start the development of Nigerian banking and propelled the growth of innovative companies such as K-Rep Bank, which is serving the unbanked in low-income and rural markets in Kenya.

Jag Johal, of CBA Capital Partners Limited in Johannesburg, who came to Africa from London in the 1990s, was surprised at the opportunities he found there. "Before I came here, the only images I saw of Africa were famine and wars," he said in an interview in Johannesburg. "I intended to be here two years, but then I saw the opportunities. Africa grows on you."

Several new funds were launched or expanded in 2007, including the creation of a $1.3 billion pan-African fund by Pamodzi Investment

Holdings in Johannesburg in August 2007. Development Partners International was launched with a target of raising $500 million. Satya, a private equity fund backed by Celtel founder Mo Ibrahim, raised $200 million in May 2007 and expected to increase the fund to $600 million in a year.[16] Renaissance Capital, building on its understanding of emerging markets in Russia, has made a major push into Africa, which it sees as the "new Russia." The company's research estimates that sub-Saharan African market capitalization will reach more than $241 billion by 2010, more than four times 2006 levels.[17] In April 2008, World Bank President Robert B. Zoellick called for government-owned sovereign wealth funds in Asia and the Middle East to invest 1 percent of their funds in Africa. This would mean an additional $30 billion for private investment in Africa.

"If you are invested in United States and Europe, it makes sense to be in Africa," said Barbara James, former managing director of the African Venture Capital Association (AVCA), in an interview with the author in August 2007. AVCA is a not-for-profit entity founded to develop and stimulate private equity and venture capital in Africa. (James took the leadership of Africa's first "fund of funds," the Henshaw Fund, when it was launched in 2007.) "If you look at the growth of different countries around the world, eight of the ten top-growing countries are African countries. Eight of the ten best performing stock markets are in Africa. These are hot spots you cannot ignore." She estimates that private equity in Africa will increase to $3 billion in five years. "It used to be that you'd have a tough time getting investors to talk about Africa, but I think that is changing now. Interest in Africa is still nowhere near the interest of China or India. But people who are looking for new opportunities, diversification, and countercyclical investment are beginning to see what is happening in Africa. They can't ignore it."

North Africa has strong connections to the Middle East, with countries such as Egypt having stronger ties to the Middle East than to sub-Saharan Africa. A common religion and history means that there are strong flows of people and resources between North Africa and the Arab world. For example, Dubai Holding is investing $14 billion in an 830-acre parcel on Lake Tunis in Tunisia, creating a location that is expected to attract 2,500 high-technology companies to the area. Dubai World has invested more than $800 million in the tiny East African country Djibouti to build a major port, hotel, and other infrastructure—in short, following the blueprint that has transformed Dubai into a major financial, tourism, and transportation hub. It is also investing in development in Rwanda. In Algeria, Emirates International Investment Company LLC has made a number of investments, including a 240-hectacre urban park aimed at halting desertification and conserving biodiversity. The park will be powered by a photovoltaic-wind system and include a center aimed at developing renewable energy. These ties continue today in a flow of immigrants from Africa to the Middle East. There are strong ties between Africa and Lebanon, with many Lebanese entrepreneurs active in forming businesses in Africa, especially in West Africa.

Private equity is allowing local successes to become multinationals. For example, the Sumaria Group started as a small trading company in Tanzania in 1957 and now has businesses that include pharmaceuticals, plastics, detergent, and dairy. Investments by Aureos Capital helped the company expand its businesses to Kenya, the Democratic Republic of Congo, Mozambique, and Uganda—making it one of Tanzania's first multinationals.

As noted in Chapter 1, "Baking Bread in Zimbabwe," investors are even flocking into areas such as Zimbabwe where the climate for investment seems pretty bleak. Others are now crowding into markets that once looked like money pits but are now attractive. Angola, swept by civil war and plagued by corruption since its independence in 1975, has suddenly become one of the hot destinations for businesses investing in Africa.[18] It has often been the faith and efforts of local entrepreneurs or expatriates that have demonstrated the potential of the market. Slim Othmani of NCA-Rouiba, a bottler of Coca-Cola beverages in Algeria, an amazing entrepreneur, helped attract investment from Tuninvest after organizing a private equity conference in 2005. This was a country in turmoil and economic decline that had looked attractive only to very brave investors or expatriates who believed in its future. Just a few years later, when I visited Slim in the fall of 2007, other investors were flocking into the market.

Financial markets outside of Africa are also recognizing the improved stability of the continent. For example, in January 2007, Nigeria's main commercial banks issued a five-year Eurobond worth $350 million at an interest rate of over 8%. This was the first time any

Nigerian institution, private or public, had approached the international capital markets since the early 1990s.[19] In late 2007, Gabon raised $1 billion on international markets through an offering of sovereign bonds, an indication of its stability and financial management.[20] As noted in Chapter 1, China and India have made significant commitments to the continent, too.

Still, the opportunities in Africa are not widely recognized, a secret that may have made raising funds for the continent more challenging in the past, but made investment opportunities less crowded. "For each person trying to do something in Africa, there are a thousand in India," said Runa Alam, who was then with Zephyr Kingdom when I spoke with her in late 2005 in Washington, D.C. (She later moved to head the new Development Partners International fund, founded by Miles Morland, who created one of the first African investment funds.) "People are excited about India, but I don't think the opportunities in Africa are much different."

### Informal Economy

Another reason the potential of Africa is often underestimated is the size of the informal economy—economic activities that fall outside of the economy regulated by formal economic and legal institutions—which means official numbers are often low. Runa Alam recalled that when Celtel opened its Congo office, it had low expectations. The country was in a war zone. The low GDP per capita seemed to make owning a cell phone an impossibility. The first day, however, they had to take the door of the office off the hinges because there was so much demand. They signed up 2,000 customers in the first week and 10,000 in the first month. All the customers paid cash.

Research by Friedrich Schneider concludes that the informal economy in Africa, on average, accounted for 42 percent of GDP in the years 1999/2000 (see Table 2-2). Zimbabwe, Tanzania, and Nigeria had more than half their economies in the informal sector, while South Africa had just 28.4 percent (below the 41 percent average for developing countries worldwide but still more than the 18 percent in developed countries). Because of the size of this informal economy in Africa, Schneider concluded that it is "more like a parallel economy."[21]

**TABLE 2-2   Shadow/Informal Economy**

| Africa: Shadow Economy in % of GNP 1999/2000 | |
|---|---|
| Zimbabwe | 59.4 |
| Tanzania | 58.3 |
| Nigeria | 57.9 |
| Zambia | 48.9 |
| Benin | 45.2 |
| Senegal | 43.2 |
| Uganda | 43.1 |
| Niger | 41.9 |
| Mali | 41.0 |
| Ethiopia | 40.3 |
| Malawi | 40.3 |
| Mozambique | 40.3 |
| Côte d'Ivoire | 39.9 |
| Madagascar | 39.6 |
| Burkina Faso | 38.4 |
| Ghana | 38.4 |
| Tunisia | 38.4 |
| Morocco | 36.4 |
| Egypt, Arab Rep. | 35.1 |
| Algeria | 34.1 |
| Botswana | 33.4 |
| Cameroon | 32.8 |
| South Africa | 28.4 |
| Average across African countries surveyed | 42.0 |

Source: Friedrich Schneider, "Size and Measurement of the Informal Economy in 110 Countries Around the World," presented at an Workshop of Australian National Tax Centre, ANU, Canberra, Australia, July 17, 2002

The informal economy also accounts for the lion's share of employment in Africa. The International Labour Office in Geneva estimated that 48 percent of nonagricultural employment in North Africa is in the informal economy, and 72 percent in sub-Saharan Africa (which rises to 78 percent if South Africa is excluded).[22] In rural areas, some estimates are that the informal sector accounts for as much as 90 percent of nonagricultural employment.[23]

In Egypt, where more than 30 percent of its GNP is in the informal economy, Minister Youssef Boutros-Ghali reduced the income tax in 2004 from as high as 40 percent to 20 percent to encourage people to declare more of their income. He was criticized by the International Monetary Fund and others for reducing the revenue base with such a drastic cut in taxes. But it paid off. Tax filings increased by nearly 50 percent, and revenues grew as a share of the GDP, despite the cuts. Egypt had expected the move to pay off in three years, but it took only one year. What appeared to happen was that with reduced taxes, more of the informal economy was declared.

There is much more to the African economy than is recognized in formal statistics. What are the opportunities to bring more of this informal economy into a formal economy by creating products and services that can compete?

## The Ricochet Economy: The African Opportunity Is Bigger Than the Continent

The GNI per capita of Africans within Africa is not the whole picture. Africa is also connected to a broad diaspora that is contributing to its future success. Dr. Titilola Banjoko, founder of AfricaRecruit, estimated that $44 billion is sent to Africa by immigrants abroad through formal and informal channels, in a 2007 conversation with the author. This is the equivalent of 5 percent of the total GNI of the continent. There may be as many as 100 million members of the African diaspora (if descendants of immigrants, including African Americans, are counted). They represent a significant force in Africa's rise. They are growing more significant every day as African nations create new channels for the diaspora to invest in Africa and educated Africans abroad come home to work, as we consider in more detail in Chapter 8, "Coming Home: Opportunities in the African Diaspora."

This "ricochet economy" (bouncing between the developed and developing world), as discussed in my book *The 86% Solution*, is driving growth in many parts of the developing world, including Africa. The ricochet economy is filling the gaps in countries facing political or economic unrest, and creating opportunities for direct investment and driving markets from tourism to hospitality to real estate. Unlike immigrants of earlier generations who cut their ties with their homelands when they immigrated, these new immigrants remain connected to their homelands. They are sending money home, making investments and contributing to charitable causes. The diaspora also creates a global market for African products. There is more to Africa than the more than 900 million Africans on the continent.

# Accelerants: Cell Phones and Banking

Finance and communications are the foundations for successful markets. The rapid growth of cell phones and banking across Africa is not only an indication of the success of these industries but also creates a platform for further growth. This can clearly be seen in the many small businesses that have been established by placing a cell phone and a microloan in the hands of industrious entrepreneurs. The growth of these two industries across Africa can help to propel further growth.

### Cell Phones

Consumers want to communicate—to connect with dispersed family members, build their businesses, or sell their crops. There are now more than 130 million Africans with cell phone subscriptions, and it is the fastest growing mobile phone market in the world. A 2007 study by the Africa Media Development Initiative found that cell phones were achieving a compound annual growth rate of 85 percent or more in 10 of the 17 African nations surveyed.[24] Because users share phones, the usage is higher than the subscription rate. The platform is there for more growth. More than 60 percent of the sub-Saharan population had access to network coverage by 2005, and this number is expected to rise to 85 percent by 2010, according to the GSM Association.[25] Major telecom companies are racing to sign up cellular subscribers across Africa and the Middle East in a market estimated at $25 billion by the end 2006. Market leader MTN of South Africa has operations in 21 African countries. Zain (formerly Celtel) grew to more than 20 million subscribers in more than 15 countries. The

Anglo-South African company Vodacom has more than 25 million subscribers in Africa. Egypt's Orascom has nearly 20 million subscribers in Africa and another 20 million in the Middle East (not surprising, given its strong connections to the region). Africa was expected to add another 184 million subscribers by the end of 2011.[26]

Although some global companies initially stayed away because of concerns about unrest, these difficult markets have proven to be very profitable. In fact, one Senegal mobile company told me they are sometimes embarrassed to release public reports on their earnings in a country where income is so low. It is an embarrassment of riches. The reason for their success was summed up by Orascom's chief executive Naguib Swiris in a *New York Times* interview: "Whether poor or rich, people still need to communicate."[27]

Nabil, a waiter at the Italian restaurant of the food court in the basement of the Grand Hyatt and its adjoining mall in Cairo, said one of the first things he did when he got his job there was to buy his three sisters cell phones. My driver in Lagos earned 18,000 naira per month, a little over $100. Yet he owned a cell phone (although he didn't always have enough money to buy a SIM card to make a call), and a television, which took him three months to save for. With rent of 3,000 naira per month (about $20), he and his family live in a small apartment where 16 families share 2 bathrooms and a single kitchen. But without finishing his high school education, he is fortunate to have a steady job. And as a driver, he needs to have a cell phone. Even in the informal developments on the outskirts of Soweto in South Africa, where there is no running water or sanitation, I saw men standing outside the doors of their cinder-block homes talking on cell phones. Before water, flush toilets, and even food and drink, communication takes priority.

Many more Africans who use cell phones don't show up in the official figures. The obvious example is the small booths where cell phone ladies charge by the call. But users also share private phones. In Senegal, I heard that it is common practice for people to buy a SIM card and use it in a friend's phone. My driver there had bought a used phone for about $5, so the cost of connecting is very low, particularly when one phone serves many.

Cell phones are an accelerant for the entire economy. Other businesses are being built upon these connections. For example, TradeNet, based in Accra, Ghana, created a free trading platform across a dozen countries in West Africa to allow farmers to buy and sell their agricultural products. Cell phones present new opportunities for getting marketing messages out. A 2005 study found that the economic impact of cell phones in developing countries may be twice as large as in developed countries. The study by Leonard Waverman, Meloria Meschi, and Melvyn Fuss concluded that an increase of 10 more mobile phones per 100 population in a developing country between 1996 and 2003 resulted in the equivalent of a .59 percent increase in GDP per capita.[28] The success of the cell phone industry could be viewed as the platform for more economic progress to come.

It might be easy through developed-world eyes to fail to see the meaning of the rise of cell phones in Africa. After all, cell phones in the West have been more of a novelty and business tool than a necessity. Consumers already have landlines. In Africa and other developing regions, cell phones are the first communications infrastructure in many areas, providing a foundation for small businesses, connecting rural areas to the world, spreading knowledge—in short, the bedrock of economic development.

## Banking

The top five African banks—Standard Bank Group, Absa Group (now part of Barclays), Nedbank Group, Investec, and FirstRand Banking Group—have capital of more than $17 billion and assets of more than $324 billion. In 2005, Barclays made its biggest investment outside of the United Kingdom and the largest foreign investment in South African history when it purchased a majority stake in Absa, the largest retail bank in the country, for 33 billion rand ($5.4 billion).[29] In October 2007, the Industrial & Commerce Bank of China Ltd. announced plans to spend $5.5 billion for a 20 percent stake in South Africa's Standard Bank, with operations in 18 African countries. But not all the activity is in South Africa, and many of these banks have moved north into other African countries. Barclays has built a network of banks across more than ten African countries, including Botswana,

Ghana, Kenya, Mauritius, Seychelles, Tanzania, Uganda, Zambia, Zimbabwe, and Egypt.

Some 28 African banks were included among UK-based *The Banker* magazine's 2006 list of the strongest 1,000 banks in the world, based on governance and other dimensions. These included institutions in South Africa, Nigeria, Egypt, and Morocco. In East Africa, Mauritius had the top two banks (Mauritius Commercial Bank Ltd. and State Bank of Mauritius Ltd.), which is no surprise given that it is among the wealthiest African nations, but there are major banks in even the poorest areas. Ethiopia boasted two banks among *African Business*'s 2007 ranking of the top 100 banks in Africa (Commercial Bank of Ethiopia, 52, and Bank of Abyssinia, 99). Banks are consolidating and implementing more rigorous policies, such as the promise by Nigeria's United Bank of Africa not to offer any more *wahala* (or "trouble") loans. Banks such as India's ICICI bank are also actively looking at this market. The coming of age of African banks can also be seen in the creation of the first African Banker Awards in 2007, honoring the continent's best banks and bankers at a ceremony at the Grand Hyatt in Washington, D.C.[30]

On a continent where only about 20 percent of families have bank accounts, institutions are beginning to draw in the unbanked. Innovators such as K-Rep in Kenya are leading the way in targeting rural and low-income customers, but mainstream banks are not far behind. Barclays is setting up its own small banks in rural Nairobi and working in Ghana with informal *susu* collectors (the country's oldest money collecting system). Standard Bank is supplying a remote branch on Uganda's Lake Victoria by dropping money by plane. Banks are creating pathways into banking for the unbanked. Within a year of the creation of low-cost Mzansi accounts in South Africa in October 2004, more than 1.5 million accounts had been opened. The accounts, named for the colloquial South African expression for "south," were offered by the country's four major retail banks (Absa, First National Bank, Nedbank, and Standard Bank) as well as Postbank. All that was required to open an account was a valid ID, and fees were low. The initiative, along with container branches in rural areas, was designed to bring the nation's 13 million unbanked South Africans into the system. It was meant to put an ATM within 6 miles (10 kilometers) of most South Africans and a full-service branch within about 10 miles

(15 kilometers). The banks added services such as low-cost money transfers and even insurance and collective investment products to attract new customers and enhance services. In discussions with Barclays in Egypt in 2006, I learned that fewer than 6 million people, or 1.2 million households, in a total population of 75 million, were considered bankable. The banks are all fishing in a very small pool, so expanding this pool is crucial.

Given the rapidly expanding penetration of cell phones and the relatively low penetration of banking and credit cards, African nations have been pioneers in moving banking to mobile devices. Prepaid minutes have become a form of currency. In markets where transferring cash is expensive, and exchange rates are volatile, minutes can be sent from phone to phone electronically. In 2005, only about 13.5 million South Africans had a bank account, whereas more than 20 million possessed cell phones. It made sense for leading cell phone provider MTN to launch MTN Banking in partnership with Standard Bank. Users could transfer money, pay bills, and buy mobile airtime from their handsets. This helped to offer banking services to a continent where many areas are without basic banking services. Uganda, for example, had just 100 automatic teller machines for a population of 27 million people in 2005.[31]

To facilitate secure telephone banking, the Union Bank of Cameroon piloted an innovative payment card, which has an acoustic chip that emits a signal at the press of a button. The user activates the sound before entering a PIN and engaging in transactions, including making remittances, paying utility bills, and transferring credit to other cards. Mobile banking, in effect, puts a branch into the hands of every individual with a cell phone. As Jenny Hoffman, chief executive of MTN Banking, told the *Financial Times*, "Our lack of infrastructure makes us leap for everything."

# Does Africa Exist?

While recognizing that markets across Africa have much in common, as noted above, we cannot gloss over their differences. There is tremendous diversity of economic, political, and social conditions in the 53 nations that make up this huge continent, as I discovered when I bought a Celtel SIM card for my phone in the Nairobi airport. I complimented the representative on the beautiful advertising on the package featuring a pair of smiling models holding a cell phone. She made a face. When I asked why, she explained that these models were not Kenyan. They were Nigerian. She didn't consider them African. Although Celtel's slogan in its advertising was "The African Dream," this dream means something different to people in different parts of Africa. To the woman at the counter at Nairobi airport, "African" meant Kenyan.

Although there are opportunities across Africa, they often are realized locally. Celtel's "African Dream" was beaten out by rival Safaricom's local approach (starting with its use of the local Swahili word *safari*, which means "travel," in its name). Yet, in spite of the reaction of the sales representative to the advertising, Celtel offers an example of a company that has created a successful pan-African strategy, as discussed earlier in this chapter.

Companies ignore this sense of national identity at their peril. SABMiller's South African beer Castle learned this lesson the hard way when it tried to enter Kenya, only to be blocked by Tusker beer from East African Breweries Limited. With its black-and-yellow elephant emblem and the slogan "My Country, My Beer," Tusker appealed to the fierce nationalism that is often evident throughout Africa, particularly in Kenya. Tusker stampeded over Castle with such force that the foreign beer was pretty much drummed out of the market. In fact, Tusker maker East African Breweries Limited took over marketing SABMiller brands in Kenya. SABMiller is one of the most sophisticated beer makers in the world, and Castle beer is one of most recognized African brands in global markets. Still it was trampled by the local Tusker elephant.

Local companies such as Société Nouvelle des Boissons Gazeuses (SNBG) in Tunisia or Hamoud in Algeria have shown that they can hold their own against multinational rivals such as Coca-Cola and Pepsi. SNBG, founded by entrepreneur Habib Bouaziz, has the dominant market share in juices and waters in Tunisia. Its local presence allows it to be responsive to local markets. It took its name for its bottled water, Furat, from a popular boy's name, recognizing that most other brands had girls' names. When popular Egyptian singer Om Kolthoum was called a "diva" by the local media, SNBG took "Diva" as the brand for its juices. It even uses temporary names to capitalize on fads and sentiments of local markets.

Similarly, Hamoud, founded in 1878, is among Algeria's oldest companies. (They joke that the company is one of the few things that outlasted French rule.) Hamoud has also tailored its juices and sodas to the local market, with popular names such as Selecto, Hamoud, and Slim. Bottlers of Coca-Cola beverages in Algeria such as Fruital (majority owned by COBEGA, S.A., in Spain) are rethinking their strategies to compete with Hamoud.

Choices between local and global brands are often quite complex. When I asked Henrietta Enumah, the attendant at the Air France lounge in the Lagos airport, about cosmetics choices, she said she preferred African herbal cosmetics and natural shampoo, or Duduosu soap made from trees and leaves that sells in a large bar for 100 naira (about 85 cents). Yet she buys European skin products such as Sunsilk shampoo from Ghana, which sells for 150 naira (about $1.25) for a small bottle. When it comes to perfume, however, she turned to Saudi Arabian scents such as Rufai, which is 200 naira (about $1.70) for a tiny bottle, and she also liked CoverGirl lipsticks from the United States. As in other markets, consumers combine local and global brands.

Just as it does not make sense to talk about an Asian market, or even an Indian, Chinese, or U.S. market, we need to be aware that discussing the African market covers up a multitude of complexities. This is also true with India, where its billion plus people are under one flag, but their distinctions at times far outweigh their commonalities in language, food, festivals, and other areas.

Despite the differences, African nations share many common experiences. As journalist Martin Meredith noted in *The Fate of Africa*, "Although Africa is a continent of great diversity, African states have much in common, not only their origins as territories, but the similar hazards and difficulties they have faced."[32] Although the differences across Africa need to be recognized, consumer markets are concerned with what is basic and universal. They address fundamental human needs for health, food, water, clothing, shelter, transportation, communication, caring for family, and having a feeling of well-being.

These basic needs and desires have been the foundation for building markets in every culture around the world.

## Diversity and Tolerance

About a third of the world's Muslim population is in Africa (see Exhibit 6 on page 4 of the insert), but everywhere I went in Africa, I had no trouble finding signs of tremendous diversity, from Hindu temples, to Christian churches of many different denominations, to Muslim mosques, to Jewish synagogues. Across Africa, Christianity dominates in 19 African nations, Islam in 13, and Hinduism in 1 (Mauritius, where people of Indian descent make up 60 percent of the population). The religious map continues to change. The rise of Pentecostalism is changing the face of African religion, with more than 15 percent of Kenyans now attending Pentecostal churches. A 2006 visit by American preacher T. D. Jakes, for example, packed nearly 1 million people into the Uhuru Park in Nairobi.[33]

The implications of these beliefs are important to understand. Outside Cairo, a cylindrical glass elevator runs through the center of the broad atrium of the five-story Star Centre Mall in the new upscale community of Star City. The mall, built by Saudi developer Abdul Rehman Al-Sharbati, could be anywhere in the world, packed with brands such as Guess, Diesel, and Ocean Pacific. But this is not your typical shopping mall. Walk into the Nike store on the fourth floor and you see the expected rows of athletic shoes, running up to more than $100 per pair (629 LE). But this could not be mistaken for a U.S. store. There is no Western music in the background. Instead, every day from 11 a.m. to noon, the music has been replaced with chanting of verses from the Koran. When I visited the Carrefour in Algiers, Algeria, in 2007, traditional Saudi Arabian *shabi* music was playing in the background.

Religion has a direct impact on business. Easter on its own accounts for 1 percent of annual sales by SABMiller in South Africa. "After the tears" ceremonies in South Africa, a big social event after a funeral, can be an occasion where Coca-Cola beverages are served and sometimes donated. Ramadan is the prime shopping season in Morocco and other parts of northern Africa (although retailers often take advantage of discounting to stockpile). In Morocco, 40 percent of desserts are sold around Ramadan. (The impact shouldn't be over-rated because the holiday season includes four to five weeks before and a couple of weeks after that actual period of fasting, a total of two to three months.) During Ramadan, Procter & Gamble releases a special scent for its Tide detergent, Musk Ramadan.

Banks in Kenya, Nigeria, and South Africa have introduced *sharia*-compliant Islamic banking, including targeting Muslim customers who were previously unbanked. Egyptian cell phone company MobilNil says to "stay close" while doing Haj, and it offers lower roaming charges during Haj time. Other mobile companies offer "Ramadan *kareem*" free minutes. (Tunisie Telecom tried offering free minutes during Ramadan but had to cancel the promotion because the network was overloaded.) In South Africa, Leaf Technologies created text services that not only transmit sports scores but also "daily bread" prayers for Christian subscribers. In Egypt, Morocco, northern Nigeria, and other countries with large Muslim populations, The Coca-Cola Company distributes meals or snacks to people returning home to break their fast during Ramadan. (This was tried in Tunisia, but was unpopular because the authorities felt it was their responsibility to feed the people. Coca-Cola supported children's education there instead. This shows that even among Muslim countries, the strategy that works in one country might not translate to another.)

Immediately after Ramadan, Egyptians flood into the movie theaters. This period is second only to the summer months in movie box office revenues, contributing about $13 million (70 million Egyptian pounds) of a total $46 million (250 million Egyptian pounds) for the year. Although traditionalist may shake their heads, television stations also gear up for Ramadan. More than ten television dramas staring famous Egyptian actors were developed for the Ramadan period in September 2006. The programs featured stars such as Mervat Amin, Ilham Shaheen, Dalal Abdel Aziz, Laila Eloui, Nadia El Guindy, Fifi Abdou, Samira Ahmed, and Shereen Seif El-Nasr. These are decidedly secular, with divorce, money, and marriage as prominent themes. The French-speaking countries of northern Africa, although Muslim, are winning international awards for their wines. Photos of American rapper Tupac Shakur hang in the market stalls of Dakar, Senegal (a Muslim country), where many local rap groups wear the same t-shirts and baseball caps as their American role models. Rap and hip-hop are musical traditions that can be traced back to West Africa centuries earlier, spoken-word music that came across on the slave ships, and now have returned home in a different form.[34]

### Headscarves and Shampoo

There are also less-direct impacts of religion. For example, what is the impact of Muslim headscarves on shampoo sales? A P&G manager in Cairo told me that the volume of shampoo sold in Egypt, with a population of 70 million people, is about the same as the volume sold to the 4 million people in Lebanon. Headscarves may be part of the reason. Because 87 percent of the potential market of 19 million women in Egypt wear headscarves, just less than 4 million have their heads uncovered. The shampoo companies are primarily competing for this small market of unveiled women, primarily Christians.

Modernization might not change this situation. Although Egyptian women want equality, they are also wearing traditional headscarves in greater numbers. A Gallup Poll across 22 predominantly Muslim countries found that the majority of women think they should have the same rights as men, *but also* that Islam's *shariah* law should be the source of national laws. The *hijab* head coverings used to be scorned by upper classes but now are donned even by the most educated women and Western-leaning Egyptian movie stars when they step offscreen.[35]

But veils create other needs. The silk or synthetic veils don't breathe and can lead to rashes, odor, and hair loss. In an attempt to reach this audience, one local Egyptian brand started advertising that its shampoo allowed women's hair to breathe. Pantene launched a campaign for a stronger Pantene with less hair loss. (One puzzle is that Saudi shampoo sales are still strong, perhaps because women tend to live in protected camps where they can walk without veils.)

In addition to consumer products, Muslim consumers in African markets also create opportunities for other products and services, such as Islamic banking. For example, Barclays in Kenya launched an Islamic bank account called a Riba, meaning "no interest," and ABSA set up an Islamic banking division in South Africa in 2006.

As these examples illustrate, there are complex implications of religion and other social differences for business across Africa. Companies need to understand these differences and tailor their products and marketing to the local market, but also need to realize that every large market has similar complexities.

# Beyond the Numbers

From the outside, Africa seems to be a dangerous place. When I was planning my trip to South Africa, my hosts from a major Western corporation suggested a driver who was also a bodyguard and who could administer first aid. A bodyguard? This was clearly a dangerous place. I figured that the Indian and Chinese companies could not do business in this way in Africa. I contacted some of these Asian firms, and through them I found a wonderful driver and car, without the bodyguard.

Of course, this is not to dismiss the true dangers. One night returning from a dinner interview on Victoria Island outside of Lagos, my editor and I were pulled over on an expressway by some young men in police uniforms holding automatic weapons. Our local Nigerian driver rolled down the window. One young man saluted a few times, expecting to receive some kind of payment, but he didn't know quite what to make of an Indian professor talking on his cell phone and my Anglo editor tapping on a laptop in the backseat. We drove off before he sorted it out. Almost every hotel I stayed at throughout Africa had security checks at the gate with mirrors run underneath the car or bomb-sniffing dogs making their rounds before I could enter. While I was in a relatively protected part of Africa through most of my travels, I also stopped to walk through the local markets and even high-density areas, but always with local guides.

Yet my first impression of the continent from the offer of a car with a driver who could serve as a bodyguard and medic was that this was a place of tremendous danger. Although the dangers are there, what is most striking about Africa are actually the opportunities. Perhaps what I needed was not a bodyguard but an investment banker. The signs of the development of the African market are everywhere.

The signs of Africa rising are apparent from almost every measure: GNI per capita, total GNI, improving business conditions, high growth rates, and rising investments. But the numbers tell only part of the story. Sometimes one photo can say more about the development of a market than a table full of statistics. In this case, a picture is worth a thousand words. Consider the photo from Kenya in Exhibit 7 (in the insert), which Richard Ponsford of Unilever shared with me shortly after my visit there. It is a woman from East Africa holding a packet of Omo detergent in her traditional home.

Reaching this market means having the right products—an expensive, large box of detergent wouldn't work here. With the right product at the right price, there is a very attractive market in Africa. There are few areas of Africa that have not been reached by commerce, and the spread of cell phones has taken the world's most sophisticated communications to the most primitive villages. Banking is going everywhere. Growth is rapid, and incomes are rising. Africa is a continent of tremendous potential. It has growing consumer markets, particularly in the middle of the market, as we consider in the next chapter. It is richer than you think.

# Rising Opportunities

- Given the relative attractiveness of the African market, are you giving it enough attention?
- How does your strategy in Africa compare with your strategies in China or India?
- How can you tap into the informal market to identify ways to create formal businesses?
- What opportunities are created by the development of cell phones and banking?

# 3

## The Power of Africa Two

*Significant opportunities abound today across diverse segments of the African market—from the elite shopping malls to the poorest rural village. And at the center of the African opportunity is Africa Two, some 400 million strong, a huge market waiting to happen.*

In almost every country where I traveled in Africa, companies divided the market into five segments (A, B, C, D, and E) based on income and other indicators, as is a common practice in other parts of the world. The exact definitions of these segments varied from country to country, and the percentages allotted to each segment varied somewhat, too, but the overall picture was the same. Most of the early focus in the market, particularly by global firms, was on the A and B class, or Africa One, who have the most disposable income and behave the most like elite segments in other global markets. This was the low-hanging fruit of the African market. However, these segments account for maybe 50 to 150 million people across Africa (see Table 3-1).

**TABLE 3-1  The Potential of Africa Two**

| Segment | Percentage of Market | Estimated Population Across Africa |
|---------|----------------------|-------------------------------------|
| Africa One | 5% to 15% | 50–150 million |
| Africa Two | 35% to 50% | 350–500 million |
| Africa Three | 50% to 60% | 500–600 million |

In contrast, the C class (Africa Two) represents about 350 million to 500 million people across the continent. It is comparable to similar segments in India or China, where there is great interest in tapping into this future middle class. (Chinese and Indian companies, who are attuned to this opportunity at home, are racing into Africa with products that appeal to this segment, as discussed later in this chapter.) The rest of the market, D and E segments (Africa Three), have their own opportunities, as explored further in this chapter.

Members of Africa Two are aspiring to a better standard of living and are upwardly mobile. They are educating their children. They are purchasing consumer products. They will be the future elite. In short, they are the future of the African market. The companies that appeal to Africa Two are connecting with rising of the market. This segment can be seen in the customers shopping in Edgars or Woolworths in South Africa, or taking advantage of the bargains on children's clothing in the Pep Stores. They are buying Chinese-made televisions and refrigerators, and are the drivers of the success of cell phone companies throughout Africa. They can be seen in the jostling crowds picking through the discount bins in the Carrefour outside Cairo, which is located in a mall primarily focused on upscale (A and B) segments. In Tunisia, I heard that going to Carrefour was like a trip to France without a visa—the experience of international travel for customers who might still find actual European travel out of reach. (Of course, this French store also sells camel and horse meat, so it is not a strictly European experience.)

## Meet Africa Two

My 55-year-old driver in Nairobi, from the Masai tribe, provides an example of this segment. He had taken retirement five years earlier as a government driver and went into private service. He earns about 15,000 Kenyan shillings a month (about $200), in addition to his pension and tips. Yet he and his wife still have managed to support three daughters living in Nairobi, paying for their education and purchasing cell phones for the two eldest. They have also sent their youngest son to a boarding school in the Kenyan upcountry.

His wife is a primary school teacher at their hometown in the Nyeri District, earning about 12,000 shillings ($180) per month, and also supplements their income with farming their 3 acres of freehold land with maize (corn) and beans. She sells milk from their 2 cows to a co-operative. They both have cell phones, although he limits the minutes on his Motorola phone, which he purchased for 5,000 shillings (about $75), to 1,000 shillings ($15) per month. He goes home for a three-day weekend to see his wife once every two weeks, taking a five-hour *matatu* (minibus) ride.

He lives very simply in an apartment in Nairobi, where he pays 7,000 shillings ($100) monthly for rent, which gives him a room with a small kitchen and private bath. Sometimes he shops at the Nakumatt supermarket (see sidebar), a Western-style supermarket created in Kenya that we discuss later in this book, but usually he shops in the local kiosks. He listens to a portable radio that he purchased for about 2,000 shillings ($30), using batteries that he replaces about once a month. He has electricity, and for the past few years it has even been fairly reliable.

## A Typical Shopping Basket

In the Nakumatt Thikaroad supermarket, my driver in Kenya walks through the aisles pointing out some of the products he buys. These include 2-kilogram (4.5 lb.) bags of Mother's Choice maize for 54 shillings (80 cents). He might buy rice for 130 to 170 shillings (about $2) for a 2-kilo (1 lb.) package, although he is more likely to scoop it out in the local kiosk or larger *duka* (a shop in Swahili) in smaller quantities. Although he usually drinks water, he also sometimes buys a 500-milliliter (17 oz.) bottle of Coca-Cola for 25 shillings (40 cents). He puts milk in his tea, so he buys a triangular package of Tuzo fresh milk for 28 shillings (less than 40 cents) for 500ml. Because he has no refrigeration, he consumes the milk with his morning and evening tea. Finally, he needs to buy batteries for his radio, which retail for 55 shillings (80 cents) for a two-battery pack. (He only needs one battery.) And occasionally, he buys a can of Kiwi shoe polish for 95 shillings ($1.40).

His biggest investment is in supporting and educating his three daughters who are living and studying in Nairobi at a cost of 15,000 shillings ($225) per month for the three of them. His oldest daughter is studying motel management, hoping to find a career in the expanding hospitality sector. Each month, he also pays about 200 shillings ($3) in tax, not to mention VAT (Value Added Tax) on purchases. His wife has a television, although she has no electricity. They took a loan from their village cooperative to buy a 40,000 shilling ($600) solar panel to generate enough electricity to provide power to their three-bedroom home, which they own. This keeps the television on for a few hours a day.

Here is a family of six with two separate addresses, and private schooling, living on about 27,000 shillings (about $400) per month, plus tips and pension. They work very hard. They are lucky to own their land in the upcountry and have steady jobs. On the surface, however, their income would not appear to be enough to support a family of six, let alone represent an attractive consumer segment. Yet they are paying for food, education, several cell phones, television, and solar panels. This is a huge opportunity that is virtually invisible from economic analysis at 30,000 feet. But many companies on the ground in Africa are seeing the potential of Africa Two and are moving to capture it.

As a younger example of Africa Two, my driver in Tunis was a third-year computer science student at the University of Tunis. Both his parents are teachers who worked hard to ensure their children received a good education. His sister is a medical doctor (education is almost free there) and owns a Ford Fiesta that she had bought on installments. Another sibling is an engineer. They live in a suburb outside of Tunis. When asked whether his family is "middle class," he replied, "No, we are *reaching* middle class." He explained that the market divides into "people who can buy and people who can't buy." This perhaps best describes the position of Africa Two. They are people who can buy.

# The Sweet Spot of the African Market

India has a similar market structure, and Indian businesses have found that they need different approaches to address this segment. Kishore Biyani, founder of India's largest retailer, Pantaloon Retail

(India) Ltd., in fact, divides that market into three segments. India One, representing about 14 percent of the market, is the elite (A and B segment). His business focuses on India Two (the C segment): the drivers, maids, and nannies who work for India One. This is roughly 55 percent of the market, or about 550 million people. India Three is the rest of the nation (segments D and E).[1]

In targeting India Two, Biyani discovered that he needed to rethink his business. Customers in this segment were turned away by the neat and orderly aisles seen in retail stores in developed markets. Instead, they wanted the crowded chaos of an informal market. He created a store that felt cluttered and cramped, with produce covered in dust, which signified freshness to customers. In fact, he spent $50,000 transforming one of his original shining, Western-style stores in Mumbai into a chaotic marketplace. He has shown that the formula for success might look nothing like the one that is successful in the West. Using this India Two formula, he had built a $600 million business by mid-2007.

What do retailers and other businesses in Africa need to do to redesign their offerings to appeal to this segment? Do they need to set aside models designed for developed markets or the elite consumers of Africa One and perhaps move to more chaotic models such as Biyani used with great success in India?

Africa Two is growing rapidly in wealth and influence.[2] Companies that can create products targeted toward these consumers and rise with them are positioned to create major businesses in Africa. With aspirations outpacing income, Africa Two is already beginning to consume products originally targeted for Africa One.

Companies across Africa are recognizing that Africa Two is their future. My meeting with Ferid Ben Tanfous of Arab Tunisian Bank (ATB) in Tunisia was typical. He explained that competition is very tough for the 4 percent to 10 percent of the population in Africa One, so he is focusing more attention on the 30 percent to 40 percent in Africa Two. Whereas Africa One customers may jump from bank to bank, Africa Two customers are much more loyal. The bank is building a reputation as a youth bank, offering products appropriate to this market and expanding its ATM networks. "The future of Tunisia is in the C class [Africa Two]," he said.

# Opportunities in Africa Two

In mid-2007, while the U.S. mortgage industry was in meltdown, a pilot housing project in Zambia was offering homes and financing to local residents. The 3,700 suburban-home development called Lilayi Housing Estate in Lusaka, Zambia, was supported by the U.S.-based Overseas Private Investment Corporation, which is also financing housing in Kenya and Ghana.[3] Helios Investment Funds created a $300 million fund aimed at companies that target the housing market. The development of mortgage markets across Africa is a reflection of the Africa Two opportunity. Banks are starting to offer credit cards, consumer loans, and mortgages; and other companies are offering services such as air travel, hotels, and financial services targeted toward this segment. Companies are creating products from retail stores to newspapers to laundry detergents for this segment. Let us examine a few of them.

## The Good Old Days

To understand the potential of this market, consider the experiences of a single company in moving from the elite markets of Africa One to the broader markets of Africa Two. Although set in Egypt, it is a typical story of market development that I heard many times in conversations across the continent. The Mansour Group, one of the biggest private sector groups in the Middle East, initially focused on A/B consumers with its successful upscale Metro supermarkets, launched in Egypt in 1998. Because the company's early executives were former Tesco managers, it was modeled after the U.K. chain. The business was very successful, but Mansour's leaders realized that with 25 stores and a footprint confined primarily to elite urban locations, there was a limit to how much the high-end Metro markets could grow. They could at most hope to reach only about 10 percent of the market.

In June 2006, Mansour launched its first discount store, called *Kheir Zaman* ("The Good Old Days") primarily targeting Africa Two consumers (see Exhibit 8 in the insert). The store sells locally manufactured products (including those under international brands). Although the stores are smaller and slightly less profitable than Metro, the market potential is much larger. By July 2006, its three stores were serving nearly 5,000 customers per day. The stores were on track to reach sales of 36 million Egyptian pounds ($6 million) for the year. By 2007, Mansour expected to have 20 stores and add 10 per year after that. While Whitney Houston played in a Metro store I visited, appealing to elite sentiments, the Kheir Zaman stores I visited played Arabic music. And although "The Good Old Days" might seem to be an odd name for a store anywhere Africa, given its complex history, the new chain of discount stores appeals not only to nostalgia but also to the most significant market segment to emerge across Africa.

## Raising the Roof

Aspirations for better homes mean demand for roofing for Mabati Rolling, part of the ComCraft Group, and this demand has carried the company from a small Kenyan start-up to the largest company in Kenya in the metal sector. Its sales of *mabati*, the Swahili word for the rolled metal roofing it produces, account for $100 million of the $180 million market for the product in Kenya.

Four-fifths of its sales come from Africa Two and Africa Three. These villagers move from a thatched roof to a rolled steel roof. A villager in Kenya might purchase the 20 or 30 mabati roofing sheets needed for an average home a sheet or two at a time, carrying them home on the top of a bus. This way, without credit, they can buy a $200 roof (15,000–20,000 Kenyan shillings) over time. Sometimes these homes are built one room at a time, starting with a single 100-square-foot room with an outside kitchen.

The homeowner who already has mabati roofing might dream of a colored roof or one that simulates a tile roof. The homeowner who already has a high-end mabati roof might be looking toward tile or a bigger home. Mabati Rolling has continued to roll out products for all segments of the market. In addition to its basic galvanized steel roof, it offered superior roofs made of zinc and aluminum, colored roofs, and metal roofing simulating clay tiles for upscale customers. Mabati built customer service centers in large cities to help assist in planning. The company introduced a new technology called ZARS in 2006, offering four times the life and better wear. It was promoted by high-tech "aliens" in space suits who crisscrossed the country by camel and other conveyances to build awareness and emphasize the high-tech quality of the product.

Mabati also exports metal products to about 50 countries around the world, including 25 in sub-Saharan Africa. Only half its revenues come from Kenya. It continues to grow by serving Africa Two.

All the houses being built and financed in Africa need to be painted, which is good for SCIB Paints in Egypt. Since it was acquired by Asian Paints of India at the end 2002, SCIB quadrupled its sales every year for four years to become the fourth largest company in the Egyptian paint market, one of the largest in the Middle East or Africa.

When I met A. S. Sundaresan in September 2006, who was chief executive at that time, he told me that they have been very successful in tailoring products for the Egyptian market. With its own development team in Egypt, it has launched seven or eight new products every year. These include very successful products such as a stain-resistant paint and decorative-effect finishes that have metallic and marble effects. While the company's cheapest paint sells for just 1.5 Egyptian pounds per liter (about 25 cents per quart), its stain-resistant paint sells for more than 10 times more, and its metallic finishes sell for about 70 times as much. In spite of the expense, these have become fast-growing new products, and the company has been successful in demonstrating value to customers. Egypt has become the leader in technology for developing these finishes across Asian Paints, with business in more than 22 countries.

Young men in Egypt cannot get married until they have a home to provide their bride, so homeownership is a point of pride. Egyptians are willing to invest in beautifying their homes. SCIB sells paint across demographic categories, from the high-end markets such as Zamelak where it offers showrooms with computerized tinting of paints to the shops of the high-density areas such as Inbaba, Warra, and Shoubra. In rural areas, customers are willing to pay extra for durability. While Asian Paints promotes its product with a lifestyle message in India ("Celebrate with Asian paints"), the appeal of SCIB is much more practical in Egypt, with a tagline that "SCIB Paints endure." While the company is only in Egypt now, there are strong potential markets in South Africa, Kenya, Nigeria, Algeria, and Sudan.

## Personal-Care Products

Two decades ago in South Africa, Unilever was primarily selling basics such as laundry powder, soap, and margarine. Now, an increasing percentage of sales is in personal-care products such as Sunsilk shampoo, Ponds facial cream, deodorants, and fine fragrances. These products targeted for Africa Two are driving double-digit growth. Retailers are also devoting more shelf space to African hair products, such as relaxants, rather than Caucasian hair products, an indication of the increased spending power of the Black Diamond consumers (discussed in Chapter 1, "Baking Bread in Zimbabwe") and other black South Africans.

I discovered in my conversations, however, that most of the shampoo in Nigeria and other parts of sub-Saharan Africa is sold through hair salons. Those who cannot afford the salons have their hair done on the streets. But most shampoo is not sold at retail. This is a serious distribution challenge for brands hoping to build markets by distributing their products through traditional retail channels.

## A $20 Washing Machine

Just as Indian retailer Biyani realized he needed to clutter up his stores to appeal to India Two, other companies have had to recognize how this segment in Africa is different. For example, in selling laundry detergents in Egypt, Procter & Gamble needed to recognize that the typical Egyptian washing machine might not be sold by a global manufacturer. Although European and Korean appliance companies in Egypt are offering washing machines and dryers, many low-income residents use semiautomatic washing machines made out of old barrels by local manufacturers (see Exhibit 9). They retail for the equivalent of $20 and are made from motors and iron leftovers. A company selling detergents in Egypt has to realize that it is going into a washer like this.

But this also raises another question: Is there a market for a very inexpensive washing machine in Egypt and other parts of Africa? If a local company can offer a machine at this price point, why couldn't a branded manufacturer? Low-cost Chinese televisions, CDs, and appliances are already expanding in Africa. It may be only a matter of time before a brand emerges to compete with these machines. There is probably already a company working on this, most likely from China or India. This branded, inexpensive washing machine could open the market for Africa Two and even lower-income segments.

Fashion retailers are moving into Africa, too, targeting consumers from Africa Two and even Africa One (because companies often have a more upscale image in the developing world). By late 2007, Zara had opened three clothing stores in Morocco and one in Tunisia. Mango had a store in the same mall as Carrefour in Tunis. Benetton had eight stores in Tunisia, one in Morocco, two in Egypt, and one in Libya. In South Africa, the Woolworths I visited in Johannesburg offered moderate luxury with a café and upscale marketplace, and leather jackets priced at up to about 800 rand ($120).

## Opportunities at Every Level

Whereas Africa Two may be the greatest opportunity in Africa, it is certainly not the only one. Tremendous opportunities exist in the elite markets of Africa One, as can be seen from the upscale shopping malls and high-end brands in every major city across Africa. There also are profitable opportunities, with the right models, in serving Africa Three.

In Nairobi, for example, Catherine Ngahu of SBO Research gave me a table of products that might be sold in the high-density area of Kibera (mostly Africa Three consumers), others for the mid-level consumers of Buru-Buru (mostly Africa Two consumers), and still others at the high end in the upscale Westlands (mostly Africa One consumers). Table 3-2 shows an excerpt from her table. It illustrates that opportunities exist in every segment of the market. Although the products for each segment differ significantly, there is more overlap than one might think.

**TABLE 3-2   Brands of Products and Services Used by Consumers in Three Areas**

| Products and Services | Kibera | Buru-Buru | Westlands |
|---|---|---|---|
| Detergent | Bar soap: Jamaa, Kipande | Omo | Toss, Omo, and Sunlight |
| Toothpaste | Small Colgate | Close-Up, Aquafresh, Colgate | Aquafresh Herbal, Colgate, Close-Up |
| Transport | Walk, bicycle, *matatu* (minibus) | Minibus—Citi Hoppa and Double M connections | Own car, sometimes use a driver |
| Clothing | *Mitumba* (secondhand) from Gikomba and Toi markets | Clothes shop (exhibitions) and secondhand | Designer shops, Woolworths, and imported clothing |
| Banking | Postbank | Co-operative Bank | Barclays, Stanchart, NIC, CBA |
| Antimosquito | Mosquito coils, mosquito netting | Mosquito netting, Doom | Mosqi chips, Odourless Doom |
| Cosmetics | Solea, petroleum jelly | Fair and Lovely | Nivea, Clarins |
| Radio | SONY (fake Sony) | National Star | LG, Sony |
| TV | National Star, black & white | Sony | LG, Sony, flat-screen/plasma TV |

Source: Catherine Ngahu, SBO Research, Nairobi, Kenya

## *Africa One: Selling in Sandton*

In the Sandton section of Johannesburg, a 6-meter (18.5 ft.) bronze statue of Nelson Mandela rises from the plaza of the square named in his honor (not far from the farm where he was arrested in 1960). The statue is surrounded by glistening shops of Gucci, Lorenzi, and more than a half dozen jewelers, and attached to the sprawling Sandton City shopping center. Nearby, Alfa Romeo, Mercedes, BMW, and Ferrari dealerships line the roadways. The first reaction on arriving in Sandton City might be: This is not Africa. But this is Africa, just Africa One.

I visited upscale malls in Lagos, Nairobi, Cairo, and other parts of Africa that are catering to Africa One. They have elegant restaurants and movie theaters that are out of reach of most of the population. I saw high-end automobile dealerships everywhere I went in Africa, including the Mercedes dealership in Harare shown in Exhibit 10. In Tunisia, the Maille Club's upscale clothing shop Mabrouk is sticking with Africa One customers in its 14 stores. It is creating brands targeting children and other segments, and waiting for the aspiring Africa Two customers to move up.

Africa's super-rich are growing at a very healthy rate, and represent an important opportunity, particularly in the short run. A study by Merrill Lynch and Capgemini reported that Africa's super-rich grew their assets by 14 percent in 2006 (compared to 11.4 percent growth globally). These wealthy Africans had a combined wealth of about $900 billion.[4] The number of high-net-worth individuals in Africa is only about a quarter of the size of that of Latin America or a third of the Middle East, but they are growing faster in size and wealth than any other region of the world except for Latin America (as shown in Table 3-3).

**TABLE 3-3   Growth Rate of High-Net-Worth Individuals (HNWI), 2005–2006**

| Region | % Change in HNWI Population | % Change in HNWI Total Wealth |
|---|---|---|
| Africa | 12.5 | 14 |
| Middle East | 11.9 | 11.7 |
| Latin America | 10.2 | 23.2 |
| Asia-Pacific | 8.6 | 10.5 |
| Europe | 6.4 | 7.8 |
| North America | 9.2 | 10.3 |

Source: World Wealth Report, Capgemini and Merrill Lynch, 2007

There are nine Africans on the *Forbes* 2008 list of billionaires, from South Africa, Egypt, and, for the first time, Nigeria. These include the first two black Africans, Patrice Motsepe of South Africa who entered the mining business after the end of apartheid and became the country's first black billionaire; and Aliko Dangote, the first Nigerian on the list, who started as a trader with a loan from his uncle and built a thriving conglomerate in businesses such as sugar, flour milling, cement, and salt processing. When I visited his company in Lagos in July 2006, there were rumors that he was among the richest men in the world, but it took a little while for *Forbes* to confirm this. There may be other African billionaires that are yet to be discovered, and certainly others are hard at work building their fortunes with Africa's rise.

### Africa Three: Least Currency Strategies

Finally, there are opportunities in Africa Three (D and E segments). These opportunities come from creating markets from scratch. As one investor described it, this is taking barefoot consumers and moving them up to inexpensive flip-flops or gel shoes. It is moving from unbranded products such as unwrapped bars of soap to bars imprinted with the brand that can be broken apart by vendors or bought whole by customers, and then moving up to branded products. This is the strategy that Unilever is following by putting laundry powder in small sachets and building innovative distribution networks to sell to hard-to-reach parts of the market. Many of the market strategies that can be used to reach Africa Three are detailed in my earlier book, *The 86 % Solution*, but we briefly consider here the importance of designing products at the right price point in meeting this market in Africa and other developing regions.

Pricing is absolutely critical in this part of the market. In particular, consumer goods firms are creating products priced at the lowest possible currency in a given market. Traditional product development starts with the product and ends with selling the price, but pricing for Africa Three begins with the lowest currency possible (a few U.S. cents) and works back to the product that can be sold for that price. Many companies are selling water in plastic bags for 5 naira in Nigeria (about 4 cents), the smallest currency there, as shown in Exhibit 11. The closest that the major companies seem to have come to this idea is a small lemon-shaped bottle produced by Nestlé under the Pure Life brand, which I saw in Lagos in 2006. With a foil cap, it could be opened and consumed in a few gulps. It retailed for 16 naira (about

13 cents) at a local Shoprite, three times the cost of the bagged water, although it contains just 33 centiliters (about 11 oz.) of water compared with 50cl (17 oz.) bags on the street. Even so, the global brand may carry more credibility, justifying the higher price. Major companies such as The Coca-Cola Company and Nestlé sell large bottles of water for those who can afford them, but the bagged water is the solution for Africa Three.

In Egypt, Rashidi's branded *halvah* (sesame dessert), selling for 15 piastres (about 3 cents) for a small package, took about 85 percent of the market from unbranded products. In Egypt, P&G is launching smaller sizes of Tide and Bonnex to target the 70 percent of the population in Africa Two and Three. In the chewing gum market in Nairobi, I saw companies pricing a piece of gum for a single Kenyan shilling (about 1 cent), which has created a challenge for global companies such as Wrigley's to position their products based on value.

By using sachets, as well as creative distribution and product design, companies can find ways to make a profit while expanding into Africa Three. To hit the rock-bottom price points, companies are also creating different delivery channels and business models, as East Africa Breweries Limited did in selling its Senator beer from kegs in rural areas in Kenya. The beer not only lasted longer without refrigeration, a scarce commodity in areas with unreliable electricity, but also could be sold by the glass at a lower price without undercutting the pricing of bottled beer.

Even the often-quoted figure that some half of sub-Saharan Africa's population is living on less than a dollar a day needs to be examined carefully. Families of five or eight people might share a single dwelling in a high-density area. This means that these households could earn $5 to $8 per day as a household, or $180 per month. This explains the thriving markets and even organized retail enterprises in these areas, such as the supermarkets I saw in the high-density area of Tafara, Zimbabwe, where branded products from global manufacturers such as Unilever were sold. The key to success, as companies such as Unilever have found, is developing profitable products at the right price points and reaching diffused sales channels such as rural markets.[5]

There is also the maid and driver effect, as discussed in my book *The 86% Solution.* Fatima Alimohamed, head of marketing for Bidco in Kenya, notes that many of the members of Africa Two and Three (C and D segments) work for Africa One employers. This means that the workers have access to products and services that might appear to be beyond their means. For example, an employer might give a cell phone to a driver, so he can be called if needed. A maid might be given clothing or a cell phone or even have schooling or medical care paid for by an employer. This means that the resources of these workers could be higher than might appear on paper. Companies need to think about marketing to employers for products and services used by their household employees.

# A Continent of Aspirations: Keep Walking

Aspirations mean that Africa Three consumers sometimes buy products designed for Africa Two, and Africa Two consumers sometimes reach into Africa One. In segmenting the market, Bidco makes a distinction between the "struggling poor" and the "resigned poor." One of the key differences is aspiration. Apiration is one of the common themes across Africa, achieving personal success against the odds. The rise of a consumer market in Africa is largely a shift from collectivism to individualism. In collective societies, the identity is your group. In individual societies, signs of status are based on personal progress and acquisition, so this is a shift in identification. Collectivism doesn't go away, but there is a stronger sense of individual initiative and connection to the market.

Rising aspirations and individualism have helped to drive the successful growth of Diageo's Johnnie Walker brand in South Africa, which posted a 25 percent compound annual growth rate over the past three years. The brand's slogan of "Keep Walking," although developed globally, seems tailor-made for the African market where the image of the striding man inspires people to keep on going, whatever the obstacles (see Exhibit 12). This is why South Africans are willing to pay 200 rand (about $25) for a bottle when less-premium brands such as

J&B sell for 80 rand ($10), or a premium bottle of brandy might go for 70 rand (less than $9). Keep walking appeals to the aspirations of the buyers.

"The desire of people at all levels to demonstrate status and wealth, through a mobile phone or a particular drink, is what will absolutely drive consumer demand across a number of African countries," said Matthew Barwell, marketing director of Diageo Africa, in an interview with the author in August 2007. He recalled a recent eye-opening visit to Angola. "If you look at the wealth emerging there and the desire to buy premium brands, it is more like Brazil or Venezuela."

To meet these rising aspirations, SABMiller in South Africa (South African Breweries) has moved from lower-priced, brown-bottled beer to launch more upscale beers in green bottles. The Coca-Cola Company and other beverage manufacturers have moved from returnable glass bottles (offered at a lower price) to PET disposables at a much higher price point. Between 2000 and 2006, sales of green-bottled beers such as Castle Light and Heineken in South Africa grew by 57 percent, jumping from 4 percent of the market to 11 percent. SAB, which has dominated the beer market, responded to the demand with the introduction of Miller Genuine Draft, Pilsner Urquell, Castle Lite, and Peroni. Consumers are trading up from brown bottles to green bottles, a sign of the rapidly growing Africa Two segment and even more rapidly advancing aspirations.

When I visited the township of Soweto in South Africa, a tavern on a side street blasted music from large loudspeakers though an open door. One refrigerated case was filled with the brown bottles of low-cost beer such as Castle. But a second case was filled with the green bottles of premium beers. Even if a group of friends could afford only one green bottle between them, they would often choose to place it in the center of their table and share a good drink rather than settle for more quantity of something more ordinary. Friends purchasing Coca-Cola beverages would often rather share a modern PET plastic bottle than buy individual sodas in cans or returnable glass bottles.

As in many parts of the developing world, even fast food is aspirational. Families go out to Mr. Biggs restaurant in Nigeria on weekends and special occasions. The quick-serve restaurants such as Mr. Biggs originally served Western menus, but they have expanded to African dishes as rising health consciousness increased demand for local foods. Now, the restaurants sell Nigerian dishes such as pounded yam *amala, eba*, beans with plantain, rice and beans, rice with plantain, *ofada* rice, and yam pottage. Mr. Biggs accounts for about half of the N39 billion ($300 million) Nigerian restaurant business.

## Conclusion: An Open Door

African markets are a study in extremes. The cost of one night at the Sheraton Lagos in Nigeria in mid-2006 was about $500 when I stayed there, greater than the average per capita GDP of the country. In a single night, executives or government officials could pay more than an average citizen earns in a year. At one extreme is an elite with liberal resources to spend at the high-end shopping malls springing up across the continent. At the other extreme are the many Africans who struggle to survive. What the economic numbers sometimes obscure, however, is the vitality and dynamism of African markets. On the streets of Nairobi, Algiers, or Lagos, the markets are bustling as products are being sold.

The doors of retailers are open to anyone. In Zimbabwe, I witnessed a woman wearing flip-flops, with a baby tied across her back, walking through the aisles of the OK Supermarket on Five Avenue in Harare. In her hand was just 400,000 in Zim dollars, worth about 80 cents at the time (based on the July 2006 currency which was revalued shortly after my visit there). Even so, she was shopping. She picked up a bag of salt for about Z$200,000, then looked at a 375ml (about 13 oz.) bottle of cooking oil for a little more than Z$200,000 before going to the soap aisle. After briefly examining the more expensive Omo soap powder, she chose a 500g "Price Breaker" solid laundry bar for Z$200,000 (about 30 cents). Finally, returning to her starting point, she left the soap and took the oil. She was trading off cooking her food over washing her clothes.

This woman is a consumer. The supermarket has an open door, and she walked through it. A combination of political reform, imports, and entrepreneurship has placed high-quality, inexpensive goods within the reach, if not the pocketbook, of almost everyone.

There are opportunities for premium products at the high end of the market and value-oriented products at the low end. But the high end will sometimes buy for value, and low-income consumers sometimes aspire to high-end goods, so these lines are not always clear. Unilever's premium Fair and Lovely skin cream is now offered in small sachets in Nigeria. The picture that emerges is a dynamic market, with opportunities from luxuries to subsistence. Driven by aspirations, these market segments are looking up. As they rise, Africa rises with them. And squarely at the center of this African market opportunity is Africa Two.

## Rising Opportunities

- What strategies do you need for each segment of the African market?
- What are the opportunities to build and serve Africa Two?
- What opportunities are there to serve the elite segment of Africa One?
- How can you use least currency strategies and other strategies to profitably serve Africa Three?
- How can aspirations drive the growth of your business?

# Part II
## Realizing the Opportunity

# 4

## Harnessing the Hanouti: Opportunities in Organizing the Market

*The African market is informal and disorganized, so creating opportunities often means looking for ways to organize the market. Companies are finding opportunities by moving informal retailing into more formal and organized stores, transforming informal and illegal markets into formal markets, and organizing secondhand markets. They are also branding unbranded products and organizing transportation and distribution.*

In Morocco, most retail sales are made through the 80,000 small, neighborhood retail shops known as *hanout*. One of the things that seems to make these mom-and-pop hanouti shops impenetrable to competition from organized chains is the credit and close relationships they offer their customers. This credit allows them to keep cash-strapped customers with no access to formal banking. When workers pick up sodas and other items on their way home, they tell the store owner to put the expense on their account. This credit is available to all members of their family. No interest is charged. A conventional retailer in a developed market, used to dealing in cash or credit transactions, couldn't offer this book of credit. It might seem that a formal chain of convenience stores would have to wait for banking, credit, and other parts of the economy to develop to move into the Moroccan market.

But entrepreneur Moncef Belkhayat, a former marketing executive at P&G and Méditel, chose not to wait. He decided to organize the market. He created the idea for a branded hanout chain (called Hanouti). Working in partnership with BCME Bank (which holds 20 percent of the investment in the project), he planned to provide credit to customers of the store. Hanouti began launching the first of a planned 3,000 stores in 2006, and is growing rapidly. The brand conveys a sense of modernity, cleanliness, and safety. The credit that had been offered informally by the owners of the traditional hanout now comes from the bank—a modern version of the old practice. The informal becomes formal. The unbranded hanout becomes the branded Hanouti. The market has been organized.

For BCME, Hanouti offers access to a large population of unbanked customers. Only 20 percent of people in urban areas in Morocco have bank accounts, and even fewer in rural areas. After customers signed up for credit at Hanouti, the bank could offer them credit cards, accounts, bill-paying services, and insurance through RMA Watanya. Many of these services are offered right at the counter of the Hanouti, or through flyers distributed in the stores, giving the bank de facto branches throughout Morocco. This is creating a market for Africa Two and Three customers (see Chapter 3, "The Power of Africa Two").

As it did in offering credit to customers, Hanouti also has organized the back end of the distribution system that feeds its stores. It created a sophisticated central merchandising system, which allowed the company to be competitive with larger Moroccan retailers.

## Organizing the Market

To transform the unorganized and informal hanout into modern retail stores, Hanouti had to bring its own banking and distribution to the table. It recognized the need to organize the market. The solution required thinking more broadly than retail to create a viable business. Other convenience stores might have waited for the market to develop to the point where enough customers already had credit, but by the time these latecomers arrive, pioneers such as Hanouti will already be well established.

The African market is informal and disorganized. The top 30 retailers in Africa and the Middle East accounted for just 29 percent of 2006 modern grocery sales in the region compared to 59 percent for Western Europe.[1] Most African retail looks like the informal market shown in Exhibit 13. Businessmen carry around stacks of cash in

Lagos, where credit systems are underdeveloped and peppered with fraud. Although credit cards have arrived, even for large purchases such as a wide-screen television or automobile, a suitcase filled with millions of naira is usually the preferred method of payment. Much of the economy operates underground in the informal economy. A manager in Nairobi might pay his auto mechanic in cell phone minutes, a transaction that never turns into currency.

As Hanouti found, by thinking more broadly about the business, companies can create opportunities by organizing markets. Companies are restructuring retail and organizing marketing and communications. They are making the informal and illegal markets formal. They are following the paths of secondhand products and unbranded offerings. They are developing public/private strategies and using companies as organized channels for sales. Entrepreneurs recognize that African markets do not arrive ready made. They must be organized.

# Organizing Retail: Shopping in Alexandra

It was a sunny Sunday morning when my driver took me along the streets of the sprawling suburbs of Alexandra, a black township outside of Johannesburg (like nearby Soweto where blacks were forced to live during apartheid). People had poured out of the rows of tightly packed cinder-block houses into the streets. Under small tents to block the rising sun, market stalls were filled with vegetables and clothing. As we passed, a young woman walked out of the open door of a small red shipping container with a row of community cell phones where callers could pay less than 1 rand (about 15 cents) for a call. The streets were dusty and crowded.

On Second Avenue, Caven Ndou worked behind the black metal bars of a traditional *spaza* shop (see Exhibit 14). This is literally a hole in the cinder-block wall of a private home, where he sold staples such as bread, snacks, and candles. He dug a Band-Aid out of a small white box as a woman waited at the door. He would sell you a single bandage, or one cigarette for 1 rand. Until recently, this was what retail looked like in the townships and rural areas. Not anymore.

A few blocks over was a new strip mall. Stepping off the dusty streets into the new Shoprite supermarket was like walking from the third world into the first. The floors were clean enough to eat from, and there was no shortage of food, as shown in Exhibit 15. Prices were posted on the well-stocked shelves of the wide, well-lit aisles that stretched in all directions. Christina Aguilera sang in the background. This supermarket could be anywhere in the developed world, and yet every checkout was crowded with local people filling up their carts with staples or splurging on one of the microwaves stacked in the aisle for just under 400 rand (about $65).

The Shoprite Group of Companies, launched in Cape Town in 1979, has become Africa's largest food retailer. It operates 825 corporate outlets in 18 countries across Africa, even making the leap above the Sahara to Egypt (unsuccessfully, as I would find out later), and east to the Indian Ocean islands and South Asia. With $5.6 billion in sales in 2006, Shoprite would rank about 408 on the *Fortune 500* list, just behind retailer Bed, Bath & Beyond ($5.8 billion) and ahead of Barnes & Noble ($5.3 billion).

In the same shopping center in Alexandra, a PEP store, which specializes in children's clothing, was selling a toddler's jacket for less than 7 rand, or about $1, as shown in Exhibit 16. Pepkor (PEP's parent) has the motto: Making the Desirable Affordable. It was started in 1965 by Renier van Rooyen as a small discount store with a focus on the very poor in his hometown in a remote village of the Northern Cape of South Africa. It was one of the first stores catering to poor black customers, a store that allowed them to see and touch merchandise. (Products were usually kept behind counters.) There are more than 1,300 PEP stores throughout South Africa, Namibia, Lesotho, Botswana, Swaziland, Malawi, Mozambique, Zambia, and Ghana. Although it serves low-income customers, it is hardly a charity. By 2008 PEP was the largest single-brand retailer in South Africa, with 14,000 employees. It sold around 400 million products per year, some of which are produced at its clothing company, which is the largest clothing company in southern Africa.[2]

In Nairobi, a smiling woman was sitting at the table at the entrance to the Nakumatt Thikaroad (on Thika Road) demonstrating Beauty 3 skin-care products from London. This was a long way from London, and this was certainly not the perfume counter at Macy's. But stepping into the supermarket was a huge stride from the humble metal-roofed kiosks of traditional retailing in Nairobi. Inside the

Nakumatt, there were gleaming aisles of food, local and international brands, a bakery, and a counter offering prepared foods. The average store is over 1 million square feet, offering products from food to furniture from 175 different countries. Nakumatt's new superstores are as large as its ambitions for Kenya and the surrounding area. Since its founding in 1991, Nakumatt expanded from 1 store to 17. Its turnover in 2006–07 was $280 million. Nakumatt was just getting started. It planned to open eight new branches in 2007, moving into Uganda, Rwanda, and Tanzania and expecting to reach $400 million before its planned IPO.

In a meeting at the company's Kenya headquarters, Thiagarajan Ramamurthy, director of operations, pointed out that their 3 percent profitability puts them on par with Wal-Mart, and the comparisons don't stop there. Nakumatt takes its name from their original product (mattresses) and the location of its first store, the town of Naku— which is perhaps an even more obscure location than Bentonville, Arkansas. Although much smaller than its U.S. role model, Nakumatt has a similar format and sophistication. The retailer has initiated smart cards, and already had more than 210,000 holders among its 1.5 million customers by 2007. It launched a co-branded credit card with Barclays in 2007. Founder Atul (Haku) Shah is its Sam Walton.

In a cash-tight economy, Nakumatt's expansion has been facilitated by a lean structure. It leases locations from landowners with the promise that they will earn back their investment from rental income within 8 years and become millionaires by the end of a successful 11-year lease. Nakumatt also stocks some of its products on consignment. This partnership allows it to organize the market while reducing its downside risks.

Nakumatt is astute in understanding customers and tapping into the global diaspora. It has connected with the aspirations of parents by allowing them to apply their Smart Points, earned through purchases, to pay their children's school fees. The retailer makes a check out to the school, adding 10 percent to the value earned. It also offers an on-line program for Kenyans abroad to send gift certificate for purchases at Nakumatt to family back home.

In Tunisia, where just 15 percent of the retail market is in the organized sector and there are 40,000 retail outlets, the market is also being organized. The Bayahi Group, with a partner, bought 52 Magasin Général stores. As a stockholder in BIAT, Tunisia's largest bank, Groupe Mabrouk is organizing the market for financial services. It also is diversifying into retail, including purchasing the MonoPrix hypermart.

Across Africa, companies such as Shoprite, PEP, and Nakumatt are organizing the market. Three South African retailers appeared on the 2006 global ranking of the top 250 retailers, including Pick 'n Pay (122), Shoprite (123), and Massmart (140). Consumers who walk into these stores can compare prices and quality with what they might find in a local store or kiosk. And they are often surprised by what they find. The prices are posted on the shelves or on large signs at the end of aisles touting sales, designed to invite comparison shopping. Informal has become formal.

Most of the market is still in unorganized spaza shops and other small operations (but this no different from India and other developing countries.). One of the more famous of such shops was run by Winnie Mandela across the street from their home in Soweto, shown in Exhibit 17. The home is now a museum, and the Mandelas are divorced, but the shop is still open. It helped support their family while Nelson Mandela was waging his long battle to reshape South Africa. Political and economic development go hand in hand.

While strip malls such as the one in Alexandra are sprouting up all over Africa, more elaborate shopping malls are also rising across the continent. In Lagos, past the jumbled stalls of street vendors that lined the highways when I visited in 2006, rose The Palms shopping mall. The Palms opened in December 2005, one of more than 20 malls planned for the country, anchored with a Shoprite and Game stores. At the center court was the Nandos Portuguese chicken restaurant (owned by Innscor of Zimbabwe, described in Chapter 1, "Baking Bread in Zimbabwe"). On the weekend I visited, it was overflowing with people who covered every available table in the restaurant and spilled out into the sunny atrium. A movie theater upstairs showed U.S. box office hits for a price of 1,250 naira (about $9) and sold Coca-Cola beverages for 200 naira (about $1.75) a bottle, more than twice the price in the Shoprite downstairs.

Only Africa One can afford such luxuries, but The Palms, billed as an "ultra modern super mall," is open to Africa Two and even Africa Three, like the couple I met in the aisles of Shoprite, who traveled an hour by bus to pick up a few staples in the clean, well-lit aisles. She was surprised that a bottle of Coca-Cola beverage in a PET plastic bottle is only 80 naira (70 cents) at the supermarket, compared to the 100 naira (86 cents) she would pay on the street. A trip to these stores is an education in pricing and consumerism.

The scene has been repeated across Africa, and there are more retail centers on the way. In 2006, the CDC (Capital for Development, the former U.K. government-owned fund for the developing world) helped set up the $100 million Actis Real Estate Investment Fund, targeting malls and other commercial developments in areas that have traditionally been ignored by international investors, including in Ghana, Nigeria, Malawi, and Mozambique. Retailing is just one of the ways the African market is becoming organized.

# Opportunities from Making the Informal Formal

There are opportunities to use the demand for even illegal knock-offs as a foundation for a legitimate business. For example, it was during walks through the *faracha* (street hawkers) of Morocco that Azbane Cosmetics founders recognized the market for petroleum jelly. They saw unbranded products and counterfeits everywhere, a clear sign of the market demand.

Based on this insight, they launched a branded product that became the market leader. They offered their products at half the price of global brands, keeping costs down by eschewing television advertising and promotions, appealing to customers who might otherwise have bought counterfeits. A 275ml (9.5 oz.) bottle of Azbane body lotion sold for about 8 dirhams (or about 8 cents), about half the cost of a European brand. The company used this initial success to move into more upscale cosmetics and perfumes. It has expanded into Spain, West Africa, Tunisia, and other parts of the world—and is even eyeing the U.S. market. Azbane also took advantage of rising tourism to sell shampoos and other personal-care products to hotel chains.

A study of mobile phones in Uganda estimated that 100,000 fake or stolen handsets are sold every year, costing the government about $9 million in tax revenues alone (Ushs 15 billion).[3] The penetration of satellite television in Egypt rocketed from 19 percent in January 2004 to 68 percent in May 2006.[4] How can it be that 68 percent of Egyptians have access to satellite TV in a country in which GNI per capita was just $1,350 in 2006? More than half of these satellite viewers don't show up on the customer lists of the satellite providers. They are not paying for their service. They pirate their signals through the widespread practice of *wasla* (or branching). Sometimes a single satellite dish might serve an entire neighborhood. In Alexandria, Egypt, 62 percent of homes are receiving wasla broadcasts, and this is more common across the poorer demographic segments of Egypt.

In Morocco, Tunisia, and other parts of Africa, I heard how entrepreneurs were doing a brisk business selling codes for European satellite broadcasts. Customers could buy a card from one of these entrepreneurs and receive access to premium channels they want (the most popular being soccer broadcasts). When the satellite company changed the code, the informal market would quickly have the new pirated codes for sale.

This piracy of satellite signals is either a huge problem or a huge opportunity. On the one hand, satellite providers are losing tons of money in subscriptions—if they believe these pirates would actually become viewers. On the other hand, these illegal viewers mean that advertising has a much greater reach than can be seen from the official numbers. Many of those who pirate signals are in the upper consumer segments of Africa Two and even Africa One (see Chapter 3), so they are a market that can afford to pay, and the scrambling of signals may actually reduce the impact of multinational advertising.

Microsoft addressed piracy and the threat of open-source software in China, in the face of rampant piracy, by making its software available free to the government. This increased the installed base and aligned the government with the company's interests. Microsoft is also addressing piracy through changes in pricing. For example, the company announced a plan in July 2007 to offer pay-as-you-go subscription copies of its Office software in South Africa, where 35 percent of all software is thought to be pirated (compared to more than 90 percent for China and 22 percent for the United States). Instead of paying $700 for a license for the professional version of the Office software suite, users can pay $30 for three months of use.[5] What other strategies can be used to organize the informal market to make it formal?

# Tokunbo: Organizing Secondhand

The *tokunbo*, or secondhand market for cars, clothing, tires, electronics, and household items is 100 billion naira (more than $800 million) in Nigeria alone. This is a huge market that doesn't show up on the balance sheets of auto or clothing manufacturers. Does BMW know how many loyal customers it has in Africa who have never walked into a showroom? Does Christian Dior recognize the African market for used branded clothing?

Secondhand clothing from the United States has created a growing opportunity in Africa. Americans give away or throw out an average of 68 pounds of clothing and other textiles per person each year. Much of it ends up in Africa. These "discards" include clothing from designers such as Bon Jovi, Calvin Klein, and Ralph Lauren. Brokers, such as Global Clothing Industries in Atlanta, Georgia, founded by an immigrant from Sierra Leone, buy the clothing for 10 to 15 cents a pound. The clothing is sorted and compressed into 1,000-pound bales for 11 cents a pound. The global secondhand clothing trade is estimated at $1 billion annually, and the industry employs hundreds of thousands of Africans in handling, distributing, cleaning, and repairing the clothing.[6]

When the Indianapolis Colts donned their championship hats and shirts after winning the Super Bowl in February 2007, the gear prepared in advance for the losing Chicago Bears was packed off to Africa. It was distributed by WorldVision to recipients in Uganda, Niger, Sierra Leone, and other struggling countries.[7] The team that lost the championship in the United States became the winner in Africa.

I found secondhand clothing markets in Nairobi. I also saw them in Tunisia and Algeria, where the secondhand clothing is called *fripe* and the stores that sell them are *friperie* (see Exhibit 18).

Along the highway in the Apapa section of Lagos, Nigeria, I stopped at a sprawling automobile lot with more than a thousand used cars and trucks stretched across the hillside. The lot was one of 27 lots organized by United Berger Motor Dealers, each with more than a thousand used vehicles. Most of the cars are imported from Europe, hence their popular nickname "Belgians." They come from all over Europe and even the United States. One of the cars in the lot still had a license plate from my home state of Texas (see Exhibit 19). They are bought by Nigerians across the spectrum, from the elite down to those just able to scrape together the cash to purchase their first car.

The cars on this lot ranged from beat-up older-model Nissans for 350,000 naira ($2,800) to a late-model Toyota Taureg with just 23,000km (14,300 miles) on it for 7.5 million naira ($60,000). A shiny BMW X5 goes for 5.5 million naira ($45,000). Because most of these sales are completed with suitcases full of cash, you would need a car this size just to carry it.

Stepping onto the dusty lot was like stirring up an anthill, as salesmen swarmed out eager to sell the one to seven cars they are responsible for. They were loosely overseen by Forster Agu and Donald Anthony. The sellers received a commission from the owner on the sale, but if they could tack on a few thousand naira to the seller's asking price, they could keep the difference. In Kenya in the east, cars are imported from the streets of Tokyo and other Asian countries, but the concept is the same as the European Belgians in Nigeria.

The formal auto industry is also growing rapidly in Africa. The Egyptian automobile industry grew by 60 percent to 150,000 new vehicle sales in 2005, with about 75 percent passenger cars. Hyundai was top in total market share. Because of high import duties, many companies are assembling locally, including Mercedes and BMW, which sell about 2,000 cars per year to the top of the market. After-sales service is a key selling point.

Although dealers do not take used cars, there is a fairly well-organized informal market in Egypt through government-sponsored lots where sellers can pay 10 Egyptian pounds (less than $2) to show their car and buyers can come and bargain. On Fridays, there are thousands of cars in the lot in Nassar City. There are also several buy-and-sell shops and small used-car shops such as Alwassit (The Broker).

As a Mercedes dealer in Senegal told me, although their sales may be lower than in Europe, margins are higher. A dealer in Paris might be grateful for 2 percent to 3 percent margins, whereas a dealer in Dakar might make 10 percent to 15 percent, and make more money on after-sales service. The market is also growing at about 15 percent per year, much faster than developed markets. Some of the most significant competition comes from the parallel market. More than one Mercedes owner has come to the dealer only to be disappointed to find that their imported car was stolen from Europe or smuggled in to avoid paying duties.

This thriving secondhand market presents a number of opportunities. For example, there is the potential to organize the secondhand market, as U.S. dealers did with certified "pre-owned" cars or companies such as CarMax did in creating a formal used-car business. The secondhand market also highlights the opportunity to create cheaper new products. For example, Ethiopian engineer Tadesse Tessema, who had imported European used cars to the country, set up his own car company with the help of Dutch investors to build a low-priced automobile based on the Fiat 131 from the 1970s (redesigned with higher clearance to navigate rough roads). Because the car is produced in Ethiopia, avoiding heavy import duties and other costs, he can offer the automobiles at half the price of a Toyota Corolla. And even though the cars are made in Ethiopia, he called his new automobile brand "Holland," an indication of the fact that "made in Ethiopia" is not a selling point compared to the high status of European brands.[8]

The new Ethiopian brand faces stiff competition from competitors from China. Chinese firms such as Great Wall, Chery Automobile Co., and Geely Group Ltd. are offering automobiles in Africa at prices that are competitive with used cars. Great Wall planned to have 30 dealerships in South Africa by 2008. Uganda announced plans in 2008 to assemble 3,000 Geely cars per year at a new plant outside of Kampala, targeting the East African market.[9] Chery started making cars in Egypt in 2006. In 2007, Chery offered zero percent financing and an entry-level car for just $12,000, about the price of a used Toyota. I also saw Chery cars in Algeria retailing for about $6,000 (as well as Mercedes for more than $90,000).

Indian companies are also selling across the African market, including Tata Motors and Maruti in Algeria and other parts of North

Africa. I also saw Tata, Mahindra, and other companies in South Africa, and other Asian manufacturers such as Korea's Hyundai and Japanese firms such as Toyota and Honda. As new car imports to Senegal have risen, imports of used European cars are beginning to fall.[10] Financing arrangements, such as the deals shown at a Mahindra and Fiat dealership outside of Pretoria in South Africa (see Exhibit 20), put these automobiles within reach of more of the population. The Fiats in the photo were offered in July 2006 for a payment of just 999 rand (about $150) per month.

As an indication of growing interest in the automobile market in Africa and other parts of the developing world, Renault-Nissan CEO Carlos Ghosn flew to Tangiers, Morocco, in September 2007 to announce plans to construct one of the largest auto assembly plants on the African continent, which would ultimately produce 400,000 cars a year (initially targeting markets outside of Africa). It also is working on plans with Indian company Bajaj Auto Ltd. to create a $3,000 car.[11] Tata Motors, which has just launched a $2,500 car of its own, is also rapidly expanding from its base in South Africa. These companies, and Chinese players, are redefining the low-cost end of the market in the way that carriers such as Southwest redefined airline travel in the United States.

The formal market is replacing the informal secondhand markets. But consumer expectations may be very high as a result of exposure to global brands in these tokunbo markets. For example, one manager in Lagos told me that he would rather have a used BMW than a new Mitsubishi car, even though their prices were comparable.

Throughout Africa, secondhand markets are filling a need for low-priced, high-quality goods. These secondhand markets could be organized, as with Goodwill or private secondhand shops in the United States. The tokunbo market also demonstrates the tremendous demand for low-cost new products with the right level of quality and reputation.

# Organizing Distribution

In Cairo, Yasser El Sayyad, chairman and CEO of Multi Service for Trade, explained how he built his business by tackling distribution for chocolate, cookies, jam, soy milk, and a range of other projects. On his table were coconut cookies and chocolate. In his refrigerator were soy milk and yogurt. To sell Mars Galaxy bars, he had to work out distribution to 40,000 stores, from supermarkets to small kiosks, throughout Egypt. Chocolate is particularly challenging because it requires refrigeration, so they had to provide refrigerators to their best retailers. Many shop owners turned off the refrigerators at night to save money on electricity. The shop owners also used refrigerators to store soda, competitors' products, or even fish. The challenge for distribution, he said, is "that the market is not mature."

Why don't the companies set up their own distribution systems? The former PriceWaterhouse executive said he had gained accounts for major Western companies because of his understanding of the local market. His company understands local consumers and the small unorganized retailers, using computer routing to find the best path through a complex and fragmented retail network. He delivered goods on trucks and even bicycles and donkeys to reach the market.

In South Africa, The Coca-Cola Company uses a combination of trucks, bicycles, and handcarts to move its sodas from the expressways of the large cities to the narrow alleyways of the high-density areas and rural villages. In Nigeria, Guinness uses small *pousse-pousse* pushcarts to sell nonalcoholic Malta. In Zambia, Gillette put some 18,000 young men on bicycles to sell small cards with five of its inexpensive double-edged blades. They took the product all over Zambia in this way and increased sales from 5,000 to 750,000 units in 2004. In Malawi, trucks carried Colgate and other products across the country, making a circuit of 600 miles once a month. In Zimbabwe, the popular corn snack ZapMax, created by a small entrepreneur and originally sold from the factory, was later offered from the back of trucks that rolled into high-density areas. The company is taking the product to the people instead of waiting for the people to come to the product.

While formal retail channels are still emerging, companies are using informal channels to reach consumers. Ghana is a country with a per-capita gross national income (GNI) of just over $500, and a poorly developed retail network and infrastructure. Yet Unilever has been able to build a multimillion-dollar business there in small packages. The company created a network of small retailers, some with stores no bigger than a large appliance box, which allowed it to reach 80 percent of the population. Then, to go the last mile, in 2003 Unilever added rural sales reps (called boreholers) to distribute products to remote villages with rotational markets (market days) that are difficult to put into coverage plans. The system may look nothing like those in other parts of the world, but it has allowed Unilever to build a profitable business there.

South African beer distribution initially depended on backyard pubs called shebeens that offered their own moonshine brews served in old jam cans. Until 1962, black South Africans were prohibited from purchasing commercially brewed beer. When the prohibition was lifted, South African Breweries (SAB) used the local shebeens and other small outlets to build its business, providing almost all the beer sold through these outlets. SAB developed a network of drivers who could deliver products along rough rural roads, often setting up its former employees in their own trucking businesses. Leaving nothing to chance, the company also needed to make sure its rural distributors had refrigerators and even generators to keep the refrigerators running.

There are also temporary markets such as the souks in Morocco, which appear for a time and then are dismantled. African markets are fragmented, dominated by small mom-and-pop shops like the hanouti in Morocco or spaza shops in South Africa. This makes distribution challenging, but the companies that can succeed in organizing distribution have a tremendous advantage in bringing their products to its remotest corners.

In crowded cities, delivery is essential for businesses from fast food to groceries. The streets are congested, and parking is unavailable. Home delivery has emerged as the most important channel for sales. McDonald's and other fast-food restaurants carry meals through traffic in Cairo on delivery scooters. Delivery accounts for 27 percent of McDonald's sales in Egypt, and as much as 80 percent for some rivals.[12] Half of the sales of the Egyptian restaurants of Americana (see sidebar) are off-premises, not drive-through windows but through home delivery. To build delivery capabilities, Americana studied best practices from Domino's and other companies in the United States, Australia, and Singapore—and then they made these practices better. Today, their delivery systems are the best in the world, and other franchisees come to learn from them. The sophisticated system integrates call centers, a routing database painstakingly developed from government data, and a network of "pilots" on motorcycles with packaging to preserve heat and freshness.

## Americana: Every Market Has Its Own Key

In the 40 years since it founding, Americana has built a $1 billion business in fast food, grocery stores, and fast-moving consumer goods (FMCG) in Egypt and the Middle East by focusing primarily on serving the high end of the market. The company has 800 restaurants for brands such as KFC, Pizza Hut (Yum Brands), Hardees (Carl's Jr.), Krispy Kreme, TGI Friday's, Costa cafes, and their local concept Chicken Tikka. Americana was founded by Mr. Nasser Al Kharafi of Kuwait, listed among the wealthiest people in the world by *Forbes*, and the company is led by CEO Moataz Al-Alfi, a respected Egyptian business leader.

The top segments of the Egyptian market (Africa One, as discussed in Chapter 3) account for just 6 percent of the population, but in a country of more than 70 million, this 6 percent is larger than the entire population of Kuwait. And if the company can penetrate down to the next level (Africa Two), who might come to the restaurant as a special treat every other month, this represents another 30 percent of the market, as mentioned in Chapter 3. The frequency of use in this segment is increasing. Americana's brands also appeal to youth, so the demographics of Egypt are also on its side, with 50 percent of the population under 25 years old. The appeal of the brands is less about income bracket and more a reflection of lifestyle. Even so, Egypt is one of the toughest markets in the Middle East. There has not been a strong tradition of eating out, although this is changing. Costs are higher in Egypt, and selling prices are about half what they are in the oil-rich countries of the Middle East. Finding real estate and reliable sources of funding has also been a challenge. Yet the challenges are worth it. "You have the opportunity to take leadership in this market," said Borhan El Kilany, the company's chief marketing officer. "If you go to the United States, everyone is killing for 2 percent market share."

The company has had to build its own infrastructure to be successful in Egypt, which is part of what has driven its move into FMCG products. To support its restaurants, it built businesses to produce frozen chicken and French fries and became the manufacturer of Heinz products in the Middle East. Its first foray into frozen foods in the 1970s was a failure because there were not enough home freezers or retail freezers to support it, and the plant was converted to canning. But the company later successfully returned to frozen foods, supplying thousands of freezers to retailers to hold its products (and ultimately those of its competitors). To emphasize the value of frozen versus fresh foods, it launched an advertising campaign.

Working in Egypt takes a lot of investment and commitment. "Take your time. Make a long-term commitment. No hit and run," said the managing director of Americana, Amgad El Mofty. Finding strong leadership is also a challenge and a critical factor in success. Mofty comes from Citibank, and other senior managers come from companies such as Hilton and Procter & Gamble. "Every door to a market has its own key," said Borhan El Kilany, chief marketing officer.

## Corporations as Markets

In many markets, multinationals and other large corporations are the most organized part of the market. The employees of large companies in Africa have jobs and access to information, making them prime segments of the market. In regions with limited marketing and distribution channels, these large companies can be a key channel for distributing products. Employers have their own infrastructure and a commitment to improving the lives of their employees. For example, Novartis developed a malaria kit for Shell employees in Nigeria, as shown in Exhibit 21, with information on prevention, testing, and pills for the treatment of malaria. This is a vital resource for workers and Shell in addressing the disease, but also a market that has already been organized by the company itself.

Companies also are serving channels for banking initiatives, as employees are paid through value cards or direct deposits to bank accounts. This may be their first introduction to banking. Infrastructure weaknesses also offer opportunities for firms that serve other companies. For example, Ahmed and Maher Bouchamaoui Group in Tunisia (Al Majd Holding) and the RedMed Company in Algeria have built some of the largest companies in North Africa by providing housing, transportation, training centers, and other infrastructure to the oil industry.

## Parallel Public and Private Strategies

Sometimes the market, particularly when it is related to a health or social issue, can be organized through the synergistic effect of public and private initiatives. Some 80 percent of the cases of malaria in the world are in Africa. This is a huge problem and an opportunity. The antimalarial drug Coartem, developed by Novartis, offers a breakthrough in treating the disease with a highly effective three-day treatment. The biggest obstacles, however, are cost, distribution, awareness, and education. Novartis addressed these challenges through a parallel public and private strategy. It offered the drugs virtually at cost to the Global Fund and World Health Organization, which distributed them to children and poor citizens in Nigeria and other parts of Africa for free. At the same time, it built its for-profit business for more affluent customers through pharmacies and doctors.

Just putting tools into the hands of people is not enough. Noelle Jude, liaison manager of the Malaria Initiative for Novartis, recalls seeing a fisherman in Senegal using a mosquito net to fish. She warned him about the need to protect his family against malaria and the potential contamination of the water from the pesticide-impregnated nets. His response: "Would you rather die of starvation or malaria?" For Coartem, Novartis has created extensive educational materials and blister packs with illustrations to encourage proper use of the drugs. The company has even created comic books in different languages for children to raise awareness of malaria and discuss its prevention and treatment.

This kind of guidance is clearly needed. At a malaria ward at a hospital outside of Lagos, which I visited in July 2006, a baby curled in a brown patterned blanket was attached to an IV tube with a malaria drug. Other children of various ages were in metal hospital beds as their mothers sit in chairs by their sides. Only one of the more than half dozen children there was receiving Coartem, even though it was offered free through such clinics, and that girl was receiving the wrong dose. Many were receiving therapies that have become less effective as resistance to the treatment built up. Rows of patients were lined up on benches in the breezeway. The hospital saw about 150 patients a day. In the coastal areas, malaria made up 80 percent to 90 percent of cases waiting to be seen by doctors during the rainy season.

The medical director of the hospital, who studied in Russia before returning to Nigeria, recognized that there is a path from charity to commerce. "Nigeria is not a poor country," he told visiting Novartis executives. "We are rich in crude oil. We are just poor in management, but we are getting better. We know donors will not always be able to distribute drugs. By the time the company is not able to give drugs for free, we will purchase them ourselves."

Because malaria is a problem that affects almost everyone in a country like Nigeria—without regard for income or education—there is a strong commercial market for effective drugs at the same time that there is a compelling need for subsidized distribution for the poor. This dual strategy helps to address both issues.

There were also competitive challenges facing Coartem. The market was flooded with cheap and less-effective products, including monotherapies. Billboards on the roadside and posters and calendars in hospital pharmacies touted these drugs and emphasized that they were "made in Nigeria." In a Lagos pharmacy, a poster read "The bitterness of low-quality drugs remains long after the sweetness of low price is forgotten." But there on the shelves, branded pharmaceuticals, many with Nigerian FDA approval numbers, sat side by side with blood tonics and other popular folk remedies such as Dr. Meyer's Anti-Gripe Remedy. Dora Akunyili, director-general of Nigeria's National Agency for Food and Drug Administration and Control (Nafdac) launched what was called the "Other War on Drugs" to crack down on an epidemic of illegal medicines. An analysis in 2001 found that more than 60 percent of its drugs were not registered with Naf-dac and that Nigerians are among the world's most frequent victims of fake medicines.[13] Many fake drugs are also coming in from China and other parts of the world.

Distribution through pharmacies in Nigeria also has many twists and turns. Many sales, even of prescription drugs, were made directly through the pharmacy without a doctor's prescription. Pricing in the market was inconsistent. When I visited, a small, unorganized pharmacy on a dirt backstreet of Lagos, sold a three-day treatment of Coartem for about 1,100 naira (about $9). A few blocks away at a larger, slightly more upscale pharmacy, the cost for the same treatment was 1,590 naira (about $13). In the hospital pharmacy at the Lagos State University Teaching Hospital (LASUTH), the cost was 1,310 (about $11), although a clinic dispensed the treatment to poor patients for free. The distribution network for the unorganized pharmacies had four layers, whereas the teaching hospital received the drug directly from the importer, but the unorganized pharmacies were still cheaper. As noted previously, reshaping such distribution systems offers an opportunity to organize the market.

As the comic books and other educational materials from Novartis illustrate, education is critical in organizing the market. Unilever is working with the World Bank on a campaign to promote hand washing in Uganda, where a 2006 survey found that only 14 percent of adults wash their hands after going to the toilet. By working with the World Bank to promote better hygiene, Unilever can improve health and also build the future market for its Lifebouy soap.[14]

Public and private strategies are always important when it comes to building infrastructure such as roads or ports, but this approach is important at a deeper level in African markets. Given the social challenges, there are opportunities to work with governments, NGOs, and other players to create infrastructure that can provide the foundation for business, as I saw in the countries I visited across Africa.

# Organizing Medicine

In addition to branded pharmaceuticals from companies such as Novartis, the generic drug market is developing rapidly. In 2001,

Indian pharmaceutical firm Cipla introduced an innovative generic combination of three antiretroviral drugs in a single pill that transformed HIV/AIDS treatment and pricing. The new triple treatment was offered for the unheard of price tag of just $350 per year initially, and it has continued to fall.[15] By 2006, the African market for pharmaceuticals was about $9 billion, compared to $6 to $7 billion in India and perhaps $12 to $15 billion in China. South African generic firm Aspen Pharmacare was founded in a home in Durban in 1997, producing drugs to treat HIV/AIDS. It grew by an average of 40 percent per year to become South Africa's leading drug maker, posting sales of more than 4 billion rand (nearly $600 million in 2007).[16] Generics account for about 55 percent of the total $1 billion market for drugs in Egypt, with another one-third from over-the-counter (OTC) drugs. More than half of sales come from local companies, and elite consumers account for most spending (Africa One, as discussed in Chapter 3).

Smugglers bring cheaper products out of Egypt to neighboring countries. To help control this, Novartis has developed its own data systems to keep track of products across a network of 23,000 pharmacists and has placed limits on sales to any given distributor without approval from a manager. Most of these pharmacists do not have their own information systems to track this information. The industry is also required to track expiration dates, and retailers will sometimes change them, so the company also has to keep close track of this. Novartis has had to organize the market.

The opportunities of the pharmaceutical market in Africa have attracted the interest of many global companies, particularly those with success in providing low-cost pharmaceuticals to developing markets. "I'm very bullish about Africa," said Ranbaxy's Ranjan Chakravarti, regional director for Africa and Latin America, in an interview in May 2006. Sales in the South African market where he is based have grown 15 times in the past 4 years, success he attributes to a strategy of localization, a product portfolio focused on emerging markets, and "patience." It takes two and a half years to register a product in South Africa. Ranbaxy entered Nigeria 20 years ago, and became the number two drug company there. Even so, competition was still a bit less intense than at home in India, with 175 pharma companies in South Africa compared to about 400 to 500 in India.

The serious health challenges in Africa and other developing countries are encouraging a number of other health-care innovations. One interesting new product is the lab-on-a-chip technology developed by U.S. company LabNow, Inc., in Austin, Texas. The chip allows HIV/AIDS testing in the field by relatively unskilled technicians without sending samples back to the lab.

## Organizing Transportation

I visited the taxi stand in Germiston, outside of Johannesburg, where "taxi" drivers queue up as early as 2 a.m. to get a spot in line for the commuters who arrived only a few hours later to begin their long journey from the townships to low-paid jobs in the cities. Some 20 workers would be packed into a white mini van designed for 9, many of which shouldn't even be on the road. The stand was a rough-and-tumble area, tightly packed with humanity, frustration, and crime. My driver said you do not want to be out here after 6 p.m.

In Nigeria, motorcycles called *okada* serve the role of taxis, becoming the most common form of informal transportation because of their low cost and flexibility in navigating congested city streets and village pathways. For the entrepreneurs who drive them, often recklessly, the motorcycles can be purchased for 55,000 to 70,000 naira ($450 to $500), but most are rented on a daily basis. Chinese manufacturer Jincheng has the largest market share with almost half the market. Because of safety concerns, Nigeria has banned the motorcycle taxis in Abuja and other cities. South Africa is working on phasing out its minibus taxis, too.

Alternatives to taxis are emerging. The Malaysian consortium Newcyc announced plans to begin construction in September 2007 on a $1.7 billion privately owned light rail system linking the township of Soweto with Johannesburg. It would replace inefficient public trains and informal, slow, and crowded taxis.

There is a tremendous opportunity for low-cost transportation throughout Africa for those who can organize the market. All these people who need to go somewhere have to have organized systems to do so. This creates opportunities for buses and taxis that are being met by companies such as Tata Motors, which is creating vehicle designs for African markets. But where is Yellow Cab? The 2010 World Cup soccer games have placed additional pressure on the South African government to strengthen and improve the infrastructure before thousands of tourists stream into the country.

There are still many weaknesses across Africa. For example, Algiers is a city virtually without traffic lights. A sea of police officers takes the place of the traffic signals that are typical in a large city. As in many parts of the continent, the expected infrastructure may be missing. This type of gap, however, can create opportunities for leapfrogging. In India and other parts of the developing world, for example, governments are moving directly to solar-powered LED lights that take advantage of the latest technology and avoid problems with unpredictable public power supplies.

## Organizing Brands and Marketing

Although it only arrived in African markets in the past decade, Korean manufacturer LG Electronics has made rapid progress by actively organizing the market. LG's experiences in Morocco illustrate its astute use of promotions and communications to organize the market. When LG arrived in Morocco in 2000, Sony was already the dominant brand, but it was sold only through traders rather than dedicated dealers. Since 2000, LG has had an annual growth rate of almost 50 percent in Morocco, driven in large part by its promotions centered on Muslim holy days. The company organized promotions for refrigerators during *Eid-al-Kebir*, or Festival of Sacrifice, when devout Muslims traditionally sacrifice a lamb, on the tenth day of the last month of the Muslim calendar. In 2007, LG sold 30 percent of its refrigerators during this period.

LG recognized that Ramadan is an important time for sales of televisions because it is a time when many new television programs are developed. LG created promotions for Ramadan, and by 2007 this holiday period made up 25 percent of its sales of televisions and other appliances. LG has also tapped into the returning diaspora. In the summer, Moroccans living and working abroad swarm back home, their pockets full of cash, so LG organized big promotions for these returning workers, family members, and other visitors. Tourism in Morocco is also driving demand for flat-screen televisions in hotels, airports, and airlines. LG now makes 12 percent of its sales during the June tourist period. The company also organizes a woman's day every year.

In discussions with Ali Lakhdar of LGE in Morocco in 2007, I learned that in addition to promotion, LG organized the market through communications and branding. It was the first to make substantial investments in media to increase brand awareness, including outdoor billboards and sponsorship of concerts and sporting events. LG became one of the top television advertisers in Morocco. In 2001, it launched the LG Soccer Cup. This helped to position the brand as aspirational, going after the top of the market and those who aspired to join this segment. In 2003, it launched the LG Hope program in Morocco with Korea University's volunteer medical team, offering free surgery to Moroccan youth suffering from cleft lip. It also built 100 branded mini-shops within electronic shops and a premium showroom in Casablanca.

LG's unaided awareness in Morocco reached 71 percent by 2006, according to Nielsen studies. By 2006, LG had captured more than a third of the market for digital displays and 40 percent of the market for digital appliances, as well as 15 percent of the market for mobile handsets.

The company also had success in brand building in other parts of Africa. In South Africa, LG was the most recognized electronics brand in the Markinor survey of brand value, surpassing more established brands such as Sony and Philips, and earned a position in the top ten of all consumer brands. Although it came into Nigeria only in 2004, two years later it already commanded 40 percent of the market for home appliances there. Its success was attributed to strong ties with local dealers, its own sales force, and marketing communications, with 60 percent of Nigerian consumers recognizing the brand. In Sudan, the company opened the largest African showroom for digital appliances in 2006.[17]

But the problem with being the pioneer in organizing the market is that it makes it easier for competitors to follow the same path. In addition to competitors, LG faced threats from smugglers who do not pay excise tax and counterfeit items from China. New low-priced brands such as Goldvision, which were manufactured in Morocco to avoid excise tax, were targeting the mid-market. (As of early 2007, LG imported its products and did not have local manufacturing in Morocco.)

LG has to keep organizing the market to stay ahead. More recently, the company focused on stepping up after-sale service in Morocco. It built 30 service centers throughout the country, organizing the service market and helping fulfill a promise to customers that if they bring in an appliance, it will be fixed within 24 to 36 hours. Outside of the city, it will be fixed within 36 to 48 hours. By organizing marketing and communications, LG has built a significant business and presence across Africa.

African markets are dominated by traders who are interested in selling products rather than building brands. This creates an opportunity for companies that make the investment, as LG did, in building brands in African markets. Some companies might consider that the markets are not attractive enough. But LG's experience shows that there are tremendous opportunities in using marketing communications, distribution, service, and an understanding of buying habits to organize the market.

## Creating Brands from Commodities

Commodities such as sugar and rice usually are sold by the scoopful in kiosks and other marketplaces throughout Africa. Soap is sold by shop owners who break off a piece of laundry soap. Another way to organize the market is to turn these unbranded commodities into branded products. For example, Nigerian-based Dangote, one of the largest trading companies in Africa, worked to build brands for its sugar and cement. Instead of the 50kg (100 lb.) bags of sugar that it sold to business customers and small retailers who would divide it up further, the company packaged its sugar in cubes and smaller bags for retail sale. Because the market is very price sensitive, the company emphasized the superior sweetening of its sugar—one teaspoon of its sugar is equal to two of competitors.

Dangote also began pushing its brand into retail, offering key retailers orange and white umbrellas (there is a five-month rainy season in Nigeria) and polo shirts emblazoned with the Dangote logo, as shown in Exhibit 22. The small shop owners became walking billboards. These promotions are aimed at Africa Two and Africa Three (the mid to low end of the market, as discussed in Chapter 3). The company was doing the same thing with cement. This has helped move undifferentiated commodity products into branded products, building a market.

Although Unilever long had offered Omo laundry detergent in Nigeria and other African markets, it introduced its new Key laundry bar in Nigeria to create a product to appeal to Africa Three. These customers usually bought unbranded laundry bars from local kiosks as a cheaper alternative to powdered detergents. The Key bar was a branded version of these laundry bars, scored into sections so that it could be cut up at resale or by consumers. But each segment was marked with the Key brand. Customers also used these bars flexibly, for both laundry and personal washing, so the company experimented with different colors, moving from the traditional green bars to pink bars with fragrance. This allowed the company to create a market for branded bars to compete with unbranded alternatives.

African markets, like most emerging markets, start out as generic markets. To establish brands, companies need to organize these unbranded markets. In South Africa, retail has reached a point where branded generics are starting to emerge. For example, retailer Pick 'n Pay offers a popular generic brand, simply called "No Name" in South Africa, targeting Africa Two and Three. But in most parts of the market, branding is just taking root. Part of organizing the market is moving unbranded products into branded products.

# Organizing Education and Training

On a Friday afternoon when I visited Suresh Chellaram's office in Lagos, he had a pillow on his couch that read "Without stress, my life would be empty." As managing director of the trading company Chellarams Group Plc, one of his biggest sources of stress was human resources. The local educational system is poor. This meant that it was hard to find employees at any level with the necessary skills. And it was hard to attract expatriate managers and skilled personnel to the country. The best expats went to work at banks or multinational firms for higher wages. The company, which was founded in 1923 in Nigeria by Chellaram's great-grandfather, who came from Sindh (in what is now Pakistan), imports or makes diverse products, including industrial chemicals, foam mattresses, cosmetics, milk and cheese, motorcycles, generators, and garments. It has even moved into service businesses such as airline catering and running airport lounges.

To meet the need for education and training, Chellarams has had to organize its own institute. The company set up a training center in a warehouse complex near the airport. It offered more than 100 training courses, from tasks as simple as attaching a nut to a bolt to business strategy. Because the market did not offer a supply of qualified employees, the company had to organize their own educational system to make up the deficit.

In Morocco, The Coca-Cola Company sponsored its own university, teaching shopkeepers how to use Excel spreadsheets and training salespeople. Many industries are facing similar challenges, although, as discussed in Chapter 8, "Coming Home: Opportunities in the African Diaspora," the diaspora is helping to fill some of the demand for experienced managers.

# The Power of Organizing Markets

African markets are not plug and play. There is almost always a missing piece of the puzzle. In the case of Hanouti, it was the ability to offer credit. For LG, it was promotion and advertising. For companies such as Novartis, Unilever, and Dangote, it was branding. Sometimes distribution systems are in disarray. Many of these infrastructure challenges create specific opportunities to fill needs for power, fresh water, and other essentials, as discussed in the next chapter. But companies also can find opportunities by thinking creatively to take informal and disorganized parts of the market and organizing them.

# Rising Opportunities

- How can you create or capitalize on opportunities in Africa by organizing the market?
- How can you organize distribution?
- How can you organize marketing communications?
- What opportunities are presented by secondhand markets?
- How can you move commodities to branded products?
- How do you need to organize education?
- How can you utilize the existing channels such as corporate employees?
- How can you use partnerships with government and other players to organize the market?

# 5

## Building Mama Habiba an Ice Factory: Opportunities in Infrastructure

*The many infrastructure weaknesses and other challenges facing African nations—from clean water to electricity to medicine—create opportunities to build businesses that profitably meet social needs.*

Africa, like many other emerging markets, is a continent in need. It has shortages of fresh drinking water, electricity, and medicine. Its infrastructure is weak or nonexistent in many areas. This may make Africa the biggest charity case in the world. Or, through a different lens, it could be the world's greatest potential market. Companies that see these problems as "opportunities in work clothes" have been able to build successful businesses and support local entrepreneurs. Many of the dark clouds of Africa offer a silver lining of opportunity.

## Providing Power and Ice

Dressed in a patterned dress and brown *gele*, the traditional Nigerian headdress, Mama Habiba sat in a chair out front of her small store on a warm day in July 2006. Her shop was in the middle of a row of small shops in the POWA market (named for the Police Officers Wives Association), which extended along both sides of the street at Falomo in the Ikoyi section of Lagos. This was the kind of day that made you want to reach for a cold bottle of Coca-Cola. Her records showed that she sold 265 cases of soda from The Coca-Cola Company in June, about 5,000 bottles, and she said sales were much higher in December, with a combination of the dry season and Christmas holiday.

A 35cl (12 oz.) returnable glass bottle sold for 35 naira (about 25 cents), and a new 50cl (17 oz.) plastic PET bottle retailed for almost three times as much, 90 naira (still a discount from the 100N suggested price stamped on its cap). These small retailers account for about 70 percent of soda sales in Nigeria.

Of course, her floor-to-ceiling Coca-Cola cooler (given by the company as a reward to shops that sell more than 30 cases per week) operated only when there was power. And Mama Habiba noted that power was sometimes out for as long as two days. When the power was off, customers drank their sodas warm, but The Coca-Cola Company was building its own ice plant to supply these small shops during power outages. Some of the wealthier shop owners in the POWA market have generators in their basements that allow them to sell cold beverages when the power fails—as it inevitably does. Others have small portable generators out on the sidewalk that serve the same purpose, if less elegantly. Outside one shop in the POWA market, a red Chinese-made Tigmax generator sits on an old automobile tire to buffer against vibrations, as shown in the foreground of the photo in Exhibit 23 in the insert). (Generators are another big market opportunity, and perhaps there is a product innovation that could replace the makeshift tire to reduce vibrations.)

The roughly 700 million people in sub-Saharan Africa, excluding South Africa, have about as much access to electricity as the 38 million people in Poland.[1] Office buildings and wealthier private homes in Nigeria typically have at least one large generator. Even in the most expensive hotels, the lights dim or flicker out momentarily as the generators kick in. In the exercise room of the Sheraton in Lagos, with every power outage, the lights would go off and the treadmills power down momentarily before a set of generators almost as big as the small gym roared to life. Some offices have twin generators because they run so much that there is a need for a backup for the backup.

In Kenya, Kirloskar of India makes larger power sources such a 20-kilowatt generator that might retail for about 500,000 Kenyan shillings (about $7,000). Competitors such as Honda, Yamaha, or Chinese firms make smaller models for shops or single homes that might retail for a few hundred dollars. In some rural areas, however, Kirloskar sells its larger generators to a groups of 30 families who pool together to buy a larger generator, sometimes with the help of financing from an NGO. A single midsize generator empowers villagers to create their own "community power plant."

While visiting an executive at a major company in Tunisia, which has a reputation for reliable electricity, I heard a boom. The office lost its electricity, and the backup generator kicked in. His computer did not even go off. He explained that he had an inverter to provide uninterrupted power to the computer between the loss of power and ignition of the generator.

Even countries with more stable infrastructures such as South Africa have found their growth threatened by limited electricity. After a series of blackouts in early 2008, the result of rapid growth and slow construction of infrastructure, South Africa instituted a program of rationing for industrial users. The shortages shut down mining operations temporarily and stopped or slowed other businesses in a country that is used to a steady supply of power. Rapid growth of the economy and delays in building the necessary infrastructure led to the shortages.[2] Along with expansion of the state-run Eskom, the government has encouraged private development, including a project led by U.S. energy company AES, which is building two plants that will generate 1,000 megawatts.[3] All this will take years, however.

This might mean that until these power plants are built there could be a growing market for generators and alternatives such as solar cells. For example, after the blackouts snarled traffic in Johannesburg, traffic officials installed solar backup systems in the traffic lights to avoid future gridlock. Solar cells also provide electricity in areas that are off the grid. With a solar cell array, a person in a rural village can power up a television or charge a cell phone. In Uganda, four remote villages near Fort Portal are using a combination of solar-powered computers, wireless networks, and cell phones to connect with the world even though the nearest landline is 4 miles away. While still pricey even in developed countries, solar power is growing rapidly around the globe, which should reduce prices. Between 2004 and 2007, the total market cap of solar companies around the globe increased from $1 billion to more than $70 billion.

Wind power is another possibility. The African Wind Energy Association notes that its equatorial location gives Africa lower wind resources than areas in more extreme latitudes, but India's rapid growth of wind power is a sign of the potential (www.afriwea.org). The Atlas Mountains in Morocco are already covered with rows of windmills, part of a plan to generate 10 percent of the country's electricity from wind by 2011. Africa has one of the world's largest reserves of uranium, so nuclear energy might be an important source of power in the future.

There are also other creative solutions. Magara Bagayogo, the mayor of Kelea in northern Mali, converted his village to locally made jatropha oil as part of a green energy initiative.[4] In Kenya, the entrepreneurial firm TechnoServe created a technology to use waste from coffee processing to make methane gas, while cleaning the highly acidic water, which can contaminate soil.

The spread of other technology such as cell phones can sometimes help address power shortages. To keep its phone network running in Nigeria, wireless company MultiLinks had to put generators on almost every cell tower. Where there is no fiber on the ground, the company needed to use satellites. Cellular companies also had to worry about the security of the towers. Celtel in Kenya allowed local villagers to tap into the electricity of their rural towers to charge their own cell phones. This is a boon to the community, but also gives them a stake in protecting the towers from vandalism. In rural areas, enterprising entrepreneurs also rig up car batteries to offer charging, for a fee, of cell phones or other electrical equipment. ASSAD in Tunisia has built a thriving business selling replacement batteries for a growing automotive industry, and other industrial batteries.

Other innovations, such as replacing incandescent light bulbs with LEDs, reduce the need for power. In South Africa, The Coca-Cola Company offers paraffin coolers where there are no power lines at all. For more upscale segments (only 6 percent of residents of Tunis, for example, have air conditioning, although 90 percent have televisions), the split air conditioner is a popular item. There is a tremendous need for new innovations and new sources of electricity.

The World Bank has increased financing of sub-Saharan power projects from $250 million in 2002 to $1 billion in 2007. South Africa plans more than $20 billion in improvements, and China and India have financed much of the $1.2 billion in upgrades planned for

Zambia.[5] The world's largest hydroelectric dam has been proposed for the Congo River in the Democratic Republic of Congo. The Grand Inga Dam would cost $80 billion and have twice the capacity of the Three Gorges Dam in China. It could produce enough electricity to serve all the 500 million Africans who currently do not have electricity. In 2008, Nigeria developed a plan to invest more than $20 billion to diverting its abundant supply of liquid natural gas, a prime export, into producing domestic power. The plan called for devoting as much as 25 to 30 percent of gas to address the country's power crisis, which is seen as a limiting factor for its growth.

At the other extreme, small-scale solutions are under development. For example, the Swiss company Solar 3, which received the European Renewable Energy Company of the Year Award in 2007, has developed a three-in-one solution that addresses the need for power, water, and education in developing markets. The device produces electricity from wind and sun, water from air humidity, and is equipped with a simple durable laptop with educational software. The company is testing its "Little Wind House" in Africa and other parts of the developing world. The Davis and Shirtliff Group has created a similar device in Kenya, a water pump that can be powered by solar panels, wind turbines, or both.

Power is a critical concern across Africa. Lack of reliable power has already reduced annual growth rates by more than 2 percent in countries with the most severe shortages, according to the World Bank. Although the deepening power shortages are dampening growth and worsening pollution, this need is also defining markets. The demand for power is leading to new investments in large-scale power projects in addition to creating markets for smaller generators, solar, wind, and other solutions.

# Water Pumps

Providing the infrastructure to take water out of the ground and move it around is also a tremendous opportunity. In Egypt, a country where water pressure is low, an Italian company, Calpeda, has become the market leader in pumps for individual homes, even though its products are two or three times more expensive than Chinese and Indian competitors. More than 100,000 of these pumps are sold in Egypt annually, a market of more than $7 million in Egypt alone.

One of the most innovative solutions to the challenge of pumping water in a world with a shortage of electricity was developed by the nonprofit organization Roundabout. It created a "playpump" that harnesses the merry-go-round play of children to pump water for rural villages in Africa. This project has provided fresh water to hundreds of thousands of Africans. The U.S.-based nonprofit organization Kick-Start has created affordable tools such as a low-cost irrigation pump. The pumps helped create more than 50,000 new businesses by November 2007, and these businesses generated an estimated $54 million per year in profits and wages.[6] The pumps are helping make farmers more productive and creating small enterprises that have helped lift thousands of Africans out of poverty.

A market also exists for larger pumps. In addition to the generators mentioned previously, Kirloskar builds water pumps, engines, generators, and drilling equipment used by businesses from flower farms to mining operations to maize mills. In discussions with Mwangi Mathai, A. M. Kelkar, and R. S. Patil of Kirloskar Kenya Limited, I found out that the total market for small engines to drive maize mills in Kenya is about $800,000 per year. The market for pumps, used by salt plants on the coast, and compressors, for the finishing industry, is about $2 million, and the market for centrifugal pumps for irrigation is about $10 million—just in Kenya. There is clearly a strong market in Africa for finding water and moving it around.

## Sanitation, Water, and Air

There is perhaps no more basic need than simple sanitation, but it is in short supply throughout Africa. Septic systems are poorly developed, particularly in the rural and high-density areas that are home to Africa Three. This contributes to disease and erodes the quality of life. Entrepreneurs have stepped into the gap by providing mobile toilets.

Isaac Durojaiye founded Dignified Mobile Toilets in Lagos in 1992 when he estimated that Nigeria had only 500 functioning public toilets, in a country that now has a population of more than 140 million.[7] There was clearly a huge need. He placed his plastic portable toilets in high-density areas such as bus stops and motor parks in major cities. Each toilet serves about 100 people per day, who pay 20 naira (about 15 cents) each, thus earning about $15 per day. Durojaiye has set up local entrepreneurs to run the toilets, allowing them to keep 60 percent of the earnings. Dignified Mobile Toilets also allows advertising on the toilet doors, which accounts for about 25 percent of its revenue, and is working on plans to recycle the waste to generate bio-gas, electricity, and fertilizer. This is just one of several similar initiatives to address this challenge in different African nations.

One-third of the world's population does not have access to modern sanitation. The World Toilet Organization, established in 2001, showed off recent innovations to address this challenge at its 2007 summit meeting in India, including an incinerator toilet that uses 1 kilowatt of electricity to produce a spoonful of ash, saving water.[8] Other innovations convert waste to bio-gas that can be used for cooking and power generation. This system, created by Bindeshwar Pathak's Sulabb sanitation movement in India, has been adopted by 15 countries in southern Africa.

A shortage of drinkable water is critical concern across Africa, which lends itself to creative solutions. Plan International, an aid organization, realized that they could sterilize water by putting it in bottles on the roofs of houses rather than heating it with wood fires. This solar sterilization saves precious firewood while offering a solution that could be used across Africa. Coastal countries are constructing desalination plants to extract drinking water from seawater. Namibia hired South African firm Keyplan to build a $140 million plant that will produce 45 million cubic meters of water per year.[9]

Clean air is also a growing concern with rising populations and urbanization. Basic cooking and heating systems present a serious health risk in developing countries. Open stoves fill dwellings with smoke. The Shell Foundation, working with Envirofit International at Colorado State University, has rolled out a stove that is more fuel efficient and cleaner burning than existing ones. The team announced plans in 2008 to distribute 10 million stoves in Uganda, Kenya, India, and Brazil over five years. This will help meet the need for stoves while reducing the estimated 1.6 million deaths that occur due to the health effects of toxic indoor air pollution.[10]

Poor sanitation and a shortage of clean water and air are not just societal needs; they are market opportunities. Where are the global innovators in sanitation? Where are the companies that recognize and can meet these pressing needs?

# Airlines

Across the continent, building the infrastructure for airlines creates channels to move people and products in and out of Africa to promote commerce and tourism. The growth of airlines is vital in linking African nations to the world and bringing goods and services from China, India, and different parts of the world. Airlines are a sign of the growth of many areas of Africa. Kenya Airways, Ethiopian Airlines, South African Airways, AirMoroc, Egypt Air, and many other carriers have built successful businesses by creating the infrastructure to weave the continent together and connect it to the world. Emirates Airlines has created a major hub running through Dubai, connecting Northern Africa and other parts of Africa to Asia and other parts of the world. Major global carriers are showing increased interest in the continent. Virgin Nigeria, launched in 2006, offers service between the United Kingdom, United States, and Nigeria, and within Nigeria and neighboring countries. Delta launched a U.S. flight between Atlanta, Georgia, and Lagos, Nigeria, in December 2007, and announced plans for flights between the United States and Egypt, Kenya, Senegal, and South Africa.

Countries across Africa are beginning to open their airline industries to increasing competition, encouraging the development of new routes within Africa and spurring the rise of discount carriers. Discount carriers, emulating Southwest Airlines and other no-frills operations, are taking off, an indication of the attractiveness and maturity of the market. Carriers such as Kulula.com, founded in South Africa in 2001, and Kenyan-based Lonrho have expanded their operations. Morocco's Jet4U offered flights from Casablanca to Paris for as little as $30 (140 dirhan). Hapagfly, one of the leading low-cost airlines in Europe, started offering four weekly flights from Cairo to Munich, Germany, for a price of 1,500 Egyptian pounds (about $270), about half the cost of legacy carriers. Another discount carrier, Jet Only, started regularly scheduled flights between Cairo and Brussels. Zambian Airways has established low-cost service to Johannesburg to carry migrant workers to South Africa for about $20, less than the cost of the bus.

Ethiopian Airlines is investing in a new cargo terminal to facilitate trade with India, China, the Middle East, and Europe. The air terminal and shipping terminals in Addis are transporting meat out to the Gulf. Ethiopian Airlines is carrying passengers to China, where it has been running flights since 1972, and bringing back inexpensive Chinese products. The airline also does a growing business in carrying flowers to Europe, returning with medicine and spare parts. By 2006, Ethiopian Airlines was carrying 70 tons a day of flowers to the markets in Holland, with plans to increase to 100 tons daily. Given how little flowers weigh, that is a lot of flowers. The new terminal will have cool rooms to keep the flowers fresh in transit. This follows the creation of one of the first modern passenger terminals on the continent in one of Africa's poorest countries, helping Ethiopian win African Airline of the Year in 2006 (named by *African Aviation Journal*). The airline is at the center of Ethiopia's strategy to increase tourism from 250,000 visitors to more than one million.

In an interview with the author in 2006, Ethiopian Airlines CEO Girma Wake explained the virtuous cycle of the flower industry and airline. "Poor farmers who otherwise have no job will have a job," he said. "Because they have employment, they will send their children to school. Their children will be better citizens tomorrow, and they can afford to do something for the country. And they probably also will fly."

Ethiopia is a landlocked country with 75 million people, 85 percent of whom live in rural areas. With a strong airline and storage facilities, however, it is connected to global markets.

Wake introduced me to some of the entrepreneurs in his country who are using the transportation networks to build thriving businesses in agriculture, textiles, coffee, and other industries. Tsegaye Abebe, who owns three flower and vegetable farms in Ethiopia, has been a driving force in helping develop the country into the second-largest flower exporter after Kenya. The country now exports $120 million in flowers annually to Europe. The success is based on a combination of government support, airlines, refrigerated facilities, and the region's naturally good sunlight. Growing at about 200 percent per year, Ethiopia expects to catch up to Kenya in this business in the next five years. The industry employs 50,000 people directly and more than 240,000 indirectly. Although they don't consume the crops they grow for European markets, they do use the income to buy other vital products. "We export strawberries, passion fruit, and green beans, and buy medicine for our people," Abebe said in an interview with the author.

In textiles, Ethiopian entrepreneur Zewde Worku is using air freight to export 1 million pieces of apparel to different sports chain stores in the United States, and is employing 600 people. An expatriate and former chiropractor in California, he returned to Ethiopia because of increasingly progressive policies of the government. He said many others are coming back. These products are joining traditional exports such as coffee, which still accounts for about half of the country's exports.

Airlines are carrying tourists, executives, entrepreneurs, and products that represent a powerful force of transformation for the continent. They bring in visitors and investors and serve Africa One and Two segments (see Chapter 3, "The Power of Africa Two") with new carriers pushing deeper into the market with low fares. As the growth of Ethiopian agricultural and textile businesses illustrates, airline infrastructure is a foundation for further growth.

## Opportunities for Leapfrogging

When Greg Wyler from Boston, Massachusetts, founded Internet service provider Terracom in Rwanda, he hoped to make the country Africa's first fully wired nation.[11] Terracom's Internet service cost about $60 per month in 2006, about a third of the average annual income in the country. Much of the country was without reliable power as it rebuilt after the genocide more than a decade ago when ruling Hutus killed more than 800,000 Tutsis.

Terracom invested more than $15 million to lay more than 200 miles of fiber by 2006, with another 700 miles planned for the following two years. Wyler had to carry tons of equipment by foot to towers on rugged mountain peaks because the air is too thin for helicopters. At a time when France Telecom and Vivendi SA scaled back operations in the Rwandan market, Terracom deepened its investments. In October 2005, Wyler spent $20 million to acquire Rwandtel, the Rwandan telecom monopoly, giving him access to cellular networks and expanding his coverage to more than 60 percent of the population. Terracom also offered cellular service for about a third of the rate of rival MTN. After its merger with GV Telecom in July 2006, the company was looking to expand its model to Nigeria, Kenya, and Congo.

### *The Rise of Internet*

Given the obstacles, Internet penetration is still very low in Africa, under 5 percent (or about 44 million users) in December 2007. This is less than the 60 million online in India and 210 million in China, but more than the 34 million in South Korea and almost 20 times the number in Singapore. Africa's online connections are growing faster than anywhere in the world except the Middle East. From 2000 to 2007, Internet usage grew by more than 880 percent across Africa, compared to 347 percent for Asia and 120 percent for North America. Among the African countries with the highest number of Internet users were Nigeria, Morocco, Egypt, South Africa, Sudan, and Kenya.[12]

Africa's first connection to the Internet was through a submarine fiber-optic cable running from Portugal to the west coast, but European and Indian companies have launched diverse projects to link to East Africa. Projects such as the East African Submarine Cable System (EASSy), Kenya's The East African Marine Systems (TEAMS), America's Seacom, the Indian-based Reliance Consortium,[13] and the South Atlantic 3/West Africa Submarine Cable (SAT-3/WASC) are linking Africa to the world. The World Bank's International Finance Corporation is investing up to $32.5 million in the EASSy project, which is expected to bring an additional 250 million Africans online by 2009.[14] Meanwhile, more than two dozen African nations signed on to invest $1 billion in a pan-African e-Network satellite project, financed through a grant from the Indian government. This project will meet the need for Internet and voice communications across Africa, particularly in remote areas.[15]

Internet cafés and schools put hardware and online access in the hands of many more people who cannot afford their own equipment or service contracts. Terracom in Rwanda has set up its own Internet cafés, where users can pay about 20 cents for 15 minutes. Beyond the cafés, the ubiquitous cell phone offers another channel onto the Internet for people without access to computers.

Some parts of Africa are leaping past the rest of the world. FGC Wireless, an indigenous company in Sierra Leone, wired the capital Freetown for wireless Internet. According to FCG Wireless, the nation's capital became the third city in the world to have citywide unrestricted WiFi/WiMax network, after Philadelphia in the United States and Taipei in Taiwan.[16] Although creating the network was challenging, it shows the opportunities in Africa to create infrastructure and systems that are equal to the best in the world.

In late 2007, Africa's largest Internet development center opened in Accra, Ghana. It was the first African site developed by BusyInternet, which specializes in markets that are traditionally underserved. The new center is an entrepreneur's dream, with a 60-seat learning center, 100 public-access flat-screen computers, and 4,000 square feet of office space where small businesses and organizations can develop Internet-related programs.

In Morocco, I heard from a Hewlett-Packard executive about how the expansion of broadband Internet (digital subscriber line, DSL) is driving the rapid growth of the computer business. DSL, offered at $10 per month, and the availability of bank financing for computer purchases have helped drive double-digit growth in computer sales. The availability of computers and Internet access has encouraged the growth of small businesses, too.

The medina (old city) of Fez in Morocco is using some of the most modern geographical information technology to plan for the city's future, including analyzing its transportation and sanitation needs. It has deployed a Geographical Information System (GIS) to manage its infrastructure on streets that are so narrow that the main form of transportation is donkey or a two-wheeler. The most sophisticated modern technology is coming to cities built in the seventh and eighth centuries.

I visited the extraordinary *Bibliotheca Alexandria* (Library of Alexandria) in Egypt, a cultural complex near the site of one of the world's greatest ancient libraries, built more than 2,000 years ago. It is now one of the most technologically advanced libraries on the planet. This library has space for 8 million books, 3 museums, 7 research institutes, several exhibition galleries, a planetarium, and a conference center. It has the latest high-tech, multimedia, and digital resources.[17] Egypt also has a contemporary museum celebrating famous singer Om Kolthoum, saving her classical music in one of the most high-tech audiovisual museums in the world.

## Wireless

A study I conducted with Alina Chircu on mobile technologies in BRIC countries (Brazil, Russia, India, and China) found that these countries have leapfrogged developed countries in data services, transaction services, media, and other areas, bridging or even reversing the so-called digital divide. These countries offer lessons about how technology can be expected to progress in Africa and other parts of the world.[18] Whereas technology depth may equal developed countries, these areas often introduce a greater number of services than some developed countries. This leapfrogging is illustrated by the Smart Village outside Cairo. When I visited in the fall of 2006, its wide avenues were lined with shining new buildings that rise from neatly manicured lawns. They were circled by cranes adding to names such as Microsoft, Vodafone, and Hewlett-Packard. It was clear that the world's best technology was coming to this nation. In a conference room in the Vodafone headquarters, Khaled El Khouly, head of Enterprise Marketing, discussed the challenges of the perception of the country as a land of pyramids and camels. "There is a problem in branding countries," he said. In fact, Egypt had 15 million cell phone subscribers when we met in 2006, and was adding 5 million connections a year in a potential market of 35 to 40 million.

Vodafone has had to rethink its phone service based on how customers actually use the phones. For example, many customers use of "paging," or "missed calls." A user who cannot afford to pay for a call rings a friend and hangs up. The recipient of the call sees the phone number and returns the call. Because the call is not completed, the provider generates no revenue. Users also use missed calls to send signals. A couple might make a missed call to say hello in the morning, or a visitor might make a missed call to indicate that he has arrived in the lobby.

Recognizing this pattern of missed calls, Vodaphone found a better way to provide this service. It set up a consumer panel to study missed calls, and created a new service called *wayak* (it's with you) that allowed users to send a free text message asking for a return call. A text message is cheaper for Vodaphone to carry than a missed voice call. The wayak service also helped build acceptance for SMS, which was initially slow to catch on in the market. Vodaphone is now selling ringtones and it introduced balance transfers of mobile phone minutes in September 2004, logging 2.5 million transactions per month two years later.

Shared phones are also popular among low-income customers. In Morocco, the MIFA Group's Iliacom (meaning "to you") has seen phenomenal growth for its satellite-based service (GSM) sold through more than 50,000 tele-boutiques throughout the country. Because this uses satellite rather than cell phone technology, it is particularly effective in rural areas. Iliacom is using microfinancing and working with the government to set up phones in small shops throughout the country. Users pay the shop owner based on a meter. Because most of these call centers are at points of purchase, the company realized it could work with other companies to subsidize the phones or generate advertising revenue. For example, The Coca-Cola Company created a phone box shaped like a Coca-Cola bottle (which also helped Coca-Cola to achieve it goal of increasing penetration in rural areas).

Bruce Cockburn, sales director of Leaf Technologies, pointed out during a meeting in Johannesburg that South Africa has some of the most sophisticated electronic banking in the world, with widespread use of automatic tellers, including wireless ATMs in remote areas. Small devices that Leaf makes use wireless signals to link a point-of-sale credit card reader into banking systems, allowing small vendors to accept credit cards. "The banking system here is probably more sophisticated than in the States," said Cockburn. "As a country, we are technology hungry. Laborers who earn 60 rand (or about $10) per day, every single one of them has a cell phone. There is deep penetration of wireless."

### Access to Millions of Books

New technologies such as electronic books could also have a major impact on Africa and other developing regions. In 2007, Amazon launched a wireless book, Kindle, that can download books to a reader through wireless networks. Although still expensive in the context of African markets (about $400), such technology and initiatives such as Google's book project could put the libraries of the world into the hands of readers across Africa. Professor Raj Reddy's Million Book Project (www.ulib.org) now offers more than 1.5 million books in 20 languages to anyone with Internet access. The Library of Alexandria in Egypt recently joined Carnegie Mellon University in the United States, Zhejian University in China, and the Indian Institute of Science in India for this project. This means that an Internet-linked computer can give a remote African village access to resources unrivaled by the largest universities.

Such innovations are particularly important because the current market for traditional books in Africa is fragmented and underdeveloped. Most publishers I talked with don't consider Africa to be an attractive market yet, although they are now moving aggressively into China and India. This is not because of lack of interest in books, and the continent has been the source of Nobel Prize–winning authors. Retailers on the ground, unlike publishers based in the United States and Europe, have recognized these opportunities. Nakumatt in Kenya, for example, has established bookstores within its stores, offering many Western bestsellers, including business books.

The weak state of bookselling across Africa is best illustrated by the fact that African authors have an easier time selling books abroad than at home. For example, *The Economist* noted in 2007 that Chimamanda Adichie's novel *Half a Yellow Sun*, which sold more than 240,000 copies in Britain, had sold just 5,000 in her native Nigeria, in part because of the weak or nonexistent distribution networks.[19] The lack of distribution becomes a self-fulfilling prophecy, because with low sales, publishers and distributors are reluctant to invest.

## High-Yield Crops

Bio-agriculture offers another opportunity for leapfrogging, although it has become very controversial. While it might lack the hype of cell phones and the Internet, there is no technology more crucial to Africa's future than agriculture. There is an urgent social need as well as an economic imperative to improve African agriculture. Even though 60 percent of the Africans are directly engaged in agriculture, a third of the population is malnourished.[20] In Kenya, the average household spends 65 percent to 85 percent of monthly income on food, compared to about 15 percent to 20 percent in Europe and the United States.

High population levels and land degradation are eroding agricultural output in many areas. Peter Rammutla, president of the National African Farmer's Union, which represents 250,000 small-scale black farmers in South Africa, said in 2003 that Africa's crop production was the lowest in the world, at 1.7 tons per 1 hectare (about 2.5 acres) compared with 4 tons globally.[21] Its productivity has stagnated for decades while Asian yield has tripled and Latin American yield has doubled. Although genetically modified foods were initially very controversial in Africa, as in other parts of the world, the need for inexpensive food and increased production for small farmers is leading to calls for a "green revolution" in Africa. This was the focus of the Summit on Fertilizer that drew together some 40 African heads of state in Abuja, Nigeria, in June 2006, part of the Comprehensive Africa Agriculture Development Programme, with a goal of raising farm yields by 6 percent by 2015.

Scientists have developed new breeds of plants designed to flourish in Africa, but there are still many logistical challenges in getting them to where they are needed. Monty Jones, a plant breeder from Sierra Leone, was named as one of *Time* magazine's 100 most influential people for his creation of New Rices for Africa (NERICA), high-productivity rices designed to flourish in West Africa. Such new seeds are the centerpiece of a green revolution supported by the Gates and Rockefeller foundations and the African Development Bank. Even so, by late 2007 the underdeveloped infrastructure of Africa—including a lack of credit to buy seeds and fertilizers, poor roads, and insufficient storage facilities for crops—had limited the spread of these new crops to only about 5 percent of the land where they could be grown.[22]

Pioneer Hi-Bred International, Inc., a DuPont business that is the world's leading developer and supplier of advanced plant genetics to farmers worldwide, has operations in South Africa, Zimbabwe, Ethiopia, Kenya, and Egypt. Its primary product is maize (corn), which is a staple food. Although the majority of South African maize is grown by large farms, most of the rest of Africa is dominated by small farmers. In Kenya, Pioneer introduced a hybrid seed in the Chura region. It also worked on improving management practices such as analyzing soil nutrients, reducing tillage, using integrated pest management, and improving use of fertilizer to increase yields. The company created 14 demonstration plots in 2004, and an additional 90 farmers bought the hybrid seed with low-cost financing from the Africa Harvest project. Africa Harvest Biotech Foundation International (AHBFI) was founded in January 2002 by Dr. Florence Wambugu, who worked on her post-doctoral studies in the United States, studying the genetically modified sweet potato. When she returned to Nairobi, the sweet potato became the first GM crop introduced in sub-Saharan Africa.

Monsanto's BT cotton, which reduces the need for pesticides, has been a great success, and today 95 percent of all cotton grown in South Africa is BT cotton. The economic impact of such advances is phenomenal, particularly for small farmers who can increase their yield and significantly decrease their pesticide use. Although originally expected to be used only by large-scale farmers, the cotton has been widely adopted by small farmers. For example, Thandiwe Myeni, a farmer, school principal, and widowed mother of five who chairs the Mbuso farmers association in the Makatini Flats in South Africa, adopted BT cotton. She had been planting 10 hectares (25 acres) of cotton in 1994 using conventional seed. By moving to BT, she increased her productivity and profitability. This allowed her to expand her farm and improve her home.[23]

High-tech solutions are also being developed for agriculture. In the dry regions of western South Africa, Pioneer has introduced neutron moisture meter technology that can make planting decisions more precise, increasing yields by more than 4 tons per hectare. This helps farmers better manage the risk of the crops and makes farming more sustainable. The African Laser Centre is designing a laser-based device that can diagnose the condition of crops, developed by Ghanaian Paul Buah-Bassuah from the University of Cape Coast, and South African Hubertus von Bergmann of the University of Stellenbosch.[24]

Of course, the use of genetically modified crops (GMOs) in Africa remains controversial. Former U.N. Secretary General Kofi Annan, president of the Alliance for Green Revolution in Africa (AGRA), ruled out the use of GMOs in its programs, sparking uproar from the scientific community both inside and outside Africa. It also shows that even though the problems of starvation and malnourishment are severe, there is tremendous caution about such innovations within Africa.

Many other opportunities exist to improve African agriculture. For example, the Indo Egyptian Fertilizer Company is using the plentiful supply of phosphates in Egypt to create fertilizer for India. The company is a partnership between 38,000 farmers' cooperatives in India that are part of the Indian Farmers Fertiliser Cooperative Limited (IFFCO) and the Egyptian mining company El Nasar. India is the biggest market for Egyptian phosphates. In India, IFFCO mobile vans go from farm to farm and test soil to recommend what fertilizer to use. The IFFCO also provides high-quality warehouses to farmers and financing, as well as help to get the best price for crops. Why couldn't a similar organization do the same for Africa?

The continent is waking up to the importance of improving agriculture. As former Nigerian President Olusegun Obasanjo wrote in a blueprint for agriculture by the New Partnership for Africa's Development (NEPAD), "After nearly 40 years of economic stagnation... African leaders are applying themselves to finding sustainable solutions to hunger and poverty. NEPAD believes that agriculture will provide the engine for growth in Africa."[25]

# Leading in Infrastructure

Although Africa has gaps in infrastructure, in some areas it also has some of the leading companies in the world. Companies such as

Alexandria Carbon Black in Egypt have proven that African companies can compete at the highest levels in global markets through advanced expertise and state-of-the-art plants.

It might be surprising to know that ships are carrying oil from Texas into Alexandria, Egypt. Africa is, of course, one of the world's most oil-rich continents, and Egypt is a stone's throw from the oil-centered economies of the Middle East. How can it be possible that Africa is *importing* oil from United States? It turns out that this oil is the best source of the highest-quality carbon black, which is produced by Alexandria Carbon Black Co. and shipped out to global manufacturers to use in products from tires to inkjet printer cartridges. Alexandria Carbon Black, part of the Aditya Birla Group of India, is one of the world leaders in manufacturing this essential product. Founded to cater to the domestic Egyptian market, it soon achieved such high levels of quality that it now exports 95 percent of its products to Europe, the United States, and other regions. Its plants produce the world's best quality product. During a meeting in Cairo with K. N. Agarwal, managing director, and other senior executives, I was impressed by the company's leadership in global markets.

Even after building the world's largest carbon black plant, by mid-2006 the company had sold out its entire 2007 capacity while three plants of competitors in Europe had shut down. The company sent as many as 50 containers a day from Alexandria, taking advantage of the fact that many ships were coming to Egypt with goods and returning empty. Africa has demonstrated the capacity to build expertise and infrastructure that allow it to compete with the best world-class companies.

Similarly, the Magadi Soda Company in Kenya (mentioned in Chapter 1, "Baking Bread in Zimbabwe") was established in 1911 and became Africa's leading producer of soda ash used in glass, detergents, and other products. By 2006, it was producing more than 500,000 tons of ash and finishing a plant that would give it the capacity to produce more than 350,000 tons of top-grade premium ash. Magadi already exports 87 percent of its ash to India, Thailand, the Philippines, and a dozen other global markets, with the local market accounting for just 13 percent of production. Like Alexandra Carbon Black, it is owned by an Indian company (Tata Group).

South Africa is even pioneering new technology to transform coal into oil. The plants heat the coal to 2,000 degrees Fahrenheit, add steam and oxygen, and use chemical reactions to transform the coal into 160,000 barrels of oil a day. While coal-to-oil plants had been considered too expensive in most parts of the world, anti-apartheid restrictions on oil imports forced South Africa to pursue the technology to use its huge reserves of coal. Coal-to-oil provides 30 percent of South Africa's transport-fuel needs, and its plant is proudly featured on the nation's 50 rand banknote. As oil prices have risen and the technology has improved, it has become increasingly competitive in other global markets. Governments and companies in the United States, China, and other parts of the world are beating a path to door of South Africa's Sasol, Ltd., which has become the world leader in this technology.

Africa is also building infrastructure around its traditional resource-based industries such as diamond mining. In Botswana, more than 15 international companies have diamond-cutting factories employing thousands of workers to polish and cut diamonds. Botswana, the world's largest diamond producer, used to just export cut stones. But companies set up programs to train workers. Building this infrastructure is helping the country move from shipping out raw materials to developing value-added products within the country, developing local skills, and contributing to local employment. This transfer from harvesting resources to building expertise is an important part of Africa's rise.

Alexandria Carbon Black, Magadi Soda, and other companies have shown that African firms can achieve levels of quality and technological superiority to lead the world. They are proving that the most valuable natural resource in Africa does not come out of the ground. Africa's wealth comes from the innovative ideas and entrepreneurial innovations of its companies and managers.

# Transforming Infrastructure: The Muthaiga Golf Club

The Muthaiga Country Club in Nairobi was the center of white elite society before Kenyan independence. As detailed by Caroline

Elkin in her shocking and well-researched book *Imperial Reckoning: The Untold Story of Britain's Gulag in Kenya*, it was one of the centers of social activity for British leaders who plotted the imprisonment and abuse of hundreds of thousands of members of the Kikuyu tribe, the country's largest ethnic group. The Kikuyu leaders had demanded their independence. Instead, they were essentially imprisoned in villages that were turned into internment camps.

When I visited the Muthaiga Golf Club in July 2006, arranged by David Mureithi of Unilever, it had been transformed. Once a center of colonial power and repression, the golf club (which spun off from the country club nearby) is now like the United Nations. On an afternoon in July 2006, there were Indians, Kenyans, and Anglos sitting around the glass tables in the clubhouse or walking across the sunny and spotless greens. The lunch steaming in silver trays on the patio was very cosmopolitan, with Indian dishes, Chinese stir-fry, fish, potatoes, and sliced carrots next to traditional Kenyan dishes such as arrowroot and a cassava flour dish called *ugari*.

"Before we used to think golf was a rich man's game," said General Manager Lawrence Muye, who said about 75 percent of the club's 1,200 members are now blacks, including some descendents of the Kikuyu leaders of the Mau Mau revolution that helped overthrow the white elite. "Today you see people in the middle class who can join if they can afford the entry fee." The fee is about $3,000 and a slightly lower annual fee. The store is well stocked with all the latest equipment from Dunlop, Nike, Titleist, and other companies.

The layered history of Africa has left behind layers of infrastructure. The colonial period helped to build roads and railroads, but also left behind its own deficiencies. Much of the infrastructure is old or designed for another era. In spite of the end of apartheid in South Africa, the entire infrastructure of the society is organized around the townships, where the poor blacks and Asians live, and the cities, where the rich live and the poor come to work. It can sometimes take a long time for the infrastructure to catch up to the society.

The infrastructure embodies the turbulent history of the past. It reflects the gaps in economic or social development. However, these gaps can be filled. Meeting these needs is sometimes necessary to do business in Africa—like supplying ice to keep Mama Habiba's sodas cool in a country with unreliable power. The gaps in infrastructure can also represent opportunities for building new businesses and even industries, as with the rapid rise of cell phones or spread of other technologies. The pressing needs for food, sanitation, drinking water, health care, and other essentials are a challenge to inventors and entrepreneurs to find ways to meet these market needs. Innovative solutions can and are being developed, creating new opportunities to serve the market. World-class organizations can and are being built in Africa. In some cases, as with the Muthaiga Golf Club, an opportunity exists to reinvent the old infrastructure to align it with the new society. This creates new promise for the future.

## Rising Opportunities

- What are the opportunities to build a market by meeting gaps in infrastructure?
- How do you need to tailor your products and services to address infrastructure weaknesses?
- What are the opportunities to leapfrog existing technology to move directly to more advanced technologies?
- How can you transform existing infrastructure for the future?

# 6

# Running with the Cheetah Generation: Opportunities in Africa's Youth Market

*Africa is one of the most youthful continents in the world, and growing younger every day. Capturing the African market opportunity means understanding and appealing to African youth—from music to milk to school uniforms.*

In the center of Harare, Zimbabwe, a two-story retail store is filled to the brim with the hopes of African parents for their children. In neat storage cubicles that line the walls of Enbee Stores are the multicolored uniforms of area schools. Parents came to this shop in the summer 2006, or the 25 other Enbee Stores across the country, to purchase what is often the best set of clothing their children will own. This is a youth market in a continent that is growing younger every day.

Enbee founder Natu Patel's father started his first retail store in Harare in 1947, importing pots and pans, blankets, soap, and other basic products, but it was in 1958 that the younger Patel had the inspiration to create a school uniform business. He was riding along the streets of Harare and saw the children coming from school. He realized there must be a huge market for school uniforms. He had his first few meetings with school principals and started producing uniforms for their students. The business spread over more than two decades to more than two dozen locations, including his primary store in the downtown, with two stories of pressed shirts, shorts, skirts, and ties in all the colors of different schools. A complete set of clothing for a starting student could run $500, and it must be replaced every other year. Each child buys several uniforms, in addition to sports uniforms and swimming uniforms, before finishing high school.

High inflation rates dampened the business in the short term, but even in a very tight economic environment, parents were reluctant to cut back on their children's education. A school uniform is a matter of pride. For workers with good jobs, employers will often contribute to school fees and costs, about 10 percent of tuition for children of a junior manager and full costs of tuition for more senior executives. Some NGOs are also pitching in. In a country with high birth rates and parents who place a premium on educating their children, Enbee's market is sure to grow.

# A Youth Market

Africa is one of the youngest markets in the world, with 41 percent of its population under the age of 15, according to the Population Reference Bureau's 2007 World Population Data Sheet. This can be compared with 33 percent for India, 28 percent for Brazil, and 20 percent for China.

Africa is ahead of any other region of the developing world in youthfulness. The developed world, in contrast, is aging rapidly. Europe has just 16 percent of its population under 15, North America has 20 percent, and Japan has just 14 percent. As Africa grows younger, adding another 900 million people by mid-century, European population is expected to decline by 60 million people in the same period. Whereas much of the developed world is worried about a birth dearth, Africa is concerned about the implications of a population explosion.

By 2050, the Democratic Republic of Congo, Egypt, and Uganda will join Nigeria and Ethiopia on the list of the 15 most populous countries in the world, bumping Russia, Japan, and Germany off the list (see Table 6-1).

At the other end of the age spectrum, the contrasts are just as stark. The percentage of the population over 65 is expected to increase to 21 percent in North America by 2050 and 28 percent in Europe, but these older citizens will account for a mere 7 percent of the population of Africa (up from 3 percent in 2007).[1] The small elderly population in Africa reflects a combination of higher birthrates and a lower life expectancy—just 53 years across the continent and 49 in sub-Saharan Africa, compared with 75 across all of Europe. (In southern Africa, the area hardest hit by HIV/AIDS, life expectancy fell from 62 years in 1990–95 to 49 years in 2005–10. It is not expected to regain the level of the early 1990s until 2045.[2])

**TABLE 6-1   Top 15 Most Populous Countries**

|    | Mid-2007 | 2050 |
|----|----------|------|
| 1  | China | India |
| 2  | India | China |
| 3  | United States | United States |
| 4  | Indonesia | Indonesia |
| 5  | Brazil | Pakistan |
| 6  | Pakistan | **Nigeria** |
| 7  | Bangladesh | Brazil |
| 8  | **Nigeria** | Bangladesh |
| 9  | Russia | **Congo, Democratic Republic of** |
| 10 | Japan | Philippines |
| 11 | Mexico | **Ethiopia** |
| 12 | Philippines | Mexico |
| 13 | Vietnam | **Egypt** |
| 14 | Germany | **Uganda** |
| 15 | **Ethiopia** | Vietnam |

Source: Population Reference Bureau (www.prb.org)

A look at the distributions of sub-Saharan Africa and the United States offers a vivid contrast between the youth markets of Africa and the graying markets of the United States, as shown in Exhibit 24 in the insert. The U.S. baby boom has been compared to a pig passing through an anaconda, but one Moroccan educator I interviewed called Africa's wave of youth a "tsunami." The real global baby boom is in Africa, and it hasn't even leveled out yet.

# Cheetahs and Hippos

These young Africans are different from their parents, and from peers in the West. Ghanaian economist George Ayittey has called these youth "the cheetah generation," because they move faster than the "hippo generation," the group that is still in power but very much mired in the past.[3] The hippos are still complaining about colonialism and imperialism, while the fast-moving cheetahs are demanding democracy, transparency, and an end to corruption. Ayittey says the future of Africa rests "on the backs of these cheetahs." This cheetah generation is not only a force that is changing politics and driving economics, it is also redefining the future of the African consumer market.

The younger generation is fast and connected. A television commercial for Siemens illustrates the impact of that cellular phone networks have had on youth. A native of a Tanzanian village returns from abroad sporting a new "leopard" hairstyle, his head painted with spots like a leopard. He calls his family on his mobile phone from the airport saying he has a surprise for them. But admirers with cell phone cameras take his photo in the city and then send the image across the country, even to his own home village. While he is in transit, all the hair salons begin offering leopard hairstyles. By the time he arrives home by bus, everyone in his village is sporting the same hairstyle. When his family asks him about his surprise, he just shrugs. Through connections and speed, the young generation has gained a different view of the world. One cheetah (or leopard, in this case), connected with a cell phone, can transform the entire society, not only in superficial ways such as hairstyle but in more fundamental ways, too.

# Speaking Sheng: Connecting with Youth

In every country, young people have their own language. To reach youth in Kenya, for example, companies are using the dialect Sheng, a hybrid of Swahili (or Kiswahili) and English along with other Kenyan dialects, with which young people identify (very much like Hinglish in India). Safaricom used *sambaza* (open) in its marketing, for example. Sheng is hip, cool, and youthful, said Catherine Ngahu, managing director of SBO Research in Nairobi. She points out that these youth are not only a large market but also early adopters of new products. Sheng cuts across different demographic segments. It is not the language of the rich teenagers or the poor. It is the language of youth.

In an article in National Geographic, Nairobi native Binyavanga Wainaina discussed the "dual personalities" of Nairobi youth. They might speak in Swahili when talking about their everyday lives but turn to English for discussions of jobs or philosophy. And Sheng is the dominant language of rappers on music videos that play on plasma screens on the newer *matatus* (the Swahili word for minibuses) that crisscross Nairobi. As Wainaina writes, "This is the tension that best defines Nairobi: to try (and often fail) to live within the worldviews of our traditional nations; to try (and often fail) to be seamless, Western-educated people; to try (and often fail) to be Kenyans—still a new and bewildering idea."[4] African youth have a complex and textured experience—connected to global trends and local traditions. Old and new exist side by side like English and Swahili, coming together to create Sheng.

# Music: The Universal Language

Music is an even more basic language of youth than dialects such as Sheng. French, English, Arabic, and Portuguese are the most common official languages across Africa (see Exhibit 4 in the insert), but the unofficial languages number more than a thousand. In Nigeria alone, there are 250 languages and an estimated 400 to 500 idiolects. A Nigerian might drive 35 to 40 minutes and have trouble understanding a conversation. This patchwork of languages means that pan-African brands and advertising have to move beyond words to emotion, music, images, and other nonverbal messages. In meeting this challenge, remember that youth everywhere speak one tongue: the language of music.

Youth across Africa are drawn to music, and this creates opportunities to build connections with youth markets. The Coca-Cola Company and music channel MTV created a marketing alliance in East Africa to create an MTV Coca-Cola VJ (video jockey) search in Kenya, Tanzania, and Uganda. The prize for the three winners was to host a new program, *MTV Coca-Cola Xpress*—a television show targeting young music lovers, the youth, and young adult community in East Africa.[5] Popular Lebanese singer Nancy Ajram is a representative of The Coca-Cola Company in North Africa and singer Haifa Wehbe, also from Lebanon, represents Pepsi.

In Ghana, Nescafé also started an annual contest similar to *American Idol* in 2004, Nescafé's African Revelation (NAR), designed to discover and nurture young African musical talent throughout the West and Central Africa. By helping to make these young musicians known, the company has built its own brands. The winning group was offered a contract to record their music and given heavy promotion via television, radio, print, billboards, and live events.

In Egypt, about 30 percent of the 250 channels on satellite are music channels, and they earn much of their revenue from viewers sending text messages to choose the music. This system for interactive television has cleverly brought together the widespread penetration of cell phones, the interest of youth in music, and satellite television. Even viewers who are stealing their signals for satellite television are paying for their SMS music selections. The pirates are forced to give up some of their loot.

Advertising relies heavily on music. An advertising campaign for Fanta in Nigeria showed a group of young people in an open-roofed four-wheel drive vehicle stuck in one of the ubiquitous traffic jams in Lagos. A girl and her father and mother are in another car. They crank up the stereo and open up bottles of Fanta. It now doesn't matter that they are stuck in traffic. It doesn't matter what life throws at you, there is always an opportunity to find music or humor in it.

The music in Africa is extraordinarily diverse, from U.S. country music to hip-hop and rap, to the Middle Eastern performers who are popular in North Africa. A small country such as Senegal has produced singer Youssou N'Dour, who played the African-British abolitionist Olaudah Equiano in the movie *Amazing Grace* about the end of slavery in the British empire.

Music is also used to engage young people in addressing health and social challenges. Population Services International's YouthAIDS project, an education and prevention initiative, uses media, pop culture, music, theater, and sports to help stop the spread of HIV/AIDS.

The project, founded in 2001 by advertising executive Kate Roberts, is designed to reach 600 million young people around the world. To treat malaria, PSI uses social marketing to make prepackaged therapies widely available and affordable through commercial outlets.

## Speaking the Language of Sports

In addition to music, sports are also the language of youth. Billboards for The Coca-Cola Company in Nigeria during the 2006 World Cup playoffs carried the tagline: "We all speak the language of football [soccer]." Sports appeal to youth in Africa, transcending dialects and culture. Vodafone used the entire Egyptian soccer team to promote its products in Egypt. Barclays in Egypt sponsored sports teams in Cairo and Alexandria during Ramadan.

In Nigeria, South Africa, Egypt, and other parts of Africa, Nokia launched the Defend Your Street (DYS) campaign, using "street" soccer to encourage youth to focus on their dreams and desires.[6] In Nigeria, players ages 16 to 25 competed in a series of 15-minute matches that led to a national playoff with a street soccer team from Brazil (the Boys from Brazil). The project taps into the growing popularity of street soccer among the youth market that is critical to Nokia's future success.

Sports also allows African aspirations to play out on the world stage. Standard Chartered Bank advertising told how blind Kenyan runner Henry Wanyoike brought home the first gold medal in Africa for the 5,000-meter event at the 2000 Paralympics in Sydney. By the age of 30, Wanyoike became the record holder of the 5,000 and 10,000 meters and gained gold medals for both distances in the recent Athens Games. He invested his prize money in knitting machines for disabled people. Standard Chartered Bank appointed him as their Goodwill Ambassador for the "Seeing Is Believing" global campaign, which aims to restore sight to a million people over the next three years.[7] These stories of sports, overcoming obstacles, and contributing to society have universal appeal.

The planned 2010 World Cup games in South Africa have created tremendous excitement, expected to bring in more than half a million visitors to South Africa alone. They are seen as a sign of Africa's development and a catalyst for developing infrastructure, tourism, and pan-African cooperation.

## Understanding Youth

African youth marketing companies such as Youth Connectivity and trend-spotting agency Instant Grass have built networks to spot trends among youth in South Africa. The network of "grasses" (young people who are vanguards of urban cool) reported on the trends they have spotted influencing local street culture and dress. Some of the most unusual finds were the nerd look (based on Urkel of the U.S.-based *Family Matters* television show) or the "rugged soul" look of rugged denim pants and t-shirts.

Companies have used such insights to create products targeted for the youth market. For example, The Coca-Cola Company created Burn, a high-energy drink for youth in Morocco, and Bank Misr created a debit card for Egyptian youth (BM Card), the first card for youth in Egypt.

## Opportunities in the Cradle of Civilization

With high birthrates, products for babies, young children, and parents are growing fast. "Pampers is a growth market," said Ihab Baligh of Procter & Gamble in Egypt, whose brand holds 76 percent of the disposable diaper market in the country, where a new consumer is born every 20 seconds. Still a relatively small market, the penetration of disposables in Egypt was only about 14 percent when I spoke with Baligh in mid-2006, primarily in the Africa One consumer segment (see Chapter 3, "The Power of Africa Two"). P&G is thus building the overall market. P&G runs hospital programs, in collaboration with the government, offering childcare education to mothers on issues such as vaccinations, breast feeding, nutrition, and diapering.

In Egypt, Sandoz has created pediatric products promoted under the logo of "Junior Products." It has held drawing contests for students on the topic of head lice, where Sandoz has the market-leading brand,

Urax. In Nigeria, where 3.5 million babies are born every year, Unilever distributes a million free samples of products such as Pears baby lotion to mothers in maternity clinics and hospitals. The company has worked with the nurses and midwives association to educate mothers about baby care.

Pears, which is made with olive oil, turns out to be uniquely suited for the Nigerian market. There is a local belief that every child born should be bathed in olive oil (even though olives haven't been grown in the region for more than a century). The belief remains that a Nigerian child bathed in olive oil will develop beautiful skin. On the other hand, if they are not given baby oil, they might end up with body odor for life. This popular belief, although not an active part of the product's marketing, certainly helps with sales of olive oil–based lotions such as Pears.

A continent with many babies and young children presents opportunities for such baby products, as well as markets for milk, cheese, and other youth-oriented foods. It also offers opportunities to tap into parents' aspirations.

### *Aspirations: "Dirt Is Good"*

Most African parents, like parents everywhere, want their children to have a better life. Tapping into these aspirations is a key part of meeting the opportunity of the youth market. One television advertisement for Unilever's Omo detergent shows a group of South African boys in white shorts headed out onto a muddy soccer field. They engage in an intense game, with the expected results that their clothing is covered in mud. But the tagline that "dirt is good" taps into parents' aspirations that their children might grow up to be accomplished soccer players—or in other ads in the series, gymnasts or scientists. The way to get to these goals might require going through a bit of dirt along the way, but it can always be washed off with the right detergent.

Previous campaigns might have touted the product's ability to remove stains. Now the brand philosophy is that the product helps children release their potential. This connects with parents' aspirations. The message is that your kids can have a better life and be more successful because Omo helps you get the stains out.

## Our Milk, Your Future

Young and growing children need milk. Companies such as Cowbell Milk are responding. With the slogan "Your Future, Our Milk," Cowbell has captured markets across ten African countries. In Nigeria, a 12-gram (about half an ounce) sachet sells for 20 naira (about 15 cents), and children pour the powdered milk directly on their tongues without water, avoiding concerns about finding fresh water. Promasidor, which owns the Cowbell brand, was launched in 1979 in the Democratic Republic of Congo (then Zaire) by Robert Rose, who left the United Kingdom in 1957 for Zimbabwe "to pursue his African dream." Rose traveled extensively across the continent as chairman of Allied Lyons Africa for more than 20 years. When he noticed a lack of availability of milk, he created a powdered milk that replaced the animal fat in the milk with vegetable fat to give it a longer shelf life. Cowbell's interest in youth doesn't end with milk. The company sponsors a high school math competition in Nigeria and sends an African student to the General Young Leaders Conference in the United States.

African milk faces challenges from international brands, however, which often are considered higher quality. When I asked a woman stocking shelves of milk in a Shoprite in the Palms shopping mall in Lagos which brand was the best, she didn't hesitate. She said the European brands were the best. Why? "Because the cows are well treated." The local brands, like local cows, do not stand a chance against such public perception. Peak Milk (see Exhibit 2) owned by Freisland Foods in the Netherlands, has dominated the Nigerian market for more than 50 years. It is sold through key distributors to a network of 500,000 Nigerian retail sales outlets.

## Biscuits and Cheese

Other products that appeal to the young are biscuits (cookies), yogurt, and cheese. Groupe Danone of France has built a thriving business in biscuits in Algeria. (Its global biscuit business was acquired by Kraft Foods in November 2007.) Danone also produces yogurt and other dairy products for the youth market.

The Bel Group, which is in Algeria, Tunisia, Morocco, and Egypt, has expanded the options in markets that once offered only high-priced imports or lower-quality local brands. Bel Group began importing French cheeses to Algeria in 2005, and was already the market leader two years later. Bel Group imported the high-end French brand Kiri, manufactured the brand La Vache qui Rit (Laughing Cow) locally, and developed local brands. Laughing Cow was positioned for children as a source of Vitamin D and calcium, with an ultra-high temperature test to ensure the product was healthy for children.

In line with this positioning, the company offered free vouchers to mothers for health clinics. Although vouchers for health care might not appeal to Africa One, the company engaged this segment by appealing to their concern for the less fortunate, sponsoring circuses and programs for sick children. In addition to importing French brands, Bel Group created its own local brand, Picon, to compete with low-cost local rivals, as shown in Exhibit 25. The company has also launched the Chef brand for use in restaurants and home kitchens. Bel Algeria has achieved a dominant share of the market in Algeria with a solid double-digit growth rate. The Algerian company has benefitted from the extensive experience of Chafiq Hammadi, an Algerian immigrant to France who returned home to build the business.

### Toys

Growing youth markets also create opportunities for the toy industry, but perhaps not the same as in the United States and other parts of the developed world. For example, the Islamic Fulla doll, created by a Syrian manufacturer, is popular in Egypt and other parts of North Africa. Sometimes nicknamed the "Muslim Barbie," it is the hottest selling doll in the Middle East. At $10, the doll was still very expensive for households in its target markets, but the manufacturer, New Boy Toys, introduced a cheaper version called Fulla Style to penetrate price-sensitive markets. At the same time, the company launched other dolls in the series along with many line extensions sporting the Fulla image, from lunchboxes to umbrellas.[8]

Companies such as Aranim Media Factory, the first comic book publisher in Jordan and one of three in the Arab world, are similarly designing products for Arab youth. The company created its superheroes after founder Suleiman Bakhit realized there were no Arab superheroes. Couldn't the same be done for African youth?

Africa represented just 2 percent of the global toy market (by value) in 2006, but it grew by more than 20 percent from the year before.[9] This makes it the fastest growing regional market in the world. By 2006, the market in Africa for toys was estimated by NPD Group at almost $1.5 billion, with 374 million children. Toys R Us had more than half a dozen toy stores in South Africa by early 2008.[10] Given the growing population of children across Africa and rising disposable incomes, this market is just starting to develop.

## Always in School

Procter & Gamble is also creating a market for feminine-care products while addressing a critical social and health concern of young African women. Young women often miss classes because of poor sanitation or during menstruation, an average of four days a month according to a study in Kenya. P&G's Always brand is helping young women from Zambia to Kenya to Egypt go to school. The company's "Always Keeping Girls in School" campaign is designed to do what the title says. In 2006, P&G announced plans to donate more than 3.2 million sanitary pads to disadvantaged girls in Kenya over a two-year period. P&G's FemCare unit inaugurated a Protecting Futures program in 2007, starting with two schools in Namibia, to build bathrooms, educate teachers, and distribute free pads.[11] It has also partnered with local NGOs to sponsor research and scholarships. Pricing and packaging are critical to success because most young women need to buy these products with their own money, which is scarce, so the price needs to be kept low. P&G gained 70 percent of the market for sanitary pads in Egypt, while allowing girls to get an education.

Marketing feminine products can be delicate in any market, but in Egypt is all the more challenging. P&G has created educational programs for schoolgirls, giving away samples and educational information. For education and promoting its Always products, Procter & Gamble started a Kalam Banat (Girl Talk) campaign to engage young girls in peer-to-peer dialogue. The educational materials used a set of three different characters—Sara, Jasmine, and Fatima—featured in a booklet with "our secret" on the cover along with product samples. In the booklet, the girls discuss health and hygiene issues. The three characters, one of whom wears a veil, are designed to relate to different groups in Egypt. Girls who read the booklet are encouraged to send their questions to one of the three characters and receive a reply by mail. The company is addressing a serious social challenge, one that interferes with the education of many young girls in Africa, while also building a market for sanitary products and its brand.

## Opportunities in Education

Rising aspirations and the demographics of a youth market have created a tremendous demand for education. This can be seen not just in the demand for uniforms, as demonstrated by Enbee's business in Zimbabwe and schools at the elementary and high school levels, but also for colleges and universities.

New technologies for education are spreading across the continent, thanks in part to public-private partnerships. The New Partnership for Africa's Development (NEPAD) launched a project to wire 600,000 e-schools in more than 16 African countries in a decade, starting with 120 schools by mid-2007. The project was designed to provide schools with information and communications technologies (ICT) equipments such as computers, TV and radio sets, and telephones with the help of corporate partners including Hewlett-Packard, Microsoft Corporation, satellite operator INMARSAT Limited, Oracle Corporation, and Cisco Systems.[12] The project would connect the schools with scanners, photocopiers, and communication terminals hooked to the Internet via satellite communication links. The goal was to equip African youth, wherever they are, with the knowledge and skills to participate in the global economy.

Nicholas Negroponte's One Laptop Per Child initiative is pilot testing putting the resources of the world (in this case, low-cost computers) into the hands of African students. In addition to such nonprofit initiatives, there are also for-profit ventures such as Intel's affordable Classmate computer, which has been installed in schools in Nigeria, South Africa, and Kenya. In a pilot project, the computers helped boost grades by 25 percent in the first three months.[13] New technologies can also be used to leverage limited computing resources. For example, the Western Cape region of South Africa, with more than 1 million students in its schools, has pilot tested technology from NComputing (www.ncomputing.com) to allow up to seven students to use a single PC at a tenth of the cost of individual PCs. This approach also lowers administration costs because there are fewer computers to repair.[14]

With a large youth market, there are also opportunities for providing pre-school education. This has been demonstrated in India by companies such as Kidzee (www.kidzee.com), which has built a successful chain of child-care centers for children in preschool and kindergarten. Kidzee is expanding rapidly across India and around the world. Africa is a natural market for such initiatives.

### Universities and Business Schools

In addition to preschool, elementary, and secondary education, demand is growing for universities. The highly selective American University in Cairo has 70,000 nondegree students and 12,000 degree students, but the nearby University of Cairo has some 350,000 students—a small city.[15] Some beginning classes there have as many as 7,000 students, and it is not uncommon to have several students with identical names. These are not classes but conventions. Still, there are not enough schools to meet demand.

Universities and business schools are expanding across Africa, although the continent is behind other parts of the world in quantity and quality. There are five African universities on Shanghai Jiao Tong University's 2007 list of the top 500 universities in the world (University of Cape Town, University of Witwatersrand, University of Kwazulu-Natal, and University of Pretoria in South Africa; as well as the University of Cairo in Egypt).[16]

There are fewer than 80 business schools throughout Africa, and only the University of Cape Town in South Africa shows up on the 2008 *Financial Times* ranking of top 100 global MBA programs (number 71).[17] In October 2005, 22 deans and directors of business schools from 10 African nations gathered in Lagos to launch the Association of African Business Schools (AABS), with the support of the International Finance Corporation's Global Business School Network (GBSN). Guy Pfeffermann, director of the GBSN, noted in a press release, "Stronger business schools can be important tools for contributing to economic growth in African countries. The new association will create opportunities for professional networking in three dimensions: north-south, south-south, and perhaps most important, among African schools themselves."[18]

Business schools in the United States and Europe are showing increased interest in Africa as they did in China and India several years ago.[19] Top U.S. business schools are inviting faculty to their campuses, setting up African exchange and degree programs, and holding alumni programs in Africa.

New business schools and universities also are being launched to meet this need. When I visited Cairo in September 2006, the American University was taking its first steps to establish a business school like the Indian School of Business, which was founded in collaboration with top U.S. schools. The African Institute of Management and the International School of Management were set up in Senegal in 1990s, the Lagos Business School was established in 1991, and the commerce faculty at the Catholic University of Eastern Africa, in Nairobi, was launched in 2003. These schools are writing local case studies and learning from their international peers.[20]

The Mediterranean School of Business, part of the South Mediterranean University in Tunisia, launched the first private, English-language executive MBA in the country. Professor Mahmoud Triki, a visionary educator and a Ph.D. graduate of Ohio State University, recognized the power of tapping into Tunisia's private sector for investment and the global diaspora to help establish the school. Whereas thousands of Tunisians earn engineering and other degrees in the United States, some 40 percent come back home, helping to bring expertise and support for education. Triki is planning to draw more than half its faculty from major U.S. and European business schools. Al Akhawayn University in Ifrane was the first American-style university in Morocco when it opened 1995, and has since started its own executive MBA program and opened an executive education center in Casablanca. These are just a few of many initiatives to fill the gap in university and business education.

Even with the launch of new universities and business schools, many high school graduates who are qualified for university cannot attend because there are not enough openings at public universities. The problem of illegal colleges, a concern in many African countries, is a sign of the magnitude of the unmet demand for universities. The Ministry of Education in Kenya, for example, closed five illegal universities in two years (2004 to 2006). These programs spring up near bars and lodgings and near commercial buildings.[21]

Innovative universities such as CIDA City campus in Johannesburg are creating new models to open business schools to even the poorest students.[22] CIDA (Community and Individual Development Association) bills itself as the first "almost free" university and even has a "clothing library" with donated suits and other dress clothes that students can borrow for job interviews. The building, books, furniture, and computer equipment are donated. CIDA recently announced plans to set up a new school in Knysna on the southern coast of South Africa, and received a $1 million grant from the foundation of former eBay president Jeff Skoll to create a "replication center" to develop plans and training for people to run similar campuses across Africa. The school launched the Branson School of Entrepreneurship in 2005 with the support of entrepreneur Richard Branson. Africa needs more such creative models to address the need of its youthful population for education.

# Fountain of Youth

U.S. parents in the top third income bracket spend anywhere from $279,000 up to more than $1 million to raise a single child up to the age of 17.[23] Although African parents have much, much less to spend, they care every bit as much about their children. And this means that as incomes rise and economies develop, spending on youth will rise. And as they grow up, these young Africans will define the future of the consumer market. What will these young people be looking for? How can companies reach them?

Oprah Winfrey was criticized for donating $40 million to build a school for girls in South Africa, instead of donating the money to the inner-city schools in the United States. She responded that the attitude of students toward education is different in South Africa. "If you ask the kids [in the United States] what they want or need, they will say an iPod or some sneakers," she told *Newsweek*. "In South Africa, they don't ask for money or toys. They ask for uniforms so they can go to school."[24] This difference in attitude may go a long way in propelling the progress of this next generation in Africa. The charitable organization Camfed International (joined by the *Financial Times*, Sofronie Foundation, and the Skoll Foundation) has focused its efforts on investing in the education of girls in Africa, as a way to address the "long-term economic, health, and social problems in Africa."[25]

Even though a youth market holds promise for the future, there are also dangers in having such young populations. Research by Population Action International shows that 80 percent of the civil conflicts that broke out in the 1970s, 80s, and 90s occurred in countries where at least 60 percent of the population was under 30. Almost nine of ten such "youthful" countries had autocratic rulers or weak democracies.[26] German anthropologist Gunnar Heinsohn has discussed how countries are more likely to dissolve into civil war or other conflict once the percentage of their populations 15 to 29 years old reaches 30 percent. Developed countries have passed through similar youth bulges on their way to lower birth rates and greater prosperity. But converting the potential of youth into productive markets depends on the right conditions and opportunities. There are many serious problems affecting youth, too, including diseases, female genital mutilation, and simple lack of good sanitation and hygiene that threaten the lives of young people, particularly young women. High unemployment means that many young people have trouble leaving home and establishing themselves in the world.

Despite the challenges, youth also represent an important market. As Charles Mbire, who runs the Ugandan division of cell phone company MTN, said of the youth market in a February 2008 *Financial Times* interview, "I am a businessman. I am happy. My market is growing." The company has grown to 2.5 million subscribers since its start in 1999, and the average age of its users dropped from 24 to 17.[27]

African youth are among the most optimistic people in the world. Although they do have interests that diverge from their parents, a study by The Coca-Cola Company found that 19-year-old pan-Africans were more conservative in their religious beliefs than peers in other parts of the world. Parents played a far more important role in their lives than ever before. Who are their heroes? African youth drew their role models from intellectual, artistic, and political leaders.

In Morocco, youth pointed to their new king; in Kenya, poets and artists; in South Africa, Nelson Mandela. Their heroes are determined by the specific value systems of their countries. Optimism may be common across African youth, but youth in different parts of Africa have different views of the world. The following figure summarizes some of the variations in these values and perspectives in a few key markets.

"East Is East and West Is West"
(North Is North and South Is South)

**Morocco:** Gender differences are very strong. Slightly more European in terms of influences. Religion is the foundation of the value system of the family.

**Egypt:** Far more conservative, parents play the strongest role out of all the countries. Success is about intellectual status.

**Nigeria:** West is best. Strong "American" influence. Religion is very important. Success is a combination between material well-being and "keeping the parents happy."

**Kenya:** Deeply patriotic, less Ameri-centric, more in tune with the African Renaissance (and cultural nuances) and aware of topical social issues (violence against women).

**South Africa:** Culturally fragmented but harmonious society. Conspicuous materialism dominates. Strong Western influence...which is then "localized." Future positive.

**Youthful optimism**

Source: The Coca-Cola Company

According to legend, European explorer Ponce de León explored North America in the early 1500s in pursuit of the legendary Fountain of Youth. Today, it is clear where the Fountain of Youth is, but one must sail in the other direction across the Atlantic Ocean to find it. It is not hard to see where the future markets—particularly youth markets—will be. Although there are challenges and dangers in African youth markets, their growth and its optimism might bode well for the future. "Imagine the kind of economy we can create in ten years time with that kind of optimism," said Lanya Stanek of Coca-Cola Africa during a review of the research in Johannesburg. "There is a sense that they have one shot in life so they need to make it count. Self-belief is very strong." Youth also recognize that with their help, the continent will be a very different place than where their parents lived. This cheetah generation is helping to create and participate in a thriving market—and this market is Africa's future.

## Rising Opportunities

- How can you find opportunities in the young population of Africa?
- How can you connect with youth through local dialects, music, and sports?
- How can you serve babies, children and parents in one of the most rapidly growing markets in the world?
- How can you address the real challenges facing youth, from disease to poverty?

# 7

## Hello to Nollywood: Opportunities in Media and Entertainment

*Africa is already a long way away from the days when most televisions could receive only two state-sponsored channels. Satellite, radio, Internet, and other media are expanding along with the meteoric rise of cell phones. Nigeria's Nollywood and other film centers across Africa are growing and gaining global recognition. From billboards on the sides of buildings to events in rural areas, there are many creative ways to get messages out to the most remote parts of the continent.*

When I met him one evening in July 2006 in Cairo, Amin El Masri was heading out the door to deal with another emergency at the hospital. He is not a doctor. He is director of several acclaimed films who was now working on a new *ER*-style hospital drama in Arabic with American producer Joseph Zito (who has directed and produced films such as *Bloodrage* and *Friday the 13th: The Final Chapter*). El Masri, of ASAP Film Production, and his partners were negotiating with two satellite stations who were interested in showing the new series in Egypt and the Middle East.

Next to a television in his office sat a videotape of the American series *ER*. Above the television was an old movie poster for *Scarface*, showing Al Pacino staring at a gun on the table, recalling El Masri's work on his own early hit movie *Mafia*, filmed in Egypt and South Africa. The film was remarkable for its production quality and box-office performance, proving that action movies could succeed in the Egyptian market where light comedies had predominated. The project also was a commercial success, netting about $3 million (14 to 15 million Egyptian pounds), more than double its cost of production.

The Egyptian film industry is a $60 to $70 million industry, second in Africa only to Nigeria's Nollywood. The investments of production companies such as Good News, Larabaya, and Elmasa-Oscar have led to higher budgets for Egyptian films. Better quality, a result of production in Europe, has helped to move the industry into global markets. Although the average Egyptian film is made for 610 million Egyptian pounds ($1 to $1.5 million), newer films with high production value are commanding budgets about twice as high. This is still inexpensive compared to the $40 to $50 million spent on a film in the United States. The bar was raised by Egyptian films such as *The Yacobian Building*, based on a popular book by Allaa el-Aswany, released in 2006, and El Masri's own film *Halim*, about the life of popular Egyptian singer Abdel Halim Hafez.

Although most popular films in Egypt are still low-budget slapstick comedies, such as *Al Limby* starring comedian Mahmoud Saad, more-artistic films have received critical acclaim at global film festivals, including Tribeca and Cannes. El Masri looks forward to the day when an Egyptian film, perhaps one of his own, might win an Oscar for best foreign film.

Africa is not a "media dark" continent. From home-grown movie industries in Egypt, Nigeria, Morocco, South Africa, Senegal, Tunisia, and other parts of Africa, to the spread of satellite television, radio, and newspapers, to the rise of cell phones and high-speed Internet connections to ubiquitous billboards, there are many channels for getting messages out. At the same time, in remote areas without access to reliable electricity or technology, companies are using their creativity to take their messages to the market through mobile vans, disk jockeys, and public events. There are opportunities in building these media channels. And, they also create unexpected opportunities for advertising and branding across Africa.

# The Accidental Nigerian Film Industry

Serious filmmaking has been active in Africa for nearly half a century. The late Senegalese filmmaker and author Ousmane Sembène is called the father of African filmmaking for his work in the 1960s on

# Africa Rising

From Johannesburg to Cairo, opportunities can be seen across the continent, as illustrated by these images, many of which are from the author's own travels across Africa.

**Exhibit 1**   An Innscor food court in Harare, Zimbabwe.

**Exhibit 2**   The future's waiting! A Saatchi & Saatchi advertisement for Peak milk taps into the aspirations of Nigerian parents—from a continent that is growing younger every day. Could one of the children from this generation really take to the heavens in an announced space program to send a Nigerian to the moon by 2030?

   Courtesy of SO&U Saatchi and Saatchi.

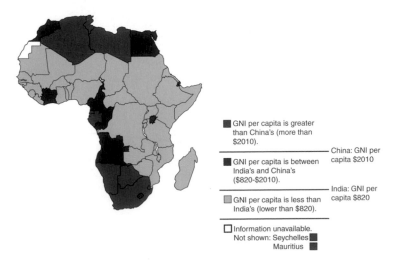

**Exhibit 3**   Africa is richer than you think. A dozen countries have GNI per capita greater than China, and GNI per capita across the continent is greater than India's.

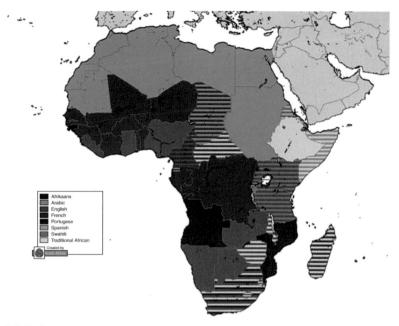

**Exhibit 4** Official languages of Africa.

Source: Arab League.

**Exhibit 5** Landlocked no longer : A map of the 22 countries, 15 in sub-Saharan Africa, served by Zain (formerly MTC), with a base of more than 42 million customers, as of December 31, 2007.

Source: Zain.com.

**Exhibit 6**   Islam in Africa.

Courtesy of University of Texas Libraries.

**Exhibit 7**   A woman holds a packet of laundry detergent in a small village in East Africa. A consumer market of more than 900 million people could represent the next big global opportunity.

Courtesy of Richard Ponsford, Unilever Kenya.

**Exhibit 8** Kheir Zaman discount store in Cairo, Egypt, targets Africa Two consumers.

**Exhibit 9** The $20 washing machine in Egypt is made by local manufacturers from old barrels. Companies making laundry detergents for Africa Two need to recognize that they might be used in a machine like this.

Courtesy of Ihab Baligh, P&G Egypt.

**Exhibit 10** Mercedes dealership in Harare, Zimbabwe. Even in the most challenging environments, there is still a market for products for Africa One.

**Exhibit 11** To reach Africa Three, companies sell products for the smallest currency in a country. For example, water vendors in Lagos, Nigeria, sell bags of fresh drinking water for 5 naira.

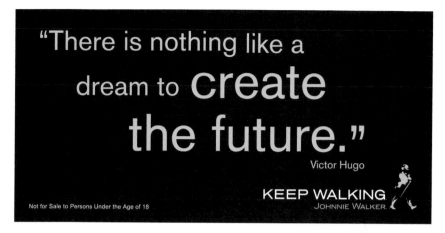

**Exhibit 12** The Johnnie Walker brand's "Keep Walking" slogan, as shown in this South African ad, appeals to the dreams and determination of Africans in looking to the future.

Image courtesy of Diageo Brands B.V.

**Exhibit 13** Informal markets in Lagos, Nigeria.

**Exhibit 14** Traditional spaza shop in Alexandra, South Africa, outside of Johannesburg.

**Exhibit 15** New Shoprite in Alexandra, South Africa.

**Exhibit 16**  Bargains in PEP: A toddler's jacket for about a dollar in South Africa.

**Exhibit 17**  Mandela spaza shop: Winnie Mandela's spaza shop across the street from their Soweto home helped support the family during her husband's long internment.

**Exhibit 18**   Used clothing sold in a friperie shop in Tunis, Tunisia, exposes consumers to top national brands. Does Christian Dior recognize the African market for used branded clothing?

**Exhibit 19**   A long way from Texas, a used car on a secondhand lot in Lagos, Nigeria.

**Exhibit 20** Financing offers a bridge to automobile ownership. A display at an auto mall outside Pretoria, South Africa, advertises low monthly payments for entry-level Fiats.

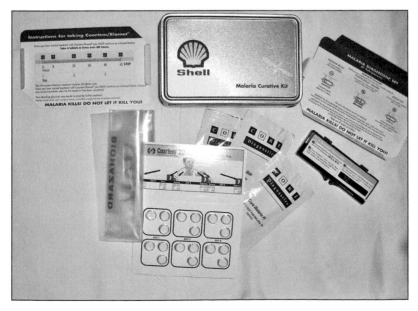

**Exhibit 21** Shell malaria kit used in Nigeria. Novartis created malaria kits for Shell employees, using the well-established corporate channels for distributing its anti-malarial drug Coartem.

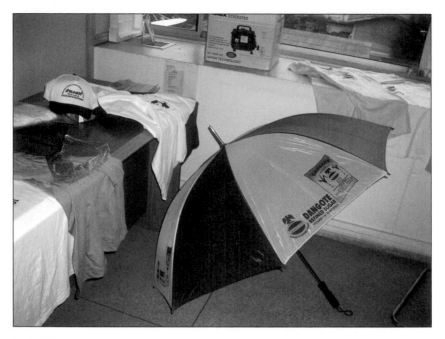

**Exhibit 22**   Dangote branding in Nigeria: Dangote is using shirts, umbrellas, and other promotional items for its retailers to help transform sugar from a commodity to a branded product.

**Exhibit 23**   Mama Habiba's and the POWA market in Lagos, Nigeria: The author, far left, walks through a strip of stores in the POWA market in Lagos, Nigeria, including Mama Habiba's (who declined to be photographed), which sells soft drinks in Lagos. Coca-Cola is building an ice factory to serve small retailers without consistent electricity or backup generators.

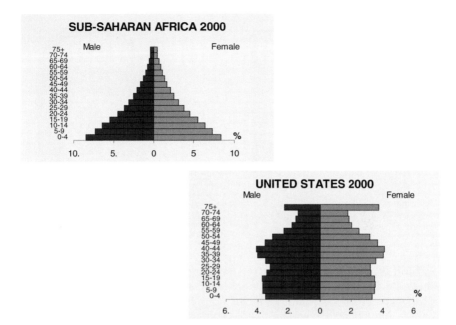

**Exhibit 24** Sub-Saharan Africa: A fountain of youth. Whereas the United States and other developed countries wrestle with an aging population, Africa is facing a population boom, creating opportunities for products and services for children and parents.

Source: Population Reference Bureau.

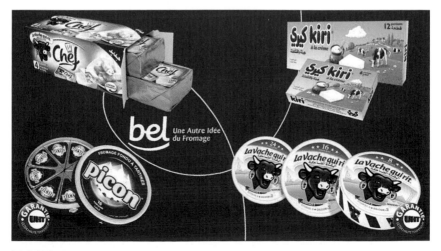

**Exhibit 25** Bel Group's portfolio of cheeses in Algeria: Bel built a portfolio of local and global brands, in part by appealing to parents.

Used with permission of the Bel Group.

**Exhibit 26** Exporting Highland tea and importing radios: By branding Kenyan teas, Highland is adding value for local farmers and contributing to development by raising funds for radios from the Freeplay Foundation, which provide information and education to tea growers.

Source for tea image: Highland Tea Company (http://www.highlandteacompany.com).
Source for radio image: Freeplay Foundation (http://www.freeplayfoundation.org).

**Exhibit 27** Tata Motors Ubuntu bus, designed for the South African market, draws together community and commerce.

**Exhibit 28**   The author with children in the Boksburg house for orphans of AIDS, part of the Thokomala project started by Unilever, and (right) outside the home with Sister Gill Harrower, who previously headed up Unilever's AIDS initiatives. It looks like a typical home in a typical neighborhood, but it is part of an innovative program that is addressing a critical challenge in a country where AIDS orphans are expected to account for 9 to 12 percent of the population in 2015.

**Exhibit 29**   Addressing AIDS by distributing condoms in Africa: A Coca-Cola truck driver distributes condoms in Zimbabwe in cooperation with Population Services International (PSI).

Photo courtesy of Coca-Cola Africa and PSI.

**Exhibit 30**    PP&G, working with Population Services International, has purified more than half a billion gallons of clean water for people in developing countries, including Uganda, Kenya, and Malawi. A PUR sachet for 7 Kenyan shillings (about 10 cents) can treat 10 liters (about 4.5 gallons) of drinking water.

Courtesy of Procter & Gamble.

**Exhibit 31**    Sign in Cape Town, South Africa.

films made in Africa that dealt with African subjects. His motion pictures focused on the lives of ordinary people and dealt with distinctly African subjects such as the impact of a foreign money order, the tensions between modern advances and traditional life, multiple wives, colonialism, racism, and the practice of female genital mutilation. He worked in film because it was accessible, and, as he said, it could be "transported to the remotest village in Africa."[1]

This tradition of serious filmmaking continues to today with productions such as the South African film *Tsotsi*, which was hailed as a coming of age for South African film production. Based on a novel by South African author Athol Fugard and directed by Gavin Hood, it tells the story of a young gang member in a South African township who adopts a baby he accidentally kidnaps during a carjacking. The film, produced by partners in South Africa and Britain, won numerous awards, including the Academy Award for Best Foreign Language Film in 2006. When it opened in South African cinemas, it broke box-office records.

Africa has made its contributions to high art (including award-winning actors such as Omar Sharif and Charlize Theron)—and then there is Nollywood, which is probably the biggest commercial force in African filmmaking. Nollywood started by accident. In 1992, Nigerian trader Kenneth Nnebue was trying to sell a large stock of blank videocassettes that he had bought from Taiwan. The entrepreneur thought he could increase the value of the tapes if he put something on them. So he shot a film called *Living in Bondage* about a man who killed his wife in a cult ritual in exchange for wealth and power, and then was haunted by her ghost. When the film unexpectedly sold 750,000 copies, along with Nnebue's videotapes, its success inspired others to follow. Nollywood was born.[2]

As a result of this happy accident, Nigeria now has the third-largest film industry in the world by revenue, after Hollywood and Bollywood, with estimates as high as $200 to $300 million. It churns out more than 2,000 films per year—more titles than either Hollywood or Bollywood. But that is where the comparisons between the Nollywood and Hollywood end. Nollywood films are notoriously inexpensive in production values and thin in plot, but millions of fans cannot get enough of them.

There are no flashy special effects, sound quality is poor, and there are few marquee actors. In a nation of few movie houses, films are released directly to video. The movies are typically filmed over a few days with a digital camera, with two-thirds in English.

The voodoo and black magic themes of the productions are sometimes seen as an embarrassment to Nigeria. The 1998 film *I Hate My Village*, which deals with cannibalism, bears a cover showing star Emeka Ani chewing on what looks to be human flesh. In another film, a controlling girlfriend shrinks her boyfriend and puts him in a bottle. Producers point out that the films usually have a good moral message, with the practitioners of witchcraft punished in the end or finding redemption through Christianity. With an overlay of ancient and modern beliefs, and a healthy dose of melodrama, these films reflect a deep understanding of the market.

While critics can debate the artistic merits of Nollywood films, no one can argue with their economic success. Films cost between $15,000 and $100,000 to make, and most have no investment from banks or the government, so the industry is self-supporting. This industry has emerged without a major studio or film school. The industry employs about a million people in Nigeria, in production and distribution, making it Nigeria's largest employer after agriculture. Aspiring actors mull around audition boards or bars in the Surulere district of Lagos, where much of the filming is centered.

The beauty of Nollywood is that no company in a developed market would have thought of it. The Nigerian market looks like a wasteland to a typical U.S. film producer, used to rolling out big-budget blockbusters in multiplex theaters and catering to sophisticated film critics. Hollywood is very concerned about the potential for loss of intellectual property. For Nollywood, an estimated half of its revenue is lost to piracy. This is a cost of doing business. Nollywood makes about as much sense to Hollywood as microfinance makes sense to the eyes of a traditional banker. It shouldn't be a profitable market, yet it is. It is a different model. And it works in Nigeria—very well. Indian filmmakers understand this environment and Bollywood films also have been popular in Africa. Some Bollywood films have been shot in African countries such as Mauritius and South Africa, and Bollywood awards ceremonies have also been held there.

# Theaters That Don't Look Like Theaters

A 2005 survey in Nigeria found that some nine out of ten had never even visited a cinema. If you look a little more closely, however, there are already many cinemas in Nigeria. They just don't look like the cinemas movie companies are used to seeing. A cinema in Nigeria or other parts of Africa is a restaurant or private home with a video or DVD player and a television. The films are sold for about $2.15—the average film sells 50,000 copies—and shown to the public for pennies in these informal movie houses. Although a lack of traditional theaters hasn't slowed the Nollywood film industry, these theaters are coming. There were plans to build 50 modern cinemas in Nigeria in 2007. In richer countries such as Egypt, 66 percent of teens already said they "go to the cinema often."

In addition to home theaters, African films also are carried on television, giving Nollywood a reach far beyond Nigeria. Satellite television company MultiChoice in South Africa, for example, offers an entire channel showing nothing but Nigerian films. U.K.-based Zenith Films launched a channel called Nollywood Movies in early 2008 on Rupert Murdoch's BSkyB pay television (www.nollywoodmovies.tv). In the United States, Nollywood films have become a multimillion-dollar industry as immigrants and other fans snatch them up, but many are bootleg copies. I rented Nollywood films at an African store run by a Nigerian family in Austin, Texas.

The cameras are rolling across Africa. The film industry in the Western Cape (including Cape Town), South Africa, contributed at least 3.5 billion rand ($500 million) to the country's economy in 2006, according to a study by the Cape Film Commission.[3] In July 2007, Botswana began shooting the first major movie filmed entirely in that country. The film, *The No. 1 Ladies' Detective Agency*, based on the bestselling novel by Alexander McCall Smith, is set in Botswana. It was directed by Anthony Minghella and financed by the Weinstein Company with the support of the Republic of Botswana.[4] Although the Botswana film industry is fledgling, a local tour operator there has added literary tours to the traditional big-game safaris.[5] Expatriates also are contributing to African filmmaking. Rachid Bouchareb, whose family immigrated to France from Algeria, directed the film

*Indigènes*, or *Native* (released in United States as *Days of Glory*), about Algerian soldiers who came to France to fight in World War II, and there is a small but vibrant film industry in Tunisia.

When I met with Ali Kettani of Sigma Technologies in Morocco, he said Morocco is a popular place to make movies, with government itself providing armies, equipment, and other support. Filmmakers have come to the country to make international hits such as *Gladiator*, *Black Hawk Down*, *The Four Feathers*, and the classic *Lawrence of Arabia*. There are also many local lower-budget productions. Sigma has been involved in creating a number of programs, including a local educational show in the Berber language called *Yaz*. Many Berbers in Morocco don't speak French. Even some foreign films have found their way unofficially into Berber versions, such as DreamWorks's hit movie *Shrek*. Kettani asked me, "Can you believe that *Shrek* was speaking Berber?" Sigma is also working on developing advertising for pay phones and other media.

In June 2007, Indian Film Academy Awards in Sheffield, England, Bollywood's version of the Academy Awards, attracted a live audience of 12,500 and a television audience of 500 million people in 110 countries. How long will it be before the African movie market is organized in this way? Not long, perhaps. The Panafrican Film and Television Festival of Ouagadougou (FESPACO), dubbed the Ouagadougou Oscars, was held in Burkina Faso in March 2007. Filmmakers from across Africa came together to compete for the Yennenga Stallion, a golden statue of a prancing horse from an ancient tale of Ghana, the African equivalent of the Oscar. Bollywood has taken its film awards around the world to where Indian immigrants live. Should African filmmakers do the same? India's Reliance Entertainment has acquired more than 200 theaters in 28 US cities, targeting US expat communities with Bollywood films. Could African companies do the same thing with Nollywood films?

Hollywood has discovered Bollywood, with studios such as Sony Pictures Entertainment producing their own Bollywood musicals, and Disney is making animated films in India to cater to the large domestic market that accounts for about 95 percent of theater box-office sales. Bollywood filmmakers have taken their companies public and also raised money in alternative investment markets (AIM) in London.

Given the large domestic consumption of films in Nigeria and Egypt, could the same opportunities be available to filmmakers there? Why is Africa being ignored?[6]

Nollywood seems unlikely to produce a winner at a major global film festival anytime soon, although initiatives such as the Nollywood Foundation in Los Angeles, created by a group of expatriate Nigerians, could change that in the long run. There are more substantial studios under construction in Nigeria. Africa is also creating prominent stars such as Genevieve Nnaji, who is a spokeswoman for Unilever's Lux in Nigeria, and Egyptian film star Mona Zaki, who represents Lux in Egypt. Nnaji's film *30 Days* was jointly produced by U.S.-based Native Lingua Films and Nigeria's Temple Productions, shows the growing appeal of such stars and films in developed markets. So, it is not so far-fetched to think that even the informal, swashbuckling industry of Nollywood might form the foundation for a more traditional motion picture industry in the long run.

# Television and Radio: Beyond Two Channels

A decade or two ago, most African nations had one or two state-run channels, if they were lucky. Now, some African viewers have access to hundreds of channels. Like cell phones, satellite television and radio do not require rewiring a nation and can reach almost across the continent. In 1986, a new satellite television service called M-Net was started in South Africa (now called MultiChoice Africa), which the company claims is one of the first two subscription television services outside the United States.[7] MultiChoice's DStv service provides locally tailored service stretching from South Africa up to Sudan and Senegal. In South Africa alone, DStv has more than 1.4 million subscribers (as of March 2007), broadcasting more than 70 video channels, over 40 CD-quality audio channels, 28 radio channels, and more than 6 interactive channels, 24 hours a day.

WorldSpace satellite radio, through which I listened to Bollywood songs in Zimbabwe, can be picked up almost anywhere in Africa. Founded in 1990 by Ethiopian-born Noah A. Samara, who had helped establish the XM satellite radio network in the United States, World-Space is a pioneer of digital satellite radio in emerging markets across all of Africa and much of Asia. It provides a wide range of programming, including sports, education, and religious broadcasts; news from CNN, the BBC, and NPR; and music ranging from rock to country to R&B to hip-hop to classical to world music.[8] CNBC launched CNBC Africa in Johannesburg in June 2007, the first 24-hour business channel to broadcast to 14 countries across Africa, replacing CNBC's European broadcast on DStv's satellite lineup.[9]

In Burkina Faso, the country virtually shuts down when the locally produced French-language sitcom *Le Nouveau Royaume d'Abou* is aired. This is in a country where the GNI per capita is just $400. The program follows the complicated, soap opera plot of Abou, a Muslim with two wives, many children, and an African mistress. He also has a mistress in Switzerland from a business trip who turns up in Burkina Faso to see him. The series cost 8 million CFA francs per episode to make (about $16,000), backed by Canal France International (CFI) and local mobile phone company Telmob, with support from the state television company. (In contrast, the average cost of a first-year drama in the United States was estimated at $2.8 million per episode in 2006.)[10] The producers are looking to export the series to neighboring francophone countries such as Benin and even beaming it to China.[11] It might not look anything like an episode of *Friends*, but from language to religion to subject matter, it has struck a chord with the viewers in this market.

In Nigeria, popular soap operas such as Super Story, produced locally, attract large audiences and advertisers such as Unilever. One of my students from Nigeria described how her mother remembered they were running low on certain household products because she saw them advertised on Super Story. By 2005, Nigeria had more than 140 television stations, including 28 state-owned stations, 14 privately owned, 2 satellite stations, and 4 digital television stations. Nigeria boasted 90 radio stations and more than 90 newspapers and 40 magazines. It also had 112 outdoor advertising firms, with almost 20,000 billboards. There is a big market for televisions, DVDs, and VCRs across Africa, for the Africa One, Africa Two, and even Africa Three consumer segments (see Chapter 3, "The Power of Africa Two").

In Kenya, Unilever uses popular radio DJs and activation events to promote its products. For example, in Nyeri, local cooks were challenged to prepare meals using the company's Royko soup cubes (used to flavor soups). The radio DJ interviewed participants, and more people swarmed in for the event to see the live broadcast. Sales of Royko cubes went up more than 25 percent in the area in the three months following the event in March 2006. With 44 FM radio stations in Kenya, radio has the greatest reach in the rural areas. And, unlike television, it can keep going on battery or hand crank even when the power is out.

# The Small Screen

On a continent with many cell phones but few movie theaters, the jump to the small screen seems inevitable. Building upon its satellite television service, DStv Mobile is testing technologies to transmit mobile television broadcasts to phones in time for the 2010 World Cup games in South Africa. MTech Communications, an African mobile content provider based in Lagos, has connected (working in collaboration with major mobile operators such as MTN, Glo, CelTel, and Safaricom) with an audience of millions of mobile subscribers across Africa. The company was founded in 2001 by Nigerians Sheri Williams and Chika Nwobi, after their return from earning degrees in computer science in the United Kingdom and United States. In the 2005/06 season, it attracted 5 million subscribers to its SMS (text-based) service focused on the Premiere League. Users can predict winners in World Cup matches, competing for a global phone, or receive news highlight from the Premier League on their mobile phones across Africa, including video and photos. MTech subscribers in Nigeria and Ghana can watch the popular United Kingdom participatory game show, *The Mint*, on their phones and call in to play the game.

In August 2007, Nigeria launched the first commercial mobile broadcast TV service, which will allow subscribers to receive CNN, SuperSport, and other DStv channels directly on their mobile phones. The service, using the Digital Video Broadcast-Handheld technology standard, means that Nigerian users will have access to the most advanced mobile technology in the world. As a sign that film directors are paying attention to the small screen, Cape Town, South Africa, hosted its first Mobfest in August 2007, with awards for the best documentary films designed for mobile phones.

Cell phones are being used to improve health in Rwanda, where the U.S. company Voxiva has built a system that allows health workers in remote villages to send reports by cell phone directly from the field. The system helps track HIV/AIDS patients and connects 75 percent of the country's 340 clinics, covering a total of 32,000 patients.[12] It can handle SMS text messages, voice messages, and input from the Internet. Clinics can also receive results of lab tests and drug-recall alerts through the system.

Cell phones are transforming agriculture. Celtel Zambia and the Zambia National Farmers Union (ZNFU) launched a commodity-price information service in 2007 for small-scale and commercial farmers. The service gives them access to pricing and other information via mobile phone. A farmer can punch in a text message such as "SMS maize" to a designated number and receive current prices from the ZNFU, allowing farmers to negotiate better pricing.[13]

Cell phones offer another channel for advertising. For example, when Guinness launched Guinness Extra Smooth in Lagos in 2006, it contacted trendsetters by cell phone and invited them to different bars. Invitees showed the invitation on their phones to get into the party. This and other promotions helped the company sell 1 million cases in the launch year. There was no need for the company to wrestle with the cumbersome postal service to get invitations out. With the rapid spread of cell phones, there are many more opportunities for such advertising that goes directly into the hands of customers.

The mobile phone is also providing the platform for the first dedicated, pan-African, 24-hour news channel, created by Camerapix in Nairobi and scheduled for launch in 2008. It builds on the success of A24 Media, a television channel that broadcasts news every hour on the hour. Mobile handsets are not only communicating news throughout Africa, but also improving news gathering. AfricaNews (www. africanews.com) is using cell phones to expand its network of reporters. Cell phone reporters cover current events in their areas, using their phones to produce video footage, written reports, and photographs. A reporter with a cell phone can be a one-person news-gathering operation.

# Print and Online

Print media and online media are also expanding rapidly across Africa, although readership is still mostly in the Africa One and Two consumer segments (as discussed in Chapter 3) of the market in many areas. In Senegal, Karim Attieh, head of Poly Krome printing, was printing a new magazine for francophone Africa when I met with him in 2007. The magazine is called *Thiof*, a playful French term that means "good-looking boy." Attieh, whose father came to Senegal from Lebanon, has stacks of magazines from Paris, but they are concerned with life in France, not North Africa. *Thiof* is published two times per month, selling about 25,000 copies for $2 each.

In a country with about 2 million households, and perhaps 40,000 in the highest-income segment (A), the magazine is already working its way across the Africa One and into Africa Two consumer segment. Readership is estimated at about 5 to 10 times sales, so a run of 25,000 might reach as many as 250,000 households. They are pricing their advertising based on readership, so the more sharing the better. This type of magazine might not have existed four years ago. By 2010, Attieh expects to be printing 50,000 copies.

Print and online media is also expanding, with the growth of magazines such as *African Business, Jeune Afrique,* and websites such as Bizcommunity.com (see sidebar). The strengthening of the broadband infrastructure across Africa is creating a platform for improved communications. Forward-looking companies are building businesses on this platform.

## Creating a Marketing Community Across Africa

Bizcommunity.com started a printed marketing newsletter in South Africa about six years ago. As interest in the initiative grew across Africa, and Africa's broadband infrastructure was strengthened, the founders created a more pan-African focused "Bizcommunity" newsletter and website in 2007. It quickly became South Africa's leading online community for the advertising, marketing, and media industry.

Three months after its launch, they had 14,000 subscribers to the free newsletter, and by late 2007 had more than 280,000 online users, adding more than 1,000 per month. The newsletter has attracted interest across Africa—including Angola, Algeria, Botswana, Côte d'Ivoire, Egypt, Ghana, Kenya, Mauritius, Morocco, Mozambique, Namibia, Nigeria, Seychelles, Tanzania, Uganda, Zambia, and Zimbabwe. It has also attracted a growing contingent of readers from outside the continent, too, including the author.

"The purchase of AfricaOnline, by Telkom SA is a keen indicator of increased broadband capacity," said Robin Parker, managing director, during an interview with the author in June 2007. "This, together with explosive mobile access (by 2010 half of Africans will have a mobile phone), motivated us to say it is time for us to get in first and look at the continent as a whole rather than isolating South Africa as we had done traditionally. We are looking at creating an inter-African marketing network and sponsoring conferences around the continent."

Building such a business has given him a distinctive view of the growth of businesses across Africa and the advantages of the continent. "One of the benefits this continent has when it comes to doing something new is the ability to leapfrog. Africa is able to take the best experience anywhere else in the world and move to the next level beyond that. We don't have to be satisfied with second best."

New media is being created, particularly targeting the rising consumer segment of Africa Two. In South Africa, the tabloid *Daily Sun* in Johannesburg went from its start in 2002 to a circulation of more than 500,000 by 2007 by focusing on Africa Two. As founder and publisher Deon du Plessis commented in an interview with the *Wall Street Journal*, "It's the beginning stirrings of what [the United States] was in the 1950s.... There are great fortunes to be made."[14]

# The Walls Can Talk

Satellite, radio, cell phones, print, and other channels offer opportunities to create profitable businesses and get messages out across Africa. Very few areas of the continent are now out of reach of communications technology, but there are still parts of Africa, particularly rural areas, that are not yet wired. Even here, there are ways to get messages out.

In rural areas outside of Lagos, every open side of a building is covered with a Coca-Cola or Pepsi logo. With limited media in rural areas, the building is the message. "Wall branding" is cheaper than buying billboard space. In Kenya, a billboard can cost 1.2 million Kenyan shillings ($18,000) per year, whereas wall branding costs a mere 25 shillings (40 cents) per square foot—for the paint. Generally, advertisers don't pay anything to the owners because the owners are happy to have their buildings painted and maintained for free.

Creativity and entrepreneurship can overcome almost any weaknesses in African infrastructure. In Monrovia, Liberia, Alfred Sirleaf broadcasts news to the community on the city's main thoroughfare every day using a battered blackboard. In the city, which has not had public electricity in 14 years, Sirleaf's board serves as the equivalent to New York City's news tickers in the developed world. Sirleaf even includes symbols for citizens who cannot read. His editorials have landed him in jail. But he continues to publish.[15] With entrepreneurial initiative, no part of Africa is beyond reach.

# Third Eye

Product packaging is also an important form of advertising. I heard in the townships in South Africa that Unilever's Handy Andy household cleaner (known as Sif in other markets) is sometimes left out on the counter for guests to see. Shiny pots and pans are also left on display. Cleanliness is so important that South Africans want to advertise within their own homes, conveying a sense of status. In this way, packaging becomes advertising for products.

The concept of the "third eye" is very important in purchase and use of products. A focus group by brandhouse—a joint venture of Diageo, Heineken, and Namibia Breweries in South Africa—found that consumers would rarely if ever think about purchasing a premium drink such as Johnnie Walker and consuming it at home. "Consumers don't want to waste the status of drinking Johnnie Walker where no one can see them. They make sure they are in a bar, where there are lots of people who can see and hear them," said Sharon Keith of brandhouse in Cape Town.

Products such as Coca-Cola's Limca and Sprite, as well as Pepsi's Mountain Dew and Miranda Orange, benefited from repackaging in Nigeria, as did Guinness with its relaunch of its Harp beer in a new bottle. In media-light rural areas, packages can shine. Retail stores serve not only as a place to sell but also as an introduction to brands.

At a clinic outside of Lagos, I met a woman coming from her village who had dressed up to take her child to a doctor. In rural areas in Egypt, residents hang their clothes out on the cliffs to show them off. Procter & Gamble's Ariel detergent used this third-party appreciation in its advertising for Ariel campaign, which showed the appreciation of a husband for the clean clothing and attention to detail of his wife. It helped Ariel become the market leader in Egypt, with more than 40 percent market share in 2006.

## Chopped Dollars and Other Surprises of African Technology and Media

The African market is more technologically sophisticated than Westerners give it credit for. One negative example of this is the infamous Nigerian letter, or 419 Internet scheme, which has netted an estimated $750 million (and perhaps billions of dollars) from unsuspecting Americans who are victims of this Internet fraud. The message usually is some variation on the theme that a very rich person in Nigeria (or Zaire or Burkina Faso) has to transfer large amounts of money abroad and requests to use the recipient's account. The American investor might be promised 20 percent to 40 percent of the transferred funds, usually millions. But then the investor has to fill out paperwork and is asked for money to bribe a local official or show good faith by making a deposit in a specified bank.

The transfer from Nigeria never comes, and the scammer pockets the money fronted by the victim. These "Robin Hoods" stealing from the developed world are celebrated in a popular song in Nigeria, "I Go Chop Your Dollar" by Nkem Owoh. Although these scams are a tragedy for victims, and blatantly illegal according to section 419 of Nigerian law (from which they derive their nickname), they demonstrate the level of sophistication of computer talent and technology that exists in Nigeria. In fact, one of the reasons these scams are so successful, besides basic human greed, is that victims underestimate how sophisticated these African scammers are.

As a more positive and practical example of how wired Africa is, I arranged for trips to several African countries almost entirely on the Internet and phone. I was able to book flights on airlines, arrange for hotels, and line up cars and drivers. I found ATMs all over in the major cities. The infrastructure is far from perfect—finding drivers who speak English in some countries was a bit more challenging than just getting a car—but I found it surprising that all this could be achieved online or by phone (usually a cell phone), and of course with the generous assistance of local hosts on the ground. Africa is much more connected than the world realizes.

The Internet also allows for more positive connections between the developed world and Africa that were not possible before. For example, the BeadforLife (www.beadforlife.org) links Ugandan women who make beads from recycled paper with North Americans who organize home parties and events to sell the jewelry. The project, founded by Devin Hibbard and Ginny Jordan, uses an online storefront from ProStores (part of eBay), one of a growing set of powerful online tools available to entrepreneurs. It generated $1.5 million in 2006. In 2007, U.S. high school students Nick Anderson and Ana Slavin used social networking sites Facebook and MySpace to raise more than $300,000 to help refugees in Darfur. Another program, founded by Jill Youse in Minnesota, has engaged more than 400 mothers in the United States who provide breast milk to children orphaned by HIV/AIDS in South Africa (www.breastmilkproject.org). Technology and other connections shorten the distance between Africa and the developed world.

These connections between Africa and the world, however, can also lead to a clash of worlds. Egyptian satellite television host Hala

Sarhan, dubbed "the Oprah Winfrey of the Middle East," created controversy by discussing issues considered taboo in Arab society, including sexual deviations, female genital mutilation, and prostitution. Critics of the show called upon the Saudi satellite channel Rotana to fire the host and cancel the show (www.no4hala.com).[16] There are also taboos in television broadcasting, particularly in Muslim countries, such as the rule that actors playing mothers and sons cannot hug on-screen because they are unrelated. The more Africa is wired, the more the old and new come together, and the more African societies have to address such clashes.

## Pirates of Jo'burg

Intellectual property protection is another challenge. Driving along the streets of Johannesburg in June 2006, I was offered copy of *Mission Impossible III* on the streets of Johannesburg for a few dollars the same week as its U.S. theatrical release, long before it came out on video. Losses through theft of intellectual property are a fact of life. Films and satellite signals may be stolen.

Local successes may change the view of intellectual property. When pirated copies of the South African film *Tsotsi* showed up on the streets—as happens with every other successful movie—there was public outrage, perhaps for the first time. The pirated copies were selling for 50 rand (about $9) based on a rough edit that had a different ending than the one released. The theft of a local film made the intellectual property concerns more personal.

The coming of the 2010 FIFA World Cup soccer games to South Africa has also ignited renewed interest in protecting intellectual property of sponsors. The event is expected to create an estimated 150,000 jobs and bring in 15 billion rand (more than $2 billon) from the 350,000 tourists who will visit the country, so there is a lot at stake, and regulators are taking the protection of brands very seriously. A successful lawsuit against Disney over the music from *The Lion King* ("The Lion Sleeps Tonight"), from the family of Zulu composer Solomon Linda, shows growing appreciation of the value of intellectual property protection. His family settled with Disney for an undisclosed amount for the use of the song written in 1939 and originally recorded by the Evening Birds. These are signs that views of intellectual property protection may be changing.

# From Michael Power to Media Power

Less than a decade ago, the shortage of high-quality television helped make black action hero Michael Power, mentioned in Chapter 1, a massive success—even though he was an advertising creation. Power, a James Bond for Nigeria, was created by Saatchi & Saatchi in 1999 to market Guinness Extra Stout beer. He was so successful that he moved out of print and television commercials to become a true star. He even had his own feature-length movie. Most movie stars go from the theater to promote products after they become famous. Michael Power started as a product promoter and went the other way to become a movie star. While doing battle with evil, he helped to double the African sales of Guinness by 2003, two years ahead of plan, and drove up Guinness brand recognition to 95 percent.

Power's legendary success was partly due to the relatively poor production quality and limited programming of television in the late 1990s, making the campaign stand out. Power also tackled distinctly African challenges, such as power cuts and fighting corrupt politicians. His tagline, "Guinness brings out the power in you," was an embodiment of rising optimism and empowerment. In one television commercial, facing a power failure that shuts down a party, he arranges for taxi drivers to shine their lights on a parking lot and crank up their radios, after calling the radio station to select the right songs. In another ad, stuck in a traffic jam on a narrow street, a common scene in African cities, he takes apart his minivan and reassembles it beyond the congestion.

The days of Michael Power may be fading, however, as African media has exploded. Now African viewers have access to high-quality entertainment—and they are creating it. Today, the production values are climbing and centers of movie production have emerged across Africa. Even Michael Power, with his intelligence and strength, may be no match for these developments (although he lasted much longer than most advertising campaigns).

There is another reason why Africa may have moved beyond the age of Michael Power (although Power continues to be involved in promoting social initiatives such as Diageo's Water of Life program). Power represented a view that Africa could be saved by a force from the outside, the superhero. This might have reflected a view that government or foreign countries would solve problems. But now, the power of Africa comes from within, from its own stories, its own entrepreneurs, its own knowledge of its own markets. "There is a belief that if things were going to improve, they would have to do it themselves," said Matthew Barwell, marketing director of Diageo Africa. This shift is reflected in the new campaign for Guinness that Diageo has launched called Greatness, with this tagline: "There is a drop of greatness in every man." One ad, for example, features the story of a successful airline pilot shown flying relief supplies to villages.

## Our Stories Are Your Stories

Right now, the developed world's view of Africa as a continent of conflict and corruption is reinforced by what people see in theaters. Recent films include *Lord of War*, about the arms trade, *Blood Diamond*, about the precious gems that fuel revolutions, and *The Last King of Scotland*, about notorious Ugandan dictator Ida Amin (for which Forest Whittaker won an Oscar). Earlier films such as *Hotel Rwanda* and *Blackhawk Down* also depict a continent on the edge of chaos. Although wonderfully produced and critically acclaimed, these films tend to reinforce the view of the African continent as a place of interminable sorrow, relentless war, brutal leaders, famine, disease, and lost causes.

As Africa begins to tell its own stories, this view will continue to change. These stories include the quirky dramas of Nollywood or the slapstick comedies in Egypt. And other stories are spreading across the world. The film *Yesterday* by director Darrell James Roodt (released in 2004) became the first Zulu-language film released internationally. It tells the moving story of a mother with AIDS struggling to raise her son. In accepting the foreign language Oscar for *Tsotsi* in 2006, director Gavin Hood noted that stories of hope and redemption are universal: "Our stories are your stories."[17]

The transformations in African media create new opportunities for companies that are prepared to build these channels, provide entertainment, or get their messages out. They have already made Africa a wired and connected continent where messages travel across countries and the heavens. Africa's more than 900 million consumers are increasingly connected.

## Rising Opportunities

- What are the opportunities from the growth of African media?
- What are the opportunities created by the growth of filmmaking, satellite television, and the Internet?
- How does the rapid spread of cell phones create opportunities to develop products and services for the small screen?
- What are the implications of the development of media for advertising and launching products?
- For rural Africa, how can you use billboards, wall paintings, and events to get messages out in areas that are not so well connected?

# 8

## Coming Home: Opportunities in the African Diaspora

*The African diaspora, with perhaps 100 million members around the globe, is investing billions of dollars annually in the continent. Africans living abroad are also returning home to lead and create new businesses, bringing the world's best knowledge to Africa. They are propelling Africa's rise and proving that the African opportunity is much bigger than the continent itself.*

Dr. Titilola Banjoko is part of the African diaspora—and a very active part. Although she was born in the United Kingdom and is a British citizen, she has maintained close connections to Nigeria, where her parents were born. "I would never show up on anyone's radar as part of the diaspora," she said in an interview with the author. She estimates that there are some 100 million members of the African diaspora, broadly speaking, and they are having a tremendous impact on the development of Africa. The diaspora is a source of philanthropy and investment, as well as an influx of remittances and other funds sent directly to relatives at home. It is also a source of knowledge and talent. And they are coming back home. Commentators have raised alarms about the "brain drain," as the best African students went to Europe or United States and stayed there (in 2005, for example, *The Economist* reported that there were more Ethiopian doctors in Chicago than in Ethiopia[1]). The return of the diaspora to the continent, however, is leading to a "brain gain" as these wealthy and well-educated Africans come back home again.

Banjoko is at the center of this activity. She founded AfricaRecruit in 1999 when a Nigerian friend living in the United Kingdom wanted to go back to Africa to work. Through the experience of her friend,

Banjoko realized how difficult it was for expatriates to make their way back to Africa. This was during the dot-com boom, but there was no way to research African jobs online. An expatriate who wanted to work in Africa had to shuttle back and forth to the continent to identify positions and interview. It was a long, frustrating process. Working with the Commonwealth Business Council, Banjoko launched the website Findajobinafrica.com, and then, in collaboration with the New Partnership for Africa's Development (NEPAD), established AfricaRecruit, a resource for African expatriates. A December 2006 survey of Kenyans in Europe, the United States, and Asia found that 78 percent considered going back home now or at a later date. It was clear that, with the right opportunities, the road to the African diaspora was a two-way street.

Banjoko realized that it was not just politics or living conditions that were pushing people to leave; employment opportunities in African businesses were not keeping up with global best practices. Many companies did not even have a dedicated human resources executive. Around the same time, the telecoms started booming, creating demand for skilled managers from the global diaspora. "Increasing numbers of Africans have gone back, and they have added momentum to those who are thinking about it," said Banjoko in an interview with the author in August 2007. She and her staff of 6 help about 500 people per year find jobs in Africa, and many others use the online resources to gather information or connect with potential employees. There also is intense interest in the website within Africa, and a growing number of private recruiting agencies have sprung up to fill jobs in Africa.

Returning members of the diaspora bring fresh ideas and capital to launch new businesses. For example, after studying engineering at MIT, Ayisi Makatiani, returned home to Kenya to launch Africa Online, which persevered against poor infrastructure and political corruption (which at one time actually cut the phone lines of the dialup service) to create a successful business that spread to more than ten countries. He went on to found Gallium Capital, which invests in technology companies. Named one of the World Economic Forum's "global leaders of tomorrow" in 1997, he is now head of AMSCO, a management consulting firm based in Johannesburg.

Connections with the African diaspora are bringing much needed skills and investment dollars to Africa. The diaspora represents a significant part of the potential for Africa, and it means that Africa has more resources than show up in the per-capital GNI figures within the continent. Members of the African diaspora are creating businesses in Africa, sending remittances home, investing in African businesses and real estate, creating development initiatives, and coming home to lead African businesses, schools, and other organizations. In China and India, the "reverse brain drain" of returning expatriates played a similar role in those countries' development.

# The Growing African Diaspora

The island nation of Cape Verde along Africa's western coast may now have more of its citizens living in the United States, Europe, and other parts of the world (500,000) than live within the country's own borders (460,000).[2] The money they send home accounts for about 12 percent of the Cape Verde GDP. About 3 million of 30 million Moroccans lived abroad as of the 2004 census, roughly 10 percent of the total population, mostly in Europe and the Middle East.[3] They send about $4 billion back home every year directly to family or to support their local villages. In the town of Taroudant in Morocco, emigrants from the area created an association to support the village, helping with local development projects and making other investments. An estimated 1.4 million South Africans are thought to be living in Britain alone.

The Migration Policy Institute estimates that there were more than 1 million African immigrants in the United States in 2006 (see Table 8-1).[4] This is only slightly less than the population of immigrants from either India or China. There are around 34 million African Americans (although many of these African Americans have little identification with the African diaspora).

The numbers are growing rapidly, as can be seen from the increase in immigrants in London, where the number of residents born in Ghana grew from 30,000 in 1997 to 70,000 in 2006. Between 1990 and 2000, African migration to the United States increased 170 percent, with the largest influx from Nigeria, Ethiopia, and Ghana. In Min-neapolis/St. Paul, the African immigrant population increased 629 per-cent in the same period.

**TABLE 8-1   Immigrant Populations in the United States (2006)**

| Country/Region of Birth | Foreign-Born Population in the United States by Country of Birth |
|---|---|
| Mexico | 10.90 million |
| India | 1.45 million |
| China | 1.39 million |
| Africa | 1.11 million |

Source: Migration Policy Institute, 2006, MPI Data Hub

The growth of the diaspora is illustrated most dramatically by the influx by boat of African refugees into Spain from North Africa. In March 2006, Spain's deputy prime minister made an emergency visit to the Canary Islands to address a record arrival of African refugees from Mauritania. More than 1,000 emigrants made the perilous 500-mile voyage from North Africa over a 10-day period, resulting in many deaths. An estimated 10,000 migrants had gathered at departure points in Mauritania in hopes of reaching Spain.[5] Among other issues, immigration became a major topic of debate in the 2008 general elec-tion in Spain.

While this inflow of immigrants is a challenge for policymakers, it is an opportunity for businesses in Europe and parts of the world where they make their homes. These immigrants are making calls and sending money home. Vodafone's Spanish subsidiary claims 40 per-cent of the nation's immigrants, many from Africa, are now sub-scribers. In one month (November 2006), the company signed up a half million new subscribers with its *Mi Pais* (My Country) campaign targeted toward the more than 600,000 immigrants who arrive in Spain annually from Africa, Latin America, and Eastern Europe. The campaign offered the equivalent of 23-cents-a-minute calls to 50 countries, and even offered reduced rates during national holidays. Although most of the immigrants in Spain are poor, they are contribut-ing to the economic growth of Spain. Some 90 percent have cell phones, and they make more international calls than locals. Because many lack bank accounts or credit cards, the company also does a brisk business in prepaid *Mi Pais* calling cards at newsstands and other outlets.[6]

African immigrants in the United States are highly educated, and 98 percent have at least a high school degree. Immigrants from Africa, the West Indies, and Latin America accounted for more than a quarter of the black students admitted to Ivy League universities, even though they make up only 13 percent of the nation's African American college-age population. This has sparked a debate about whether these admissions are masking low admission rates for U.S.-born African Americans.

# From Nigeria, With Love: An Engine for Investment

The United Nations estimates that total remittances to sub-Saharan Africa reached more than $20 billion in 2006, but the actual numbers might be much higher, because these numbers include only official transfers. Banjoko, who has worked extensively with the diaspora, estimates that remittances to Africa could be close to $44 billion for the entire continent. In 2006, remittances to Nigeria hit $2.3 billion, to Sudan $1.4 billion, and to Kenya nearly $500 million, according to the World Bank. In most parts of Africa, they are growing rapidly, with many areas experiencing double- or triple-digit growth. Remittances jumped by 4,000 percent in Guinea and more than 1,000 percent in Guinea-Bissau between 2000 and 2006.[7]

The flow of remittances into Africa is clear from the ubiquitous presence and rapid growth of money transfer firms such as Western Union, MoneyGram, and others. On the streets of Lagos, I saw billboards for MoneyGram targeting workers headed abroad with the tagline "From Nigeria, With Love." Western Union, which seems to have an office on every corner of Lagos, had a similar approach. An ad showed a man, woman, and child, with the tagline "He's sending his love." (Following global migration patterns, Western Union now has five times as many locations globally as McDonald's, Starbucks, Burger King, and Wal-Mart combined.)[8] The operator of the small

Western Union office I visited next to the BIAT Bank on Habib Bour-
guiba Avenue in Tunis said he handled about seven transfers a day, av-
eraging about 300 dinars per transfer (more than $200). Traffic
increases during Ramadan when they have a *Ramadan Mubarak* (Ramadan Greetings) promotion. A 2007 ad in *African Business* showed
a pilot with his wife and daughter, reading "He is sending her to new
heights," emphasizing the role of remittances in preparing the next
generation for success. MoneyGram is growing at 40 percent per year
in Africa, with 3,200 agents across the continent. With an estimated 2
million of 17 million Senegalese living and working abroad, the evi-
dence of remittances can clearly be seen in the growing business of
Western Union and the Senegalese firm Money Express. Remittances
often take the place of formal banking systems.[9]

Workers abroad make a significant impact on their home countries. Ghanaians living abroad sent back $800 million to the country in
2005—more than Ghana earned from cocoa or gold.[10] Remittances accounted for a quarter of the GDP of Somalia in 2005, and for more
than 20 percent of the GDP of Lesotho in 2006. Nigerian remittances
were estimated at about a third of oil earnings in 2005, before oil
prices rose. The diaspora may be one of Africa's most valuable natural
resource and drivers of wealth.[11]

Money transfers are not just from outside of Africa but also from
the urban to rural areas within countries, and from country to country
within Africa as workers send money back to their families. For example, in South Africa, some six million residents transfer an estimated
12 billion rand ($1.8 billion) in cash annually, mostly to rural areas.
This reflects the rapid urbanization of Africa. There are significant
population movement and financial transfers within Africa, with 17.1
million international immigrants within Africa in 2005, according to
U.N. estimates. Although some of this movement within Africa is
driven by the search by immigrants for opportunities and income,
many Africans are also forced to flee famine and conflicts, with an estimated 3 million refugees across Africa in 2005.

Policymakers and private businesses are creating more efficient
channels for transferring money, to increase the flows from the diaspora. Sites such as www.sendmoneyhome.org (which publishes comparisons of the cost of money transfers through different channels) are
improving transparency and encouraging lower pricing.

Safaricom in Kenya launched its m-Pesa service in 2007, a free account that allows users to send money via cell phone. Within 2 weeks of its launch, more than 10,000 people had registered and transferred more than $100,000. Some African countries, recognizing the importance of remittances to their economies, require expatriate workers to send remittances home. Mozambican mineworkers must repatriate 60 percent of their income for half the year, and Lesotho mineworkers have to repatriate a third of their income for three months and 15 percent for the rest of the year.

## ATMs, Letters, Groceries, and Cell Phone Minutes

While formal channels for remittances from workers abroad are growing by leaps and bounds, there also are many informal transfers that fly under the radar. A household survey by the World Bank found that 80 percent of Ugandan remittances were through informal channels. Only 20 percent were being tracked through formal channels. A study by Johannesburg-based Genesis Analytics concluded that fewer than half of remittances in South Africa were carried by formal financial service providers.

There are many ways to get funds home. I heard how a manager in Harare would receive foreign currency in letters from an aunt in London. I also spoke recently with a Moroccan taxi driver in Houston, Texas, who had developed his own method of sending money to his mother in Marrakech. He had given her an ATM card linked to his account in his U.S. bank. As any international tourist knows, his mother can use the card and PIN number in almost any machine in Morocco. It costs him $1 per transaction. He puts the money in the bank in the United States and it comes out in Morocco. The only downside is that he usually receives a phone call from his bank, checking on suspicious activity. Relatives also give their family credit cards using the same mechanism. There are many informal channels for money transfers, such as *hawala* (using brokers around the world to make exchanges without any formal records).

The nature of remittances, with many small transfers and an incentive for people making the transfers to stay under the radar, makes them hard to track. In fact, the actual numbers could be double the official figures.[12] Including hidden remittances means that Senegal probably received around $1.7 billion in 2006, about a third of the national budget.[13]

Sometimes the transfers are not even converted to cash at all. Why send cash when you can send groceries? Through Sadza.com (www.sadza.com), people in the United States and other parts of the world can send food to relatives in Zimbabwe. Instead of wiring cash, which could be worth less by the time it arrives, given rapid fluctuations in exchange rates, the website offers groceries and medicine that can be bought online and delivered within Zimbabwe. The site in the United States forwards the orders to contacts in Zimbabwe by e-mail, where they deliver the food or medicine, often by the next day. The price is guaranteed not to change during the transaction, and as many as 30,000 people use this site and similar ones to send food to Zimbabwe—an informal relief operation in a country hard hit by shortages.

Recognizing the power of the diaspora, Kenyan retailer Nakumatt offers a program so that relatives anywhere in the world can buy vouchers online for use in the company's retail stores. The MamaMike's website (www.mamamikes.com) allows immigrants or relatives in the United States, Europe, Australia, Asia, or South Africa to go online and purchase vouchers in denominations as small as 500 Kenyan shillings (about $8) for Nakumatt or other stores in Kenya and Uganda, using a credit card (Visa or MasterCard) or by sending a money order. The retailers send an SMS message to the recipients letting them know the vouchers have been bought and can courier them to recipients in major cities. The vouchers can be used for groceries, appliances, furniture, and other goods in the retail store. Senders can even set up regular monthly vouchers that are sent automatically, or give mobile airtime, delivered directly to the recipients' phones.

In a world of increasing cell phone penetration, there is no need to go to a bank or even a Western Union office to transfer money. Tunisie Telecom is offering wireless access for expatriates in France, who send $1 billion back home every year. The GSM Association launched a pilot project in February 2007 with MasterCard to allow international migrant workers to send money back home using mobile networks. The group includes 19 mobile operators with more than 600 million subscribers in more than 100 countries, including Africa. GSM and MasterCard estimate this new channel could expand the value of remittances globally to more than $1 trillion by 2012. The system would allow migrant workers to use their cell phones to trigger financial transfers at local banks, and their families back home would be notified of the transfers via their own cell phones.[14] As such services are developed, immigrants and their families back home may have the equivalent of a Western Union branch in their pockets.

# Investments and Charity

In addition to sending money home, members of the diaspora are investing in Africa and contributing to charitable activities. A study of Kenyan expatriates by AfricaRecruit found that even though 82 percent sent remittances home for sustenance purposes, half were also bringing money home for business or investment purposes, contributing an estimated $2.6 million per year to the Kenyan economy alone (about five times the World Bank estimates). Investment conferences in Africa and London are encouraging investors to consider opportunities in Africa, in addition to the growing number of private equity funds focused on Africa.

New investment vehicles and channels are being developed to facilitate these investments. Nigerian-based United Bank for Africa Plc offers banking services for nonresident Nigerians. It provides accounts that can be opened by Nigerians living abroad, mortgages for buying properties in Nigeria, international account-to-account remittance services, assistance for buying and selling shares on the Nigerian stock exchange, and investment products—all without having to return home.

The enthusiasm of the diaspora can sometimes overcome many obstacles to build markets. For example, Kamal Driss, whom I spoke with in the fall of 2007, earned his MBA at New York University before returning to Algeria in 1991. Driss, who had worked for Citigroup in the United States, brought the company to Algeria. When he realized that no one was investing there, he published his own Algerian Investment Guide. He showed me a copy when I visited in Algiers, and it clearly showed that GDP declined from 1989 to 1996. It was evident why no one was investing in Algeria at the time, yet Driss remained bullish on the market. He brought in David Gibson, a senior executive from the corporate office, to Algeria and convinced him that this was a good investment. Driss points with pride to a neon sign for Citibank on the roof of the building. Some said it would make them a target for anti-American sentiment, but instead the sign ultimately became a beacon for others to follow. His investments in the government-owned Algerian oil company have paid off handsomely, and now that the economy is picking up there are more opportunities. Citicorp/Citibank now has more than $7 billion invested in Algeria. As a pioneer, it is one of the most respected foreign commercial banks there, and they are using this strength to begin developing retail banking.

In addition to investing in African businesses, expatriates are founding businesses that support local development. Ghanaian-born Tralance Addy, who retired as a senior executive at Johnson & Johnson in the United States in 2001, founded WaterHealth International, Inc. It provides low-cost purified water to West Africa, India, Mexico, the Philippines, and other parts of the developing world. Today, more than half a million people in 500 locations worldwide have access to clean water provided through WaterHealth filtration systems. An estimated 9 million people in Ghana, about 50 percent of the population, lack adequate water supplies, and 70 percent of all illnesses in Ghana are related to waterborne contaminants.[15] WaterHealth sees its operations in Ghana as a gateway to West Africa. Addy holds dual citizenship in Ghana and the United States, connecting developed-world expertise and business models to the needs of the developing world.

The diaspora also makes direct philanthropic investments. For example, Houston Rockets basketball center Dikembe Mutombo fulfilled a lifelong dream by donating $15 million to set up a hospital in the Democratic Republic of Congo in honor of his late mother. His 64-year-old mother died in 1997 when she was unable to get to the hospital because streets were closed due to civil unrest. The Biamba Marie Mutombo Hospital and Research Center opened in September 2006, a 300-bed hospital that will provide health care to people in the capital city of Kinshasa, where Mutombo was born. The hospital is desperately needed in a country where one in five children dies before the age of 5 and the average life expectancy is only 42 for men and 47 for women. Mutombo's goal is to get 100,000 people to contribute $10 a month on his website to support the hospital and its research, a $29 million project. It is one of countless philanthropic gifts that are coming to Africa from the diaspora. John Dau, author of *God Grew Tired of Us*, noted that the first thing he did when he came to the United States after fleeing Sudan was to send money home. He is now building the Duk Lost Boys Clinic in Southern Sudan.

Indiana University–Purdue University Indianapolis (IUPUI) basketball coach Ron Hunter has collected more than 30,000 pairs of shoes to send to Africa. He went barefoot and encouraged fans to do the same to draw attention to the many African children who have no shoes. Hunter, an African American, worked through a North Carolina charity called Samaritan's Feet, founded by Nigerian native Emmanuel "Manny" Ohonme, who received his first pair of shoes at age 9 from a U.S. missionary. Ohonme, who went on to play college basketball at Lake Region State College in North Dakota, has set a goal of contributing 10 million pairs of shoes in ten years.

# Coming Home: Tourism

All these emigrants abroad come home regularly, helping to drive the rapid growth of African tourism. In 2006, tourism in Africa grew by 8 percent, faster than any other region of the world for the second year in a row.[16] Between 2000 and 2005, international tourists arriving in Africa swelled from 28 million to 40 million. This growth rate of 5.6 percent outstripped the 3.1 percent growth of tourism worldwide. This is much larger than the 4.4 million tourists who visited India in 2006, but less than the nearly 50 million who went to China.[17] Africa's international tourism receipts more than doubled, from $10 billion to $21 billion, in the same period between 2000 and 2005. In Egypt, tourism brought in nearly $7 billion in 2005, about a quarter of the country's foreign currency revenues, more than revenue from the Suez Canal. In 2007, more than 10 million tourists visited the country. It is not just the direct income from tourism that benefits the economy. Tourism builds other industries, too, such as airlines, hotels, and other parts of the service economy.

Recognizing that tourism and foreign remittances were the largest source of income for Morocco, the country set up a ministry for Moroccans living abroad in 2002 and stepped up investments in its tourism industry. In 2006, more than 3.5 million non-Moroccans came to visit, and more than 1 million Moroccans returned home, bringing about $5 billion total into the country. In announcing his Vision 2010 for Moroccan tourism, King Mohammed VI, called for the creation of an infrastructure to house 10 million tourists by 2010. By 2010, Morocco will have 250,000 hotel beds.

This influx drives commerce during the tourist season. Money-Gram in Morocco sees sales spike by 20 percent in the summer when Moroccan emigrants return home. The Kitea home furnishing store in the Hay Ryad shopping mall in Rabat sees its sales go up 45 percent in the summer months as emigrants return home and purchase furniture and other goods for their Moroccan homes. Kitea is helping to furnish some of the 100,000 new homes built in Morocco each year (many by emigrants abroad). Kitea has opened more than 20 stores since its founding in 1992 and planned a superstore for Casablanca to open in 2008. My driver in Morocco had a brother who ran a store in Philadelphia. One of the first things his brother in Philadelphia did when he saved some money was to buy a big apartment back home. My driver in Cairo has a brother in Italy who also owns an apartment in Egypt, so this is a very familiar story.

To respond to these emigrants and other tourists, the hotel industry is growing rapidly across Africa. Chains such as Accor (with 124 hotels in 21 African countries) and Protea Hotels (with more than 25 hotels in Africa) have expanded rapidly across Africa, and raised the standards of the hospitality industry. Global chains are moving into Africa rapidly, with new hotels created by companies such as Sheraton and InterContinental. They join Serena, created by the Aga Khan Fund for Economic Development (AKFED), which has hotels in Kenya, Uganda, and Mozambique, and built the first four-star hotel in Rwanda. Saudi Arabian-based Kingdom Holding, with a goal of earning 20 percent returns on its projects, has invested in hotels in Africa and the Middle East. The International Finance Corporation has committed more than $100 million to the African hotel sector in 14 countries.[18]

Tourism also benefits other industries. Volvo and Renault are building buses for tourists in Morocco, and Tata Motors is building trucks, buses, and cars for the South African market. Tata Motors entered South Africa in 1994 and started its subsidiary in 2000. Its commercial vehicle business grew by six times in four years, driven by a commitment to performance, reliability, and service, as well as a booming local economy. Tata is working with a Spanish partner to build buses in Morocco, and using this operation as a base for expanding the business into Algeria and Libya, with plans to move into Tunisia in the future. Tata also set up a bus plant in Senegal after winning a major government contract to replace vehicles for public transportation. The purchase of 350 new Tata buses was supported in part by a loan from the government of India of almost $18 million. In this way, the Indian government is supporting Africa development while advancing Indian brands. Every year, during Senegal's Independence Day festivities, there is a huge parade featuring the Tata buses, adding to the stature of Indian products in Africa.

Moroccan tourism indicates the complexity of African tourism, however. As a French-speaking Muslim country, more than 40 percent of Morocco's tourists come from France (it is just a few hours from Paris to Casablanca), and 19 percent are returning Moroccans. Morocco offers Western-style beaches to French tourists, but also provides more conservative resorts to Arab visitors. To cater to the needs of the various groups, the country has set up six tourism zones throughout the country, each under the control of a different developer. AirMoroc has arranged for direct flights from Europe to each of these regions.

India and Thailand have become centers of medical tourism, thanks to the development of sophisticated hospitals systems such as Apollo in India and Thailand's Bumrungrad International. They have attracted Western-trained medical doctors back to their home countries. Medical care is cheaper in India than in the United Kingdom, United States, and other developed countries, even with the cost of airfare. Given the growing airline and hospitality industry in Africa, could there be an opportunity to build facilities for medical tourism? Could there be a day when tourists will come to East Africa or South Africa for a safari and elective surgery?

# Serving the Diaspora Abroad

A British television advertisement for Unilever's Royko soup cubes shows a brother and sister from Nigeria living in London. Their dress is clearly Western. They miss home. A package comes from their mother, and a pack of Royko soup cubes tumbles out. The siblings switch from speaking the Queen's English to speaking the pidgin English that might be heard on the streets at home. Even though they are in England, they are home again.

In addition to the opportunities the African diaspora creates within Africa, companies are targeting products such as hair care, coffee, and entertainment to African immigrants and African descendents in Europe, the United States, and other parts of the world. Sky Channel 148, "Ben TV," was launched as the first African-Caribbean channel in the United Kingdom and has more than a million viewers. It appeals to viewers' involvement in Africa. As its advertising said, "Don't forget this year 2007 is the 200th year since the abolition of the slave trade. What role are you playing?"

The connections between Tunisia and France are so significant that Tunisian marketing research firm Sigma is setting up an office in Paris to study the behavior of immigrants from Tunisia and other Maghreb countries living in Europe. It will use the information to help clients promote the many African brands that are popular with the diaspora.

A variety of companies cater to the African hair market, including Africanhair.com, Afrohair.com, Blacklikeme.co.uk, and African-braids.biz. African Braids was started by a U.S. immigrant from Nigeria living in Minnesota, who had lived in Africa for 25 years before coming to the United States. It sells braids that can be woven into hair and hair-growth cream, products designed for the African diaspora.

*Tiro* magazine, focusing on African fashion and entertainment, was founded by Helen Eferakorho, a Nigerian immigrant in the United States. The name is from the Nigerian tribal languages of Urhobo and means "a woman who is full of grace." As the magazine's website notes, "The majority of fashion and entertainment magazines on the market today are primarily concerned with fashion trends in the Western world, ignoring the uniqueness of the African fabric and its impact on the Western world." This is one of many titles designed to appeal to the African diaspora.

Many African stores cater to immigrants. Yomi Alimi, for example, owns the Austin International Market on Pampa Drive in Austin, Texas. Through its doors come thousands of immigrants every year from Nigeria, Ghana, Liberia, Sierra Leone, Equatorial Guinea, South Africa, the Ivory Coast, Burkina Faso, Senegal, Malawi, Kenya, Morocco, Ethiopia, Zimbabwe, Zambia, Angola, Uganda, and other parts of Africa, as well as from the Dominican Republic, Puerto Rico, and the Bahamas. They buy African newspapers and magazines, foods such as Nigerian spices, mashed yams in a tube, dried stock fish, and fresh goat meat. He carries a wide stock of DVDs from Nigeria and Ghana available for rental at $5.50 for three days. Customers buy phone cards or transfer money back home; he used to be a Western Union representative. His wife, a nurse, runs a hair salon upstairs.

In the Harlem section of New York City, Senegalese immigrants dominate small vendors. They are sending an estimated $100 million from New York to Senegal every three months. Although vendor licenses are hard to obtain in New York, these immigrant entrepreneurs represent the majority of vendors, particularly unlicensed vendors, as can be seen in estimates that Senegalese immigrants account for about 90 percent of the 1,300 vendor arrests annually.

Not all these businesses founded by immigrants remain small. Patak Indian food company has become one of Britain's most successful brands, in large part by catering to immigrants with authentic Indian food. Founder L. G. Pathak (who dropped the *h* in his company's name) arrived in the United Kingdom nearly penniless from Kenya in 1956, and the company's products are now distributed in more than 40 countries.[19] In the United States, energy company CAMAC International, Inc., in Houston, founded by Nigerian-born entrepreneur Kase Lawal, became the second black American company to generate receipts of over $1 billion in 2002. (With revenues of nearly $1.5 billion, it ranked 272 on the *Forbes* list of the largest privately owned companies in 2006.)

The African diaspora is a huge global market for goods from Africa and goods designed for Africans. It is a relatively wealthy and well-educated segment, often looking for connections to Africa. This diaspora creates additional markets for movies, magazines, food, and other products as well as services such as money transfers that connect the world with Africa.

## Door of Return: The Complex Diaspora

The African diaspora is tremendously broad and deep. An apartment fire in New York that killed members of an extended family from Mali in March 2007 drew attention to the growth of a close-knit community of immigrants from Mali in New York. A U.S. bridge collapse in the summer 2007 highlighted that Minnesota has the largest population of Somalis in the United States. (They began arriving as refugees in the 1990s, and a decade later there were more than 11,000 people of Somali descent living in the state, including a large community near the site of the collapse.)[20] U.S. Senator Barack Obama returned to Kenya, where his father was born, before declaring his candidacy for U.S. president.

The African diaspora includes Africans of Indian descent, such as the more than 75,000 expelled from Uganda under Idi Amin in 1972. Film director Mira Nair's classic film *Mississippi Masala* highlights some of the complexity of the African diaspora when the Ugandan-born Indian heroine falls in love with an African American carpet cleaner played by a young Denzel Washington. Uganda is still the second home for Nair and her husband, a Columbia University professor who was born in Uganda. She has set up an annual workshop for filmmakers called *Maisha* (meaning "life" in Kiswahili) in Kampala to train screenwriters and film directors in East Africa. Her goal is to expand the project into a permanent art and culture center.[21] Many Indian immigrants who became multimillionaires in the United Kingdom are also from African descent, having emigrated from Kenya or Uganda.[22]

Even the darkest moments of African history are the basis for connection. Countries such as Ghana are building connections with families taken from the country in the slave trade, encouraging descendants to return to visit, invest, and even retire in Ghana. The country has renamed its infamous "door of no return" at the fort of Cape Coast, the last sight of Africa for many taken onto slave ships, as the "door of return." It is offering descendants of former Ghanaians lifetime visas and relaxed citizenship requirements. Ghana honored Dr. Martin Luther King Jr., W. E. B. DuBois, and other prominent African Americans in a 2007 celebration marking the two-hundredth anniversary of the end of the trans-Atlantic slave trade by Britain. Tourists from around the world come to Goreé Island off Darkar, Senegal, once the center of the West African slave trade. (I was so moved by this place, particularly when my guide who was raised on the island and lived in a cave apartment, described how he had picked up several foreign languages from tourists, and how his wife, through an international program, was studying medicine in the United States. In two centuries, here was a daughter of Africa who has gone to America under different conditions.)

In *The Grand Slave Emporium*, William St Clair estimates that 11 million people born in Africa were carried across the ocean between the mid-fifteenth to late-nineteenth century, the greatest forced migration in history (estimates vary from 11 million to 25 million).[23] Among the most famous was African Prince Ab-dul Rahman Ibrahima Ibn Sori from West Africa who was captured and sold into slavery in the United States, as commemorated in the book by Terry Alford and the 2008 PBS documentary *Prince Among Slaves*. The continent is beginning to build other connections to the African American community in the United States, from stars such as Danny Glover, who is investing in the African film industry (including his Louverture film company), to talk show host Oprah Winfrey, who has built a school for girls in South Africa. When actress Whoopi Goldberg had a DNA test showing she was of Papel descent, a tribe that makes up most of the population of Guinea-Bissau, she received an impassioned invitation to come to the poor nation with a population of just over 1 million. The country also began playing her movies on its two television channels.[24] Countries across Africa are recognizing the importance of strengthening their connections with the diaspora.

African immigrants in the United States have created organizations such as the All African Peoples Organization in Omaha, Nebraska; the Nigerian-American Chamber of Commerce in Miami; the Tristate (Ohio, Indiana, and Kentucky) Cameroon Family (TRISCAF); the Nigerian Women Eagles Club in Cincinnati, Ohio;

and African Heritage Inc. in Wisconsin. San Francisco opened a new Museum of the African Diaspora in December 2005. The opening wall asks visitors "When did you discover that you are African?" with a mosaic of more than 2,000 photos of people from all over the world. A similar Museum of the African Diaspora has opened in Paris, where the *Musée du Quai Branly* in Paris also attracts a steady stream of immigrants from countries such as Algeria, Senegal, Tunisia, Congo, and Gabon to see African artifacts.[25] Members of the African diaspora are playing increasingly prominent roles in global businesses. Among the CEOs of Fortune 500 companies are Altria Group's Louis Camilleri of Egypt, Alcoa's Alain Belda from Morocco, and Eli Lilly's Sidney Taurel of Morocco.

## Strengthening Connections

Kwesi and Yvonne Nduom went to the United States for education and work before returning to their native Ghana in 1991, when they were in their late 30s. Kwesi, a consultant for Deloitte, initially worked to build the company's business in West Africa. Like many expatriates, he was able to bring insights from the United States to Africa and open up the African market for his company.

But this was just the beginning. The entrepreneurial couple launched a number of businesses when they returned to the country with their young children. The Nduoms had acquired the experience and resources to make investments in start-ups, including a securities exchange firm. They purchased land on the coast to develop a seaside resort called Coconut Grove Beach Resort in Elmina, putting up their U.S. home in Virginia as collateral. At the time, there was little resort development in the country, so coastal land actually cost less than inland.

They used those assets to build a chain of four hotels, but they still faced a challenging banking system. To purchase other properties, they had to put up collateral valued at four times the value of the land and pay interest rates of more than 40 percent. Their resorts have attracted visitors such as actor Will Smith and former U.N. Secretary

General Kofi Annan. The Nduoms have not only built value for them-selves, but point proudly to the fact that their enterprises now employ 500 people. Their civic mindedness extends beyond their own enter-prises. Kwesi Nduom, active in politics (including serving as minister of state), was preparing to run as one of three candidates for president of Ghana in the December 2008 elections.

"The diaspora is making a difference back home," said Yvonne Nduom in an interview with the author from Washington, D.C., in February 2008, where she and her husband were raising support for his campaign. "For me, the third world is the last frontier. It is full of opportunity, but you have to have some form of tenacity. If you perse-vere, you will be successful. In addition to our education, there was something else that we brought back home—the can-do attitude of the Americans. If God gives you lemons, you make lemonade. If all us were to go back with the experience we acquired, we would be able to transform Africa in no time."[26]

There is growing activity across Africa focused on the diaspora, such as the founding of the Diaspora Africa Forum during a meeting of Africa Union heads of state in July 2007. There have also been investment forums for the continent and specific countries such as Rwanda. Countries are creating diaspora offices or offering dual citizenship. The Homecoming Revolution (www.homecomingrevolu-tion.co.za), a nonprofit organization sponsored by First National Bank, encourages and helps South Africans living abroad to return home. It offers advice, financing, and other services.

There are many other opportunities to deepen these connections, as shown by the activities of Mexico in supporting connections with its diaspora, particularly in the United States. Mexico has created a strategic alliance with convenience store 7-11 to use its stores as of-fices for wire transfers, putting such offices on virtually every street corner. Mexico has consular offices throughout the United States. Ac-cording to former Mexican President Vicente Fox, the $14 billion in annual remittances to Mexico from immigrants in the United States between 2000 and 2004 was a key factor in achieving a 16 percent de-cline in families living in poverty at home. Could Mexico be a role model for Africa? India also has created events such as the annual Pravasi Bharatiya Divas and prizes to recognize and engage members of the Indian diaspora. Could this also be a role model for Africa?

The African diaspora is already playing a critical role in the development of the continent, and this role can be expected to broaden and deepen in the years ahead. There are millions of Africans abroad, most of whom have greater income and education than relatives back home. This is a tremendous resource and a powerful engine for future progress across the continent.

## Rising Opportunities

- What are the opportunities to encourage remittances and other investments from the diaspora in Africa?
- What products or services could you offer to the African diaspora?
- How can your business create direct channels for expatriates abroad to purchase products for relatives at home?
- What are the obstacles to participation by the diaspora in Africa, and how can you address these obstacles to encourage the involvement and investment of the diaspora?

# Conclusion: Ubuntu Market

*A few decades ago, few outsiders believed that India would make the economic leaps it has made. This required entrepreneurial initiative and political courage. Africa stands at a similar threshold today. The best hope for Africa is entrepreneurship and market development. Building successful enterprises will build wealth by increasing political and economic stability and offering better quality goods and services to African consumers. But to create these enterprises, we need to first look beyond Africa as a charity case to see it as one of the world's most important emerging markets.*

After graduating from Columbia Business School in 2002, Kenyan-born Wanja Michuki initially thought of setting up a business importing coffee. But after seeing Kenyan coffee in Starbucks, she decided on tea. After all, it was tea that had helped put her through graduate school. The Highland Tea Company, LLC, was founded by her mother, Watiri, in Kenya in 1991. Her 30-acre tea garden at the base of Mount Kenya (called *Karurumo*, which means "little treasure" in Kikuyu) had helped support and educate Wanja and her five siblings. "My mother is a very enterprising woman herself, and she is a strong role model for me," the younger Michuki said in an interview with the author in 2007.[1]

Most of the tea sold in Kenya—the world's largest tea exporter, shipping more than 300,000 tons per year—is sold as a commodity on the Mombasa auction market, ending up under labels such as Twinings and Tetley. Michuki saw an opportunity to create a Kenyan brand, under the Highland name. The company set up a factory in Kenya for the tea, commissioned Kenyan artwork for packaging, and built branding and distribution in the United States. Through her base in Montclair, New Jersey, she now sells teas under the Highland brand through upscale specialty stores and supermarkets such as Whole Foods and Kings.

She is building a "social enterprise," creating a viable business and helping small farmers in Kenya. To deepen the impact of the business, she has teamed up with the Freeplay Foundation to supply hand-cranked and solar radios to Kenyan farmers for education and information, sharing a common vision, as shown in Exhibit 26 (see page 14 of the insert). The relationship started when there was a shipment of radios stuck in the port in Mombasa, and she helped get them released. Now, Highland encourages donors in the developed world to hold tea parties, to sample the Kenyan teas, and raise funds to supply radios to the farmers. The tea collection centers in Kenya, which draw together local farmers, form a natural focal point for listening, so a radio in the collection center can be used by about 40 people, magnifying the impact. This is another example of how the diaspora is reaching back to benefit communities back home, as discussed in Chapter 8, "Coming Home: Opportunities in the African Diaspora."

Because her focus is not just on building Highland but on supporting Kenyan tea growers, she is even helping its competitors. For example, Michuki invited the CEO of Tazo Tea (owned by Starbucks) to accompany her to Kenya to learn more about the tea industry there. Why would she help her competitors build a Kenyan business? It helps fellow tea farmers—and builds recognition of Kenyan teas. "The commitment we have is to add value for these tea farmers, and if that means we are selling to other packers, that is fine," she said. "We are working on behalf of farmers who are locked into this auction market. Besides, competition is good. If Kenyan teas are sold in Starbucks, that makes more consumers aware of Kenyan tea, and that works for us."

The company follows Fair Trade principles to ensure the sale of teas helps the farming communities in Kenya. "You're engaging in a virtuous cycle," Michuki said. "You pay a premium price and that goes into a fund that supports a program that helps meet needs such as education that the farmers feel are most important to them. Our belief is that the best approach to sustainable poverty eradication in Kenya is by adding value where we have a comparative advantage."[2]

It is such initiatives large and small that are propelling Africa's rise—creating successful businesses and improving local communities. Across the continent, local economies and societies are being transformed by such sustainable market development projects that are building successful enterprises while contributing to local development, as well as the initiatives of inspired social entrepreneurs and the corporate social responsibility projects of large corporations. These initiatives draw upon the entrepreneurial spirit within Africa and the knowledge and connections of the new "Cheetah generation" who are working within Africa and outside on behalf their homelands. Companies such as Highland are transforming the way Africa is viewed in the world. And they are building community at the same time that they build their companies. These enterprises are attracting more outside investment to the continent, and economic development is creating a new urgency for political reform. There is so much to be found in the bottom of a cup of tea.

# The Power of Ubuntu

South African Nobel Prize laureate Bishop Desmond Tutu has described the Zulu word *ubuntu* as meaning "I am because you are." It represents humanness, sharing, community, or humanity toward others. According to the Zulu maxim, "A person is a person through other persons" (*Umuntu ngumuntu ngabantu*). Success in the African consumer market comes from meeting basic human needs. It comes from recognizing and meeting the needs of African communities. Customers, employees, and business partners come from these communities. Success comes from building businesses that strengthen communities, as Highland has done in supporting Kenyan tea growers while building its global business. Unless you take care of the farmers, you will not have any tea. By increasing the income of farmers, you create resources that can support the growth of other businesses and the education of their children. Businesses flourish when they address real human needs, and nowhere is this more true than in Africa, where the needs are often so great. In an economic sense, businesses recognize that "I am because you are."

Africa is a market that faces serious political and economic challenges. Zulu is just one of more than 1,000 languages spoken across this complex continent. But beyond the headlines and divisions, humanity is what makes Africa an attractive future market. It is basic human needs for food, shelter, clothing, and communication that are driving progress in Africa. It is the human desire of parents to create a better world for their children. It is the indomitable spirit of entrepreneurship and optimism that is overcoming the challenges and drawing the continent together into one of the world's most important future markets.

This recognition of humanity is driving charitable work on the continent, but also is the bedrock of consumer market development. Companies and entrepreneurs that are responding to these human needs already are building profitable enterprises for the future African market. They are creating this "ubuntu market." The concept of *ubuntu* has resonated in the speeches of many individuals including Bill Clinton, as well as in products such as a community bus designed by Tata Motors for the South African market, called Ubuntu (see Exhibit 27). The wealth of Africa is in its entrepreneurs and consumers. If you don't recognize what is going on in the community, you cannot be successful. The power of ubuntu, and the wealth of Africa, is in its people.

# Building Community through Corporate Social Responsibility

Companies in Africa are making a direct and indirect impact on the serious challenges facing the continent. On a winding road in Boksburg, just outside of Johannesburg, I pulled up to a small, well-kept house in a quiet neighborhood. Sister Gill Harrower who was then head of the Unilever HIV/AIDS Resource Centre led the way inside, where a bevy of small children were gathered around Gloria Nontsikelelo, the foster mother of the house. All of these children, ranging in age from 4 to 14, had lost both parents to AIDS (see Exhibit 28). This house is part of the Thokomala project (which means "warmth" or "caring" in Zulu), started by former Unilever Chairman Niall Fitzgerald. He raised the initial funds, 1 million rand (about $150,000), while running the London Marathon in 2002. In contrast to a large orphanage, the project provides a home atmosphere and more normal childhood for the children. The funding for this particular home was donated by a Muslim donor from the United Kingdom, and it is located in a neighborhood near a mosque. Caring for these children cuts across ethnic and religious lines.

The impact of AIDS in South Africa is startling. When researchers from a market research firm in South Africa surveyed a poor area of

Johannesburg on the use of glass bottles, they inadvertently discovered that 45 of the 60 houses on one street were headed by children. Their parents had died of AIDS, and the older children stepped in to take care of the younger ones. The issues facing these communities went far beyond the choice of glass or plastic bottles, and this was research that no company could ignore. In 2005, 1 million South African children lost their mothers to AIDS. By 2010, the number will climb to 2.5 million, and these orphans are expected to make up 9 percent to 12 percent of the South African population by 2015. Children as young as 9 have been left as heads of households in South Africa.

In the face of this need, the Thokomala homes containing a half-dozen children may seem like a small victory. The homes are a model that can be replicated in neighborhood after neighborhood. Unilever has a goal of establishing 100 homes by 2010. Each house also is a center of support for other AIDS orphans in the area, who are living with relatives or on their own. Roughly 450 children are supported by each home in this way.

Given the intense needs of the continent, building any successful business needs to go hand in hand with addressing the challenges of Africa. This is not only the right thing to do, but the people affected are the company's employees and customers.

"The previous era was about aid for Africa, but aid for Africa is not going to bring Africa out of its dependence," said Gail Klintworth, chairman of Unilever South Africa, during a meeting in Durban in May 2006. "The secret is going to be trade in Africa, but you can't sell basic consumer goods to people and not recognize what is going on in their personal lives."

Virtually every company or organization I met with or spoke with in Africa had some kind of social program designed to address the serious challenges of its customers and employees. In an age of rising attention to corporate social responsibility, it almost goes without saying that companies have to take an active interest in social and environmental outcomes of their businesses, in addition to the traditional focus on financial returns. This "triple bottom line" recognizes that the role of business extends beyond generating returns for shareholders.

### Distributing Coca-Cola and Addressing HIV/AIDS

Working with Population Services International and other organizations, The Coca-Cola Company is using its highly developed networks to distribute condoms throughout Africa to fight HIV/AIDS (see Exhibit 29). With 900,000 retail outlets across Africa, the company has unmatched reach in carrying products and messages to the African people. These channels, developed for private-sector businesses, can be used for community projects.

Coca-Cola has initiated a health-care plan to provide antiretroviral drugs to employees and families with HIV/AIDS. All the employees of bottlers of Coca-Cola beverages in Africa are either participating in existing health-care programs, or have joined the joint Coca-Cola Africa Foundation/Coca-Cola Africa Bottlers Healthcare program. The Foundation and bottlers already support HIV/AIDS campaigns in more than ten countries and have entered strategic partnerships with UNAIDS, UNICEF, and other nonprofit organizations to strengthen the delivery of public health services across the continent. Companies such as The Coca-Cola Company have a far-reaching impact on Africa.

### Providing Fresh Water

More than 300 million people in sub-Saharan Africa are without access to clean drinking water. As part of its Water of Life program, Diageo launched the "1 Million Challenge" in 2006 to provide an additional 1 million people in Africa with access to clean drinking water. Procter & Gamble has distributed its PUR powder for water purification, shown in Exhibit 30, part of a clean water initiative with Population Services International that prevented an estimated 11 million deaths from diarrhea around the world in 2005 alone. P&G has provided more than half a billion gallons of clean water to people in developing countries such as Uganda, Kenya, and Malawi. PUR is sold for 7 Kenyan shillings (about 10 cents) for a sachet that can treat 10 liters (about 4.5 gallons) of drinking water.

When I met Clarice Odhiambo in the summer of 2006, with a group of executives of The Coca-Cola Company at the Serena Hotel in Nairobi, she was headed to Atlanta to extend her work as manager of the company's Africa Water Partnership. She helped Coca-Cola create the Global Water Challenge in 2005, along with partners, including CARE, UNICEF, Proctor & Gamble, and others. "A healthy consumer means a healthy business," she said. "There is nothing more sensible than to try to give back to the community. In rural Africa, 74 percent of the population doesn't have access to safe water and sanitation. These areas are so sparsely populated; even a borehole with piping is not practical. You need innovative solutions."

Among the innovative solutions, she has worked with local women to redesign their traditional clay pots for storing water. To replace the wide-mouthed pots or bowls from which water was dipped with dirty hands, they created new designs with narrow mouths and spigots to preserve water quality. The company has also engaged in water purification, drilling wells, and wastewater treatment projects. A chemical engineer, she is a graduate of the University of Nairobi with a Master's degree from the University of Rhode Island. Odhiambo served as a research scientist for Betz Paperchem Inc. in Florida (where she earned two patents) before she joined The Coca-Cola Company in Kenya as an engineer 1997. "The African people are very passionate, very determined, and very willing to help themselves," she said. "They even know what solutions will work for them. They just need facilitation. Given the opportunity, as Coca-Cola has given me, we will come up with our own solutions."

Water purification systems are also an opportunity. The Life Straw, for example, offers a $3 water filtration system that can be used just about anywhere. There are other potential opportunities. For example, Richard Heinichen in Dripping Springs, Texas, has created a sophisticated system for filtering and bottling rainwater. From his collection center in Tank Town, Texas, he was bottling 5,000 bottles a week of his "cloud juice" by 2005. He also had worked with local businesses to produce branded rainwater with their logos.[3] This is currently a product targeted for U.S. markets, but couldn't there be an opportunity to create a similar business in Africa?

## Addressing Diseases

Some 3,000 children age 5 or younger die every day from malaria in Africa.[4] As noted in Chapter 4, "Harnessing the Hanouti: Opportunities in Organizing the Market," Novartis is addressing malaria with a powerful drug through a public and private strategy. SC Johnson also has sponsored major malaria-prevention programs in South Africa and other parts of Africa at the same time that it has built a commercial business for Raid and mosquito-control products. I had the pleasure of speaking with Maude Christian-Meier, Ph.D., a senior research scientist with SC Johnson in Racine, Wisconsin, about her mosquito trap program to study and reduce malaria in Africa. Christian-Meier, who grew up in Ghana before coming to the United States for her education, has returned to Ghana every six months to oversee the project in the village of Tafo. The innovative mosquito traps emit a small amount of carbon dioxide, similar to human breathing. The mosquitoes that are attracted are then vacuumed up into a net, allowing evaluation of the trap's performance. Initial results, based on data collected at the local clinic in the test area over several years, show that there were one-third fewer cases of malaria in 2005 than in 2002. In an area where one in ten children under the age of 5 typically dies of malaria, they have recorded no deaths. The trap doesn't use any of SC Johnson's commercial products, so it doesn't have a direct commercial benefit, but it is the right thing to do. The study is helping the community of Tafo while building knowledge about the new approaches for preventing this deadly disease.

Other initiatives are also having an impact. Africa Partners Medical (APM) is a group of American and African doctors, nurses, and other health-care professionals committed to improving medical care in Africa. APM (www.africapartnersmedical.org) does so by sponsoring educational conferences in Africa and establishing long-term partnerships with indigenous African health-care personnel. The faculty of Africa Partners Medical includes physicians and nurses from Mayo Clinic, Scott and White Clinic, Harvard Medical School, Stanford University Medical Center, Children's Hospital of Philadelphia, among others, who volunteer their time. Since 2000, APM has brought an annual medical education program to a total of more than

900 physicians, residents, nurses, and emergency medical technicians in Ghana, Nigeria, Kenya, Ivory Coast, Burkina Faso, and Mali.

A recent study by McKinsey, reported in the November 2007 *McKinsey Quarterly*, concluded that Africa's dire shortage of health-care professionals could be addressed through new models. With one-quarter of the world's diseases and just 3 percent of its health-care workers, the capabilities in Africa are mismatched with the challenge. But the study found that by adopting models used successfully in other developing countries, Africa could better meet its health-care needs. These strategies include using 1) more nonphysicians such as nurses and community health workers, 2) adding private-sector education to public medical training programs, and 3) creating an environment that encourages broader collaboration with NGOs and the private sector.[5] In December 2007, the World Bank's International Finance Corporate announced a $1 billion fund for health care in Africa, which will include private-sector initiatives.[6]

Sometimes, nonprofit initiatives can be more effective than commercial ventures. Studies in Kenya, Ethiopia, Ghana, Rwanda, and Zambia by the World Health Organization on behalf of the Global Fund found that it was more effective to give away mosquito nets for free than to sell them. This contradicted the view that charging a nominal price for such public health solutions makes purchasers take them more seriously, increasing their effectiveness.[7] Sometimes the best solutions may be free.

There are some positive signs of improvements in health in Africa and other parts of the world. For example, the United Nations reported in September 2007 that infant mortality rates have dropped sharply, including a steep decline in sub-Saharan Africa. This is a positive sign of progress toward the U.N. Millennium Goal of cutting the 1990 infant mortality rate by two-thirds by 2015.[8]

### Environment: Doing Well by Doing Good

Steve Fitzgerald built Conservation Corporation Africa (CC Africa) into one of the largest African safari and eco-tourism companies by keeping one eye on catering to wealthy tourists and another on improving local communities and the environment. CC Africa has more than 35 safari camps across South Africa, Botswana, Namibia, Zimbabwe, Kenya, and Tanzania. When it set up a new game park in Zululand, it faced a community claim on its land. Rather than dispute the local claim to the land, which would have led to a long legal battle, the company conceded the land to the community and then struck up a deal for a long-term lease of the property. The community wins by receiving the rental income and employment, and CC Africa ensures good relationships with its neighbors, who help protect the animals from poachers and other threats. Through its Africa Foundation, it has raised more than $4 million for projects in five African countries, an initiative that both serves the continent and adds to the company's reputation among its altruistic clients.

Africa is now one of the fastest emerging tourist destinations, but these tourists not only want to see wild animals and sweeping vistas; they also want to make an impact by protecting wildlife and supporting local communities. During a meeting late one evening at their headquarters in Johannesburg, Fitzgerald commented that he's been advised by marketing experts to change the organization's name, since its sounds more like a nonprofit organization than a safari business. But "conservation" is essential to its mission, so the line between for-profit and nonprofit is not always so sharp. "We are doing well by doing good," he said during the interview in his office in Johannesburg. "We make more money by thinking differently, through community-based tourism."

Similarly, Jake Grieves-Cook set up the Gamewatchers Safaris in Kenya, with funding from Aureos Capital, working with the local Masai tribes to set up a safari tour in a rustic yet comfortable bush setting. The local tribes receive a lease fee and a fee for each visitor, providing much-needed income. The clients receive a less-commercial safari experience, staying in real tents, and meeting with the Masai. Shearwater Adventures in Zimbabwe (owned by Innscor) taps into conservation concerns of its 80,000 visitors per year by selling walks with lions or the artwork (footprints) of elephants, in addition to helicopter rides over Victoria Falls. With declining revenues due to the Zimbabwe economic crisis and growth of tourism from Zambia on the other side of the falls, finding ways to generate additional revenue from each visitor has become essential to survival.

Public and private strategies are vital anywhere in the world in building infrastructure such as roads or ports, but this cooperation is important at a deeper level in African markets. Given the social challenges, there are opportunities to work with governments, NGOs, and other players to create infrastructure that can provide the foundation for business.

## Providing Seed Money

The spirit of joining development and business building is embodied in the Aga Khan Development Network (AKDN), which has built schools, universities, and hospitals at the same time that it has developed successful businesses such as hotels, banks, insurance companies, and manufacturing enterprises. "Our philosophy is development for the country and improving the quality of life for people," said Anil Ishani, resident representative of the Aga Khan Development Network (Kenya) in an interview with author in 2006. They have initiatives in Kenya, Uganda, Tanzania, Congo, Ivory Coast, Mali, Burkina Faso, Angola, Mozambique, and Madagascar. AKDN literally has given "seed money" to 30,000 small bean farmers northeast of Nairobi who were provided with seeds and a market to buy their crops at the end of the season. AKDN also provided education, medical facilities, microfinance, and other support for the initiative. The end result was a quality product that could be exported to European markets and a huge boost to the standard of living of the farmers.

Companies are also providing private financing for public initiatives. Goldman Sachs, several European countries, and the World Bank joined together to launch a major initiative to vaccinate children in developing countries, using an innovative $1 billion bond in November 2006 to fund the health programs of the GAVI Alliance (formerly the Global Alliance for Vaccines and Immunization) in 70 of the world's poorest countries, including many in Africa. The International Finance Facility for Immunization (IFFIm) is expected to protect 500 million children in the next decade, saving an estimated 10 million lives.[9] It was the first time bonds were issued to support a specific objective related to health and immunization.

Even in addressing issues such as health care, which have typically been seen as public-sector challenges, the World Bank and others are

designing private-sector solutions. This is recognition that on a continent where governments have been ineffective in addressing health-
care crises, investing in entrepreneurship may be the best hope.

Donations are becoming more strategic. Millennium Promise, a
project co-founded by economist Jeffrey Sachs, has provided investments in dozens of sub-Saharan countries to create community-based
economic development activities. Working with the United Nations,
Millennium Promise makes strategic investments in agriculture,
health, education, roads, electricity, and other areas to help break the
cycle of poverty. For example, providing fertilizer to a small village in
Tanzania can help farmers be more successful, giving them the resources to make further investments in their own farms and the community's development.[10] The Clinton Foundation is supporting
projects such as one in Neno, Malawi, where they have built a hospital and worked with a group of 1,200 local farmers to form a cooperative and secure loans for fertilizer to grow winter wheat. The
cooperative also allowed them to build a mill to process the wheat.[11]

### Creating Markets through Social Entrepreneurship

Social entrepreneurs are building markets and encouraging entrepreneurship at the same time they are addressing social challenges.
Organizations such as the Draper Richards Foundation are encouraging "social entrepreneurship," to help "outstanding people create wide-
reaching social change." Among the fellows supported by the
foundation were Matt Flannery and Premal Shah, founders of Kiva
(www.kiva.org), the world's first person-to-person lending marketplace
for the poor. Flannery was inspired to create the concept after he and
his wife observed how growing a small business could drastically alter
the lives of low-income entrepreneurs in Uganda. Shah, a product manager at PayPal, became a pioneer in Internet microfinance after a sab-
batical in India before he joined Flannery to create Kiva. Kiva's goal is
to reduce global poverty by creating a platform where Internet users
can lend to and connect with a specific developing-world entrepreneur
online. The Draper Richards Foundation also is supporting social ventures such as the One Acre Fund (www.oneacrefund.org), working with
poor farmers in Rwanda and Kenya; Living Goods (www.livinggoods.
org), using an Avon-like model for essential health products in Uganda;

and the Scojo Foundation (www.scojofoundation.org), which is empowering local entrepreneurs who sell affordable reading glasses in Africa and other parts of the world.

Ashoka, founded by Bill Drayton in Washington, D.C., in 1980 has been a pioneer in social entrepreneurship, supporting the work of more than 1,800 Ashoka fellows in more than 60 countries. Among its fellows is Victoria Hale, a former U.S. Food and Drug Administration employee, who has created the first nonprofit pharmaceutical company in the United States to capitalize on U.S. drug research that could be of value to Africa and other parts of the developing world. Hale's OneWorldHealth is using innovative models to develop drugs for diseases such as malaria and cholera.[12]

Grameen Bank's innovative microfinancing and its entrepreneurial phone ladies illustrate how social enterprises can lay the foundation for markets. Now cell phones have become so widespread, even in the smallest villages, that there is less demand for the phone ladies. Microfinance has been picked up by mainstream banks. Grameen founder and Nobel Prize winner Muhammad Yunus, working with Danone, has helped start a yogurt factory in Bangladesh that has created a new model for development. The fortified yogurt would address malnutrition while supporting dairy farmers and microvendors, providing income for an estimated 1,600 people in a 20-mile radius of the plant. Such "social business enterprises" present a model that could be repeated in many parts of Africa and with different products, building on Danone's strong presence in many parts of Africa.[13]

Governments can also play an important role. In Morocco, the government is providing low-interest loans to create a housing market. It is tearing down high density areas called *bitonville* (rubbish), the largest of which is in Sidi Moumen in the suburbs of Casablanca, which had been home to some 170,000 people. It is replacing them with public housing, with mortgage loans at 4 percent interest.

The encouragement of entrepreneurship and development of consumer markets can build up local economies. Sustainable market development can go hand in hand with social development. As a sign I saw in Cape Town, South Africa, succinctly put it: "Shop till unemployment drops" (see Exhibit 31).

## Designing for Africa

From agricultural innovations to household products, new designs are needed for Africa and other parts of the developing world. These designs need to be tailored to the specific demands of Africa. I visited an exhibit on "Design for the Other 90 Percent" (http://other90.cooperhewitt.org/) at the Smithsonian Institution's Cooper-Hewitt National Design Museum in New York City in early 2007. It offers important examples of the opportunities to rethink the designs for the developing world, from low-cost prosthetics to water filters to sanitation to computers.

An example is the Q-drum (www.qdrum.co.za), a plastic, donut-shaped container that can easily transport 75 liters (about 20 gallons) of clean drinking water by rolling it along the ground with a rope through the center of the drum. It is so easy, even a child can transport water for many kilometers. In many rural areas, people live far from a reliable source of clean water, leaving them vulnerable to cholera, dysentery, and other water-borne diseases from closer water supplies. Another example of design for Africa is the Kenya Ceramic Jiko, a portable charcoal stove that can reduce fuel consumption by 30 percent to 50 percent, saving the consumer money, reducing toxic gas and particulate matter, and resulting in better overall heath for the user. The stove is now used in more than 50 percent of all urban homes and 16 percent of rural homes in Kenya and is spreading to neighboring African countries.[14] (As noted in Chapter 5, "Building Mama Habiba an Ice Factory: Opportunities in Infrastructure," this is just one of the innovative solutions that have been developed to address the challenge of increasing efficiency and reducing environmental impact of cooking stoves.)

In addition to its hand-cranked radios, the Freeplay Foundation has created a foot-powered generator called the Weza (which means "power" in Swahili) that it has distributed in Rwanda, where 95 percent of the population does not have access to power. The Weza can be used to charge cell phones, supply lights, or even jump start cars. The foundation set up "Weza Pioneers," local entrepreneurs who can distribute fee-based power to their rural communities. The micro-enterprises are expected to be profitable within a year.[15]

Large corporations are also encouraging a fresh look at designs for Africa. Nokia asked consumers in shantytowns in Accra, Ghana (in addition to Mumbai and Rio de Janeiro), to design their own "dream phones." The company unveiled the designs in London in April 2008, with truly innovative designs that addressed local needs. For example, one phone offered slots for multiple SIM cards, reflecting the need of African users to access more than one network operator to get reliable coverage.

In 2006, GE Healthcare challenged students at the Art Center College of Design in Pasadena, California, to come up with innovative solutions to Africa's health-care challenges. Among the ideas that were turned into prototypes were a radio bracelet that would allow communication between patients, midwives, and clinics; a field microscope that would simplify the search for parasites; a fetal ultrasound belt that would require less training for technicians; and a scanner to detect malaria by looking through the skin of a patient's hand.[16] In countries that do not have great financial resources, it is essential to spend imagination and create products tailored to local challenges. GE is also pushing its own designers to create products for Africa and other developing markets, such as a portable ECG machine offered in 2008 for a fraction of the cost of its standard machines.

These are wonderful examples of how we can create innovation solutions to address the challenges of developing markets, but why should "Design for the Other 90 Percent" be a special exhibit? Why isn't there an annual conference on this topic, similar to the annual Comdex conference that used to define the future of computing? Can China, India, or Africa take the lead on this?

# Trade Not Aid: Beyond a Continent of Victims

As noted in Chapter 1, the West has given unprecedented attention to providing aid to Africa. Performers such Bono have kept attention focused on the continent. The Gates and Clinton Foundations, among many others, have announced project after project on the continent. Gwyneth Paltrow and David Bowie declared, "I am African," in campaigns to combat AIDS. Austrian actor Karlheinz Böhm founded *Menschen för Menschen* (Humans for Humans) in 1981 for humanitarian work in Ethiopia. Bono and Alicia Keys raised money for AIDS through their recording of "Don't Give Up (Africa)" and the Keep a Child Alive initiative. Major companies such as Gap, Converse, American Express, and Dell, along with many celebrities, are championing a campaign of "Red" products that are providing millions of dollars for fighting AIDS, tuberculosis, and malaria in Africa while allowing these companies to make a profit.[17]

There is intense debate about the impact of the hundreds of billions of dollars in aid that has been pumped into Africa. Former World Bank economist William Easterly commented in his book *The White Man's Burden* that the true tragedy of aid for the poor is that "the West spent $2.3 trillion in foreign aid over the last five decades and still has not managed to get 12-cent medicines to children to prevent half of all malaria deaths."[18] Taking an historical perspective on the economic evolution of societies, Gregory Clark of the University of California at Davis argues in *A Farewell to Alms* that changes in behavior rather than charity have been the key to economic advancement in our post-industrial world.[19]

Research on the impact of aid by the International Monetary Fund (IMF) concluded that billions of dollars of aid did not boost growth and may have adverse effects on competitiveness such as dampening the export sector of recipient countries. Authors Michael Homan and Greg Mills point out that an estimated $580 billion of Western aid for Africa over the past 50 years has had little impact. They note that if saving rates in Africa were doubled in 5 years to 30 percent of GDP, this would create a pool of $100 billion for investment.[20]

There are two challenges in particular. First, the aid can cast the recipient as a victim rather than an active worker in driving change. Second, the pleas for aid for the continent reinforce the global perceptions of the problems there. The more the world focuses on disease, malnutrition, corruption, and other problems, the more the view of the continent suffers. Charity campaigns inadvertently contribute to the negative public perception of Africa. As Uzodinma Iweala, author of *Beasts of No Nation*, commented on the "I am African" campaign showing Western celebrities bearing tribal face paint: "Such campaigns, however well intentioned, promote the stereotype of Africa as a black hole of disease and death. News reports constantly focus on the continent's corrupt leaders, warlords, 'tribal' conflicts, child laborers, and women disfigured by abuse and genital mutilation."[21] You want the world to be sympathetic about the challenges facing Africa, but seeing the continent as a basket case undermines interest in building businesses and making investments there.

Aid projects have become more focused and rigorous with initiatives such as the Gates Foundation and Clinton Foundation, or thoughtful approaches such as that used by the Novartis Foundation (see sidebar). The United Nations Millennium Project, the U.K.'s Commission on Africa, and the U.S. Commission on Capital Flows to Sub-Saharan Africa have concentrated intense attention on the needs of the continent, as did the Live 8 concert designed to encourage G8 leaders to focus on Africa. In fact, in July 2006, the leaders of the G8 countries agreed to double international aid to $50 billion by 2010, half of which would go to Africa, and cancel $55 billion in debt to 18 countries, 14 of which are in Africa. (By 2007, it was reported that many of these countries had already fallen behind on their pledges to Africa.)[22]

Although the external support has helped, remember that the transformations in China, India, and Vietnam were based on internal reforms in addition to external aid.[23] As the former cultural minister of Mali wrote to French President Jacques Chirac in April 2005, "The fight against poverty amounts to begging and submissiveness, leading to reforms that make us even poorer."[24] Tony Blair's Commission for Africa concluded in its 2005 report that "Africa must drive its own development" with support from the international community, "If Africa does not create the right conditions for development, then any amount of outside support will fail."

We need to move beyond charity to sustainable market development. These are projects that improve living conditions and produce a profit, which makes them viable business investments. As the slogan emblazoned on Andrew Rugasira's Good African Coffee in Uganda states, "Africa needs trade not aid to fight poverty."[25] Rugasira pointed out in a 2005 article in London's *Telegraph* that when Uganda gained its independence from Britain in 1962, the country's GDP was equal to Malaysia's (which had gained its own independence from the United Kingdom just five years before in 1957). Now, Malaysia's GDP is 20 times greater than Uganda's, a result that Rugasira attributes only partially to the repressive and despotic regime of Idi Amin. Malaysia created economic incentives and policies that encouraged its industrialization.[26]

Rugasira has followed his own advice. The company built a global coffee-exporting business by sharing profits 50/50 with its 10,000 farmers and their communities, most of whom are in the Ruwenzori Mountain area of Uganda. He and others have proven that Africa is not a charity case. He is creating successful farmers. They are among the more than 900 million consumers on this continent who represent a major global market opportunity and are contributing to Africa's rise.

## Novartis Foundation: Beyond Simplistic Views

The Novartis Foundation for Sustainable Development, created in 1979, serves as a think tank and a networking vehicle as well as a philanthropic initiative. It is "like an NGO for the company." Along with other innovators, it is developing a new model for an "enlightened private-sector" view. "Ten years from now, we will have a totally different kind of development assistance for a variety of reasons," said foundation president Klaus Leisinger in a phone interview with the author in October 2006.

The foundation conducts research to provide advice to Novartis on making investments that will have the most impact. It collaborates with NGOs. It has addressed issues from malaria to AIDS, and has created innovative programs such as a groundbreaking program to provide health insurance to Africa's rural poor and an educational program to help destigmatize leprosy in Tanzania and Madagascar.

In the latter project, researchers realized the most significant stumbling block for leprosy patients could not be addressed by giving drugs away. They needed to address the stigma that prevented patients from seeking help. This was done through training and social marketing, involving village elders and midwives to get the message out. They used bullhorns and television soap operas. They needed to "sell" the idea that leprosy can be cured the way companies sell soap and soft drinks.

For malaria, the foundation "looked at how much was spent on malaria and how little was achieved," Leisinger said. Interviews with patients found that they were poor at spotting the symptoms so that only one out of three patients being treated for malaria actually had the disease. Most were self-diagnosed. Working eight hours in the African sun might lead to the dizziness or headaches associated with malaria. Researchers also found that patients were not taking the full course of treatments once they started feeling better. Simple packaging innovations such as blister packs could have a dramatic impact. Blister packs prevented drugs from being lost or ruined by dirt or water, and also made it easier for patients to remember to take the right doses. Finally, health-care workers could monitor compliance by asking for patients to return the empty blister packs before receiving their next dose.

The foundation also helped launch a private health-care plan in Mali, starting with ten villages near a Novartis research station there. Many developing countries are moving away from free or subsidized health care, which has hit rural areas the hardest. The new health insurance in Mali costs individuals about $2 per year. Members can go to local clinics, and there is an emphasis on vaccinations and prevention. Again, education was important in getting members to accept it. "They were not used to insurance thinking, spreading risk among many," said Leisinger.

By the third year, they had enrolled 1,500 people in the Mali program (of a total population of 20,000 in the villages where the pilot program was launched). The initiative could actually break even in five years, and could then be expanded to Tanzania and other areas. Why hasn't a private insurance company done this? "A lot of people don't want to get involved in complicated things, yet if you look at real issues, they are complicated," said Leisinger. "People have to seriously address the complexity and contextuality of most health issues. If we can get away from simplistic views, then we can achieve a lot."

As Jason Pontin, publisher of *Technology Review*, commented in an editorial in the *New York Times*, "In truth, Africa will need both investment in entrepreneurialism and aid, intelligently directed toward education, health and food."[27] The aid is crucial to solve immediate problems while business development will build sustainable wealth in the long term.[28] Homan and Mills recommend using "aid specifically for humanitarian purposes" and building African economies through more land ownership, increased foreign direct investment, private-sector growth, and tighter banking policies to stem illegal transfers.

# Rebranding Africa

Leaders across Africa have recognized that the public image of Africa has not kept up with the optimism reflected on the continent. "We should do the branding properly to tell this very, very positive story," said South African President Thabo Mbeki during the 2006 World Economic Forum on Africa in Cape Town. Countries have taken steps to rebrand themselves, and the continent more broadly. Uganda, for example, has become "Africa's Friendliest Country." Ethiopia claims "Thirteen Months of Sunshine," and Nigeria is positioning itself as the "Heart of Africa." Some African countries already have developed valuable national brands. The Anholt Country Branding Index and Financial Branding estimated that South Africa's brand was worth an estimated $94 billion in the fourth quarter of 2005, or 44 percent of the 2004 GDP. Egypt's national brand is estimated at $67 billion, or 21 percent of its GDP. The brand value per capita of South Africa ($2,282) and Egypt ($976) exceeds the per capita value of the country brands of China ($549) and India ($270).[29]

As discussed in the book, African entertainment, music, and literature are gaining larger global audiences and increased recognition. African art is also attracting rising attention and prices, as illustrated by the extensive collection of contemporary African art by Italian businessman Jean Pigozzi. The world is changing the way it looks at Africa.

Part of this rebranding is addressing the real serious challenges facing the continent, and dealing with issues such as corruption and poor leadership. One senior executive I spoke with dubbed the continent portrayed in the Western media as "CNN Africa." While this coverage highlights real challenges of disease and political disruption, it does not show the whole picture of Africa. Don Cheadle, the actor who portrayed the hero in *Hotel Rwanda* and co-authored *Not on Our Watch* about the Darfur crisis, said in an interview with *Time* magazine that the greatest need of the African people is better public relations. "The news loves to talk about all the terrible situations, but it is very resistant to talk about the success."[30]

Initiatives such as the Diageo Africa Business Reporting Awards are helping to change these perceptions. These awards were established in 2004 to stimulate and promote a more accurate and widespread understanding of the business environment—and opportunities—in Africa. Diageo believes this change in perception is critical to attracting more investment to the continent. The company, which provides 4.5 billion servings of its products every year in Africa, recognizes the strength of the market.

African countries and entrepreneurs are also creating branded products such as Highland Teas from Kenya, to capture more of the value of their exports. This recognition of the value of branding led to a showdown between Starbucks and Ethiopia. Ethiopian coffee, for which farmers were paid about $1.45 per pound, retailed at Starbucks in the United States for around $26. In 2005, Ethiopia filed to trademark the names of three Ethiopian coffee-producing regions with the U.S. Patent and Trademark Office (Yirgacheffe, Harrar, and Sidamo). The problem was that Starbucks had already applied to trademark Sidamo with its "Shirkina Sun-Dried Sidamo" brand. This led to a dispute between one of the world's top coffee producing countries and one of the world's leading coffee retailers. They hammered out an agreement in 2007, and Starbucks announced plans in November 2007 to open a center in Ethiopia to help farmers improve their profitability. This trademark dispute shows how African countries are beginning to recognize and capitalize on the value of their brands.[31] They are not willing to part with them lightly.

San Francisco–based startup TCHO has developed a sophisticated system for analyzing and classifying cocoa beans—a key African export. In addition to branding, this could make the chocolate industry more like the wine and coffee industries, allowing producers to recognize more value.

# A Call to Action

The market of more than 900 million consumers in Africa has tremendous implications for businesses (on the continent and outside), investors, policymakers, and philanthropists. Africa is on the move, but much work still remains to be done. There are opportunities to continue to build Africa into one of the world's most important emerging markets. But rising to this opportunity presents a challenge for diverse stakeholders who have an interest in the success of African markets. All of them need to be focused on balancing social development with sustainable economic progress.

## *Private Sector*

As discussed previously, companies know that the people they are helping in Africa are their customers and employees. No company can operate in Africa, as in other emerging markets, without being concerned about health, education, and other welfare issues that directly affect their communities. The needs are great, but so are the opportunities, because companies have the most developed infrastructure for communication, distribution, and innovation in meeting these needs.

There are many opportunities in Africa that have not been seized. Although local players such as Mr. Biggs in Nigeria or Innscor in Zimbabwe and many other areas have built thriving restaurant businesses, major players such as McDonald's and Pizza Hut have little presence in sub-Saharan Africa. When I had asked Marcel Portman of the International Franchise Association in Washington, D.C., to introduce me to U.S. restaurant companies in sub-Saharan Africa (outside of South Africa) in 2006, he could not. They just were not there. Instead, he introduced me to African-based companies such as Innscor, discussed in Chapter 1, "Baking Bread in Zimbabwe."

Companies that are in Africa need to consider moving their headquarters to Africa. Many are still based in the United Kingdom or France, but as the airlines and other infrastructure improve, it might be time to run the continent from the continent. If you want to sell in Africa, go there. Many countries have still not figured out how to do business in Africa.

As noted previously, companies need to create products designed for this market. They also can organize parts of the market that are disorganized, as discussed in Chapter 4. For example, a company in India, Babjob.com, has created a social networking site to connect maids, cooks, and drivers with employers. The company, founded by an ex-Microsoft employee, is organizing a market that was informal. Could the same be done in Africa?

We also need to expand pharmaceutical research in Africa. Could we set up new research labs and institutes in Africa to research diseases on the continent, perhaps with the help of major pharmaceutical companies both from the developed and developing world? If the diseases are in Africa, how productive is it to research them in the United States? We also need innovations in pricing and marketing drugs. For example, Wal-Mart announced in 2006 that it would offer a 30-day supply of 150 generic drugs for just $4 in U.S. markets, and Target quickly matched the offer. If this can be done in the world's richest country, why can't a major retailer do this in Africa?

Companies need to improve the quality of data about African markets (see sidebar). Africa is a continent that is data poor. Chambers of commerce throughout Africa are helping provide education and information to their members. Africa needs a resource like the Marketing Science Institute (MSI) in the United States, a Boston-based institution sponsored by a number of companies that deals with urgent consumer behavior and marketing issues. Many companies are funding their own research in South Africa, but if they were to pool their data, there might be a more accurate picture of the African market and how to reach it. The identification of the "Black Diamond" segment by the Unilever Institute at the University of Cape Town in South Africa is an example of how research can help draw attention and resources to meet this growing opportunity. Is it possible for the universities and companies across Africa to support the establishment of a broader initiative such as MSI that can encourage research on African consumers and markets?

There have been some important steps toward filling the data gap. The African Development Bank along with OECD is now producing country reports every year on most African countries in a standard format that facilitates comparisons, although it doesn't offer specific industry information. Investment companies such as Renaissance Capital are also building sophisticated research and analysis operations in Africa to guide investments.

## Shortage of Data

There is a shortage of reliable market data in Africa. This creates a need to get out into the streets. When Deepak Karcher of Far East Mercantile Co. Ltd. wanted to understand the tire market in Nigeria, as importer of Firestone tires in the country, he sent agents out to physically inventory the brands of tires on 18-wheelers. They took worksheets and identified the brands of tires on each of the 18 wheels. He recognized that without reliable data, you need to get out to where the rubber meets the road. The legwork allowed them to expand Firestone's business from $256,000 in 1995 to more than $2 million in 2006.

Similarly, the German consumer goods firm Henkel entered Algeria through its French division, by acquiring a government-run detergent company Enad in 2000 with a well-known product, Isis. Over the years, it launched several new successful products to appeal to various market segments of the population and to compete with new multinational competitors. In an interview with the author, Michel Katlama, current managing director, said that one of his major issues was the lack of market information. He had no idea of what the market was for their products. Although it was next to impossible to get good information at the time, his perseverance and belief in the market helped them build a successful business and develop their own market information. He was naturally reluctant to share this hard-won information when I spoke with him in 2007.

When Bhudeb Mukherjee started marketing Indo Mie Noodles in Nigeria in 2000, he would take off his tie at the end of the day and, posing as a humble researcher, go door to door in Lagos to find out how families were eating noodles. This was how Mukherjee recognized that the product was seen as a snack for children, not a family meal. It was not that Nigerians were opposed to eating noodles.

They just did not see them as a meal. Based on this insight, the company changed the positioning of the product to emphasize family meals. Sales took off.

Danone faced similar data issues when they started manufacturing biscuits (cookies) in Algeria in 2004. Danone's Claude Joly told me in an interview in Tunis in 2007 that one of his major issues was to obtain reliable and accurate estimates of the market size and the market share of local competitors and even his own. Over the years, he has created a very successful organization, by manufacturing products locally and importing other products from Tunisia. To get better data, they worked with AC Nielsen, setting up a panel at some of the retail stores to collect more accurate market information.

Although these heroic efforts are impressive and served these entrepreneurial managers well, there is a tremendous need for better data across Africa.

## NGOs and Activists

Activists need to recognize the power of the African people to help themselves and harness that power. They need to encourage entrepreneurship at the same time that they address immediate needs. Some NGOs are partnering with the private sector to address issues such as promoting hygiene or empowering women.

NGOs need to be careful to consider how their actions might encourage dependence. There may come a day when African nations, like India after the tsunami in December 2004, may turn away international aid to build up their independent capacity for responding to such disasters. Assistance needs to be focused on removing obstacles and building sustainable enterprises. In this, public and private actors can be completely aligned.

## Educators

Africa desperately needs new schools, particularly to build technical and business skills, as discussed in Chapter 6. Major universities are considering setting up new business schools, but roughly 80 business schools for a continent of more than 900 million people is still far too few. Why can't Harvard, Wharton, and other top schools, working with private-sector leaders, develop a school in Africa similar to the Indian School of Business or schools in Shanghai, Argentina, and other parts of the world? (I expect that such an idea, whose time has come, may already be in discussion, but there is a need for many such schools.) Where there is such a great need for knowledge and such a high concentration of young people, there is an opportunity to build new institutions that will have a tremendous impact on the development of Africa. The planned investments by the International Finance Corporation in the South Mediterranean University in Tunisia, as well as the involvement of the Tunisian diaspora, offer an example of the potential of concerted effort to improve education across Africa.

Major African and non-African entrepreneurs and foundations should be thinking about establishing professional institutions in Africa. Monterrey Tech, a world-recognized university in Mexico, was started by a group of businessmen in 1943 to develop talent for the Mexican economy. Turkish billionaire Hüsnü Özyegin has invested more than $50 million in building a network of 36 primary schools and dormitories in the poorest parts of Turkey.[32] There are many opportunities for the private sector and even private individuals to make an impact on education in Africa.

Governments can also play a role, as shown by the collaboration of the French and Algerian governments in founding *L'Ecole Supérieure Algérienne des Affaires* (ESAA) in Algeria, with faculty drawn from French schools. To understand the impact of government initiatives, consider the Indian Institute of Technology (IIT), which was started by Indian Prime Minister Jawaharlal Nehru in 1950 to give the country the skilled engineers needed to drive its progress. By 2007, there were more than 100,000 graduates, a quarter of whom lived in the United States. In July of that year, more than 3,500 IIT alumni gathered for a reunion in California that was sponsored by Google, Microsoft, and General Electric (which employs 1,500 IIT graduates) and featured keynotes by GE CEO Jeffrey Immelt and Senator Hillary Clinton (by satellite).[33] IIT is intensely competitive and is seen as a global leader in engineering. Couldn't a similar initiative be created in Africa? Where is the African version of the Indian Institute of Technology or the Indian Institute of Management? The planned Nelson Mandela African Institute of Science and Technology, modeled on the IIT, is a step in this direction, but more schools like this are needed.

African students also need more opportunities to study abroad. International students collectively brought an estimated $14.5 billion into the U.S. economy in 2006–07, led by India and China. India sent the most students to U.S. schools (83,833) followed by China (67,723). The only African nations among the top 25 countries sending students to U.S. programs were Kenya, with 6,349 students, and Nigeria, with 5,943, according to the annual "Open Doors" report by the Institute of International Education (IIE) and the U.S. Department of State's Bureau of Educational and Cultural Affairs. Indian graduates of American schools have made a major impact back home. With more than 900 million people in Africa, why aren't American universities doing more recruiting of African students? The African American Institute, which has provided scholarships for undergraduate, graduate, and professional training abroad for Africans since 1953, has made important contributions in this area. But much more needs to be done.

There are also serious needs for education of children before they reach college. Investments in primary and secondary schools are crucial. India has privatized schools there. Government cannot keep up, so the private sector has taken up the initiative and companies have started their own schools. Although there are private schools in Africa, many more quality schools are needed. It is also vital to support initiatives that remove obstacles to education such as P&G's "Always in School" initiative.

## African Diaspora

The African diaspora is emerging as one of the primary drivers of progress on the continent, as discussed in Chapter 8. No segment of the world has a better understanding of the opportunities there and the unique challenges that can be met through investments and new enterprises. No group has a greater stake in the success of Africa. Members of the diaspora need to recognize that their investments make sense not only from the standpoint of humanitarian support for their homelands but also because there is a real opportunity to invest in very promising enterprises focused on African markets.

As these investments are treated more like investments and less like charity, a broader group of diaspora investors—including African Americans, for example—might be attracted to these markets for economic and cultural reasons. In India and China, the diaspora played a significant role in their development, offering resources and knowledge that was not available at home. Couldn't the same thing happen in Africa?

## Media

The challenge for media is to show the full picture of Africa, not just to focus on the negative headlines that reinforce existing stereotypes. There is some movement in this direction, with Diageo's business reporting awards, reporting by Charlayne Hunter-Gault on NPR (and her book *New News Out of Africa*) and Carol Pineau's television series and documentary "Africa Open for Business" (www. africaopenforbusiness.com). New direct sources of information from Africa are helping to fill in the gap, including *African Business*, the French-language *Jeune Afrique*, and Bizcommunity.com, showing a dynamic continent with thriving businesses. Recent articles by Thomas Friedman of the *New York Times* have also highlighted positive stories of entrepreneurship and business on the continent. We need to change the way that we see Africa. As Stephen Cohen of the Brookings Institution said of India in an article in the *Financial Times* in August 2007, it is "no longer a large, exotic basket case."[34] The same transformation needs to be made in our views of Africa.

## Leaders

As Mo Ibrahim recognized in creating his leadership award, leadership in business and politics will shape the future of Africa. By rewarding leaders, he is helping to align economic incentives with better government. While Rwanda and other countries hope to play the gateway role of Singapore in regions of Africa, they need to recognize that part of the secret of Singapore's successful reforms was that govern-ment began offering competitive salaries to government employees. Without this type of change, anticorruption initiatives will face an up-hill battle.

Lack of political stability is very costly. Armed conflicts in Africa cost an estimated $284 billion between 1990 and 2007, which is about equal to the amount of aid major donors gave in the same period, ac-cording to a 2007 study by Oxfam International and two nonprofit arms-control groups. (The good news, however, was that the study found Africa experienced fewer of these wars than five years earlier.) But political leadership and stability are essential to economic progress.

There is a need for more political leaders with vision and compas-sion, as well as business leaders with the drive, knowledge, and per-spective to lead their enterprises through the many challenges they face in Africa. We need leaders who demonstrate the kind of compas-sion and commitment shown in distant Bhutan, by Her Majesty the Queen, Ashi Dorji Wangmo Wangchuck. She literally walked through rural villages in the remotest parts of the country, going to places where even the NGOs didn't go, which led her to establish the Tarayana Foundation to serve her people. She set a national goal to have a happy and poverty-free Bhutan through programs to deliver education, health care, and other services by involving youth. The country is transforming itself in other ways, becoming a constitutional monarchy on its own, with the king stepping down in favor of his son. The country held its first elections in March 2008. If a small country of modest means like Bhutan can do this, it is possible anywhere. All that is needed is a champion.

We are seeing more of the skilled leaders that Africa needs to progress. Ngozi Okonjo-Iweala, former finance minister and foreign minister of Nigeria, was named managing director of the World Bank in October 2007. She helped lead economic reforms in Nigeria, in-cluding attacking corruption, and now will lead the bank's work in Africa, South Asia, Europe, and central Asia. An economist educated at Harvard University and the Massachusetts Institute of Technology, she is one of a new set of leaders who are making an impact within Africa and now in an organization that is playing a major role in African development. We need more leaders like this. Goldman Sachs launched a major initiative in 2008 to help ensure they will be prepared. The "10,000 Women" initiative, backed by a $100 million grant from Goldman Sachs and the collaboration of more than a dozen top business schools and universities around the world, will help develop the business skills and leadership of women in developing countries, including Kenya, Tanzania, Nigeria, and Rwanda.

The World Economic Forum on Africa is drawing together global and African business and government leaders to address issues facing the continent. Its seventeenth forum meeting in Africa, held in Cape Town in June 2007, examined Africa's progress and challenges, including the need for capacity building and improved implementation.[35] It has provided a critical forum for discussing issues, providing information, and drawing attention to the continent. The Commonwealth Business Council in the United Kingdom, founded in 1997, is also encouraging informed study, cooperation, and investment between the developed world economies and Africa. When the African Venture Capital Association, which has focused global attention on African investments, held its seventh annual meeting in Botswana in March 2008, the conference title was "Africa Rising." This is another sign of the growing interest and optimism about investing in Africa.[36] The new African Business Awards, established by *African Business* magazine in 2008, are designed to celebrate entrepreneurial excellence, promoting world-class best practices in business (www.theafricanbusinessawards.com). By recognizing leadership, these initiatives will encourage its development.

# Bridging the Divide

In 2006, Americans spent $41 billion per year on pet food. This was nearly equal to the amount that immigrants outside of Africa send home in remittances (if informal transfers are included). This is a striking statistic. It indicates how much more wealthy the United States is today. On the other hand, when I visited Harare in the summer of 2006, there was cat food on the shelves of the supermarket. Someone there was buying pet food in a country where most consumers are hard pressed just to purchase enough to stay alive.

Although U.S. statistics show how far Africa has to go, they also show the potential for growth.

We have seen in many developed nations how quickly they can be transformed by what have been called "economic miracles." In fact, these so-called miracles are the product of enlightened policy and entrepreneurial energy that unlocks the potential of the nation. That type of entrepreneurial energy already can be seen across the African continent, and the policy changes are coming. It is unlikely that any African nation will create wealth to rival the United States, Europe, or Japan in my lifetime. But it is also clear that, given the population demographics and their growth rates, these markets are the future. Does the continent have the potential to demonstrate the same level of growth as India and China? I think so.

We live in a world that has changed in fundamental ways. The connections between the developed and developing world are stronger. The flow of immigrants and ideas is going both ways. Markets are connected in new ways. This can be seen in the rise of open source software that is changing the view of businesses and commerce. In fact, one of these new open source, community-developed operating systems has a surprisingly familiar name: Ubuntu. This free Ubuntu software (www.ubuntu.com), an operating system for desktops, is emphasizing the power of community in advancing development and offering resources to the developing world.

In Africa, as has been in the case in other developing areas such as India and China, despite different styles of public governance, the best hope for sustaining progress may be economic development and entrepreneurship. As a continent, Africa has many problems. But entrepreneurs recognize that problems are also opportunities and they are seizing those opportunities—from small enterprises fueled by microfinance to pioneering African and multinational companies. There is a rising spirit of optimism and determination on the continent, particularly among the growing population of youth. As SAMA-award winning South African singer Simphiwe Dana said in a 2008 interview in the *Financial Times*, "My hope for the children of the African continent is that where their parents have failed, they might succeed."[37]

# Reinventing Africa

*Chak de India* is a slogan of encouragement in India, as well as the title of a hit Bollywood movie telling the fictional story of an underdog women's hockey team and a dishonored coach who went on to win the world title. It means, roughly, "You can do it, India!" A colleague of mine says perhaps we should be saying "Chak de Africa!" I agree, and this sentiment is being heard across the continent, although not specifically in those words. There is a new sense of optimism.

One of the things that struck me most during my visits to Africa and conversations with an amazing cross-section of entrepreneurs, chief executives, and others leaders in the nonprofit and private sectors is the resilience of Africa. It has the capacity to reinvent itself time and again.

There are layers upon layers of civilizations existing side by side, like the eyes of the Sphinx peering toward the modern buildings of Cairo—and in the distance, a new Carrefour department store. Khan Al-Khalili in Cairo is one of the world's oldest bazaars, founded more than a century before Christopher Columbus made his journey to the new world. Walking through its narrow streets takes visitors back into the past. Yet it is also home to a modern, five-star restaurant, the Naguib Mahfouz restaurant, named for the Nobel Prize-winning author, who was a frequent visitor. The restaurant, run by Oberoi Hotels from India, is a modern addition that feels at home in the midst of the bustling ancient bazaar. The company is also running one of the finest hotels in the shadow of the pyramids in Cairo, one of the most luxurious resorts on the Red Sea, and some of the finest cruise ships on the Nile.

One of the more striking examples of the inclusiveness of African society, particularly South African society, is the imposing Voortrekker Monument. It is a monumental tower between Johannesburg and Pretoria that commands a stunning view of the countryside. This memorial commemorates the journey of the Dutch from the coast of the Cape of Good Hope into the heart of South Africa. The paintings in the basement museum show pioneers in battles with the Zulus, a battle that the European settlers won at first, but ultimately lost with the end of apartheid. This museum is still here, peacefully absorbed into the rich tapestry of the nation's complex history.

The El Djazair Hotel, where I stayed in Algiers, is more than 100 years old. Originally called St. George Hotel, it was host to kings, dukes, and other dignitaries. In 1943, during World War II, General Dwight D. Eisenhower made the hotel his headquarters from November 1942 to December 1943. When I stayed there, I asked to look into Eisenhower's room. He would be surprised to see it today. When you walk past the plaque commemorating his stay there, the first thing you see is a large Samsung flat-screen television. Eisenhower could never have imagined, during a time when the Allied forces were at war in Asia, that the room would be furnished with a product from a Korean company. It is a sign of the tremendous changes in the world, but also in Africa.

Moulay Idriss in northern Morocco is one of most ancient and holy cities in the country. Many Muslim pilgrims come each year to visit the tomb of its namesake, an imam and the great-grandson of the Prophet Muhammad. And yet in this holiest of cities in Morocco, I saw traders right outside his burial place peddling pirated Bollywood movies and shoes, clothing, and other products from China. These Asian traders have penetrated into the heart of the oldest and most holy cities. This is a sign of the depths of the transformation of African markets.

Africa is full of such unexpected surprises, as we have seen time and again on this "consumer safari" described in this book. Former war zones become stable centers of commerce. Companies such as Samsung, and many others, are finding opportunities across Africa, not just in providing televisions to five-star hotels such as El Djazair, but also in the streets of the poorest high-density neighborhoods. Africa is growing, changing, and progressing, despite its manifold challenges, more rapidly than many expected.

If you have written Africa off, it is clearly time to take a look. "Walk the market" as we have done in this book. It is clear in the streets and in the parliaments that Africa is moving, rising. There is passion in the voices of the entrepreneurs, growing interest and even excitement among the leadership of global companies, determination in the words of members of the diaspora, and optimism among Africa's youth. The African market is on the move. If you are not invested or involved there, it may not be too late to participate in Africa's rise. As an old African proverb says, "The best time to plant a tree is 20 years ago. The second best time is now."

## Rising Opportunities

- What are the opportunities to participate in Africa's rising?
- What are opportunities to build business in Africa while addressing social needs? How can you do well by doing good?
- What are entrepreneurial approaches to addressing medical, water, hygiene, and other needs?
- How are you contributing to the triple bottom line?
- What are the challenges in participating in Africa's rise and how can you meet them?

# Endnotes

## Preface

[1]Ramachandra Guha, "Great Expectations," *Financial Times*, April 6, 2007, W6.

## Chapter 1

[1]*New York Times*, May 2, 2006.

[2]"At African Waterfall Visitors Confront a Tale of Two Cities," *Wall Street Journal*, December 29, 2006, A1.

[3]"Africa's Top 1000 Companies," *African Business*, April 2006, 34.

[4]"Kroners for Cronies," *The Economist*, July 26, 2007, 47.

[5]"Zimbabwe: Heinz Sheds Its Interest," *New York Times*, September 4, 2007.

[6]"Zimbabwe's Battle of the Brands," *African Marketing*, www.bizcommunity.com/Article/410/82/16734.html.

[7]Desmond Walters, "SA Retailers Rough It Out in Zim," July 25, 2007, Bizcommunity.com, www.bizcommunity.com.

[8]Sarah Childress, "Investors Go to Treacherous Places Seeking Returns," *Wall Street Journal*, November 17, 2007, B-1.

[9]Michael Bleby, "Black Middle Class Drives Demand," *Financial Times*, May 22, 2007.

[10]Jenny Wiggins, "Diageo to Expand Guinness Sales in Africa," FT.com site, July 25, 2007.

[11]Laura Blue, "Life in the Land of a Thousand Welcomes," *Time*, September 6, 2007.

[12]"As Its Brands Lag at Home, Unilever Makes a Risky Bet," *Wall Street Journal*, March 22, 2007.

[13]Jonathan Guthrie, "The Emigrant Empire-Builder," *Financial Times*, June 14, 2006.

[14]"China, Filling a Void, Drills for Riches in Chad," *New York Times*, August 13, 2007.

[15]William Wallis, "Drawing Contours of a New World Order," *Financial Times*, January 24, 2008, special issue, 1.

[16]"Egypt Sees China Replacing US as Top Trade Partner by 2012," *Wall Street Journal*, September 7, 2006, A8.

[17]Harry G. Broadman, "Africa's Silk Road: China and India's New Economic Frontier," Washington, DC: *The World Bank*, 2007, 2.

[18]Celia W. Dugger, "In Africa, a More Business-Friendly Approach," *New York Times*, September 6, 2006.

[19]Anver Versi, "Donald Kaberuka: Africa's Unique Window of Opportunity," *African Banker*, Summer 2007, 16.

[20]"Going on Down," *The Economist*, June 8, 1996.

[21]Nicholas Kristoff, "Optimism and Africa," *New York Times*, October 3, 2006.

[22]Andrew England, "Rwanda: The Task of Rebuilding A Nation," *Financial Times*, December 5, 2006.

[23]"Oil Could Break or Make Africa's Largest Country. But At the Moment There Is More Breaking Than Making," *The Economist*, December 9, 2006.

[24]www.moibrahimfoundation.org.

[25]Mo Ibrahim, telephone interview with author, August 16, 2007.

[26]Patrick Awuah, telephone interview with author, May 30, 2007.

[27]Lydia Polgreen and Marjorie Connelly, "Poll Shows Africans Wary, but Hopeful about the Future," *New York Times*, July 25, 2007, A6.

[28]"2004's Nobel Peace Prize Winner Looks Back," CNN, www.msnbc.msn.com/id/9533147/.

# Chapter 2

[1]www.diplomatie.gouv.fr/en/country-files_156/north-africa_5493/france-and-maghreb_5495/france-maghreb-relations_8837.html.

[2]Communication with the author, e-mail, December 17, 2007.

[3]www.bizcommunity.com/Article/410/78/19999.html.

[4]Paul Collier, *The Bottom Billion: Why the Poorest Countries Are Failing and What Can Be Done About It*, Oxford University Press, 2007.

[5]Peter Wonacott, "Lawless Legislators Thwart Social Progress in India," *Wall Street Journal*, May 4, 2007, A1.

[6]"The Good, The Bad, and The President," *The Economist*, January 3, 2008.

[7]*2007 African Development Indicators*, International Bank for Reconstruction and Development, The World Bank, October 2007, vii.

[8]Neil Ford, "African Growth Will Hit 6% This Year, Says Report," *African Business*, October 2007, 72–73.

[9]"2007 World Population Data Sheet," Population Reference Bureau, www.prb.org/pdf07/07WPDS_Eng.pdf.

[10]"Foreign Direct Investment Reached New Record in 2007," UNCTAD, January 8, 2008, www.unctad.org/Templates/Webflyer.asp?docID=9439&intItemID=2068&lang=1.

[11]Stephen Williams, "The Henshaw Fund's Barbara James," *African Banker*, Autumn 2007, 15–16.

[12]Neil Ford, "South Africa Joins Elite FDI Destinations," *African Business*, March 2008, 26–27.

[13]Neil Ford, "Record FDI for Africa," *African Business*, January 2008, 24.

[14]"Once Bitten, Twice Shy," *The Economist*, June 7, 2007.

[15]The African Venture Capital Association reported that investments in the continent hit $948 million in 2005.

[16]Kate Burgess, "Private Equity Explores the Sub-Sahara," *Financial Times*, August 10, 2007.

[17]Omar Ben Yedder, "Neil Harvey of Renaissance Capital," *African Banker*, 1st Quarter 2008, 24–27.

[18]Alec Russell, "Angola Turns into Investors' Hot Spot," *Financial Times*, August 23, 2007.

[19]"Nigerian Bonds: No Laughing Matter," *The Economist*, January 25, 2007, 77.

[20]"On Safari," *The Economist*, December 15, 2007, 84.

[21]Friedrich Schneider, "Size and Measurement of the Informal Economy in 110 Countries Around the World," presented at a Workshop of Australian National Tax Centre, ANU, Canberra, Australia, July 17, 2002.

[22]Men and Women in the Informal Economy. International Labour Organisation (2002).

[23]"Forces for Change: Informal Economy Organizations in Africa," War on Want, 2006, www.waronwant.org/forcesforchange.

24"Mobiles Lead Growth in African Media," *African Business*, March 2007, 8.

25"Buy, Cell or Hold," *The Economist*, January 25, 2007.

26www.bizcommunity.com/Article/410/78/16382.html.

27Abeer Allam, "Egyptian Mobile Phone Provider Treads Where Others Dare Not," *New York Times*, February 13, 2006, 6.

28Leonard Waverman, Meloria Meschi and Melvyn Fuss, "The Impact of Telecoms on Economic Growth in Developing Countries," Vodafone Policy Paper Series: Africa: The Impact of Mobile Phones, No. 2, March 2005.

29Jane Croft, Peter Thal Larsen and John Reed, "Barclays plans integration after Absa bank deal," *Financial Times*, May 9, 2005, http://search.ft.com/ftArticle?queryText=barclays+purchases+absa&y=0&aje=true&x=0&id=050509005334&ct=0.

30www.africasia.com/resources/pressreleases/AfricanBankerAwardsWinners.pdf.

31John Reed, "Mobile Users Branch Out," *Financial Times*, October 6, 2005.

32Martin Meredith, *The Fate of Africa: From the Hopes of Freedom to the Heart of Despair*, New York: Public Affairs, 2005, 14.

33"Hallelujah!" *The Economist*, July 22, 2006, 46.

34James McBride, "Hip-Hop Planet," *National Geographic*, April 2007.

35"What Muslim Women Want," *Wall Street Journal*, December 13, 2006.

# Chapter 3

[1]Eric Bellman, "In India, a Retailer Finds Key to Success Is Clutter," *Wall Street Journal*, August 8, 2007, A-1.

[2]The C class is different from definitions of the "middle class." The World Bank estimates that there will be 43 million people in the official middle class in Africa by 2030, more than tripling from 12.8 million in 2000. However, the World Bank defines the middle class globally as individuals with incomes between about $4,000 and $17,000 (PPP), between the per capita incomes of Brazil and Italy. With just over four people per household globally, this translates into annual household earnings of $16,800 to $72,000 (PPP). This creates a very high threshold for the middle class and does not necessarily reflect the true market dynamics. See, "Global Economic Prospects, 2007: Managing the Next Wave of Globalization," The World Bank, Washington, D.C., 2007.

[3]Michael M. Phillips, "In Africa, Mortgages Boost an Emerging Middle Class," *Wall Street Journal*, July 17, 2007, A-1.

[4]"Africa's Rich Grow Richer," *African Business*, August/September 2007, 8.

[5]Haig Simonian "Nestlé Charts Low-Income Territory," *Financial Times*, July 12, 2004.

# Chapter 4

[1]Oliver Heins, retail analyst, Planet Retail, "A Race for Opportunities: Top 30 Grocery Retailers in Africa & the Middle East, 2006," http://planetretail.net.

[2]www.pepkor.co.za/index.html.

[3]www.bizcommunity.com/Article/410/78/17144.html.

[4]Sherif Coutry, FP7egypt.com.

[5]Clark Boyd, "Pay-as-You-Go Software for the Developing World," *Technology Review*, July 25, 2007.

[6]Dan Chapman, "Your Cast-offs, Their Profits," *Atlanta Journal Constitution*, December 24, 2006, A-1.

[7]http://abcnews.go.com/WNT/story?id=2851172&page=1&CMP= OTC-RSSFeeds0312.

[8]Jason McClure, "The Makings of Motown in Addis Ababa?" *BusinessWeek*, September 10, 2007.

[9]"Uganda to Assemble Chinese Cars," *African Business*, January 2008, 8.

[10]John W. Miller, "Africa's New Car Dealer: China," *Wall Street Journal*, August 28, 2007, B1.

[11]David Gauthier-Villars, "Ghosn Bets Big on Low-Cost Strategy," *Wall Street Journal*, September 4, 2007, A8.

[12]Michael Arndt and Caroline Ghobrial, "Knock Knock, It's Your Big Mac," *BusinessWeek*, July 23, 2007, 36.

[13]Andrew Jack, "Lethal Doses," *Financial Times*, April 7, 2007.

[14]Barney Jopson, "Unilever Looks to Clean Up in Africa," *Financial Times*, November 15, 2007.

[15]Michael Fleshman, "Global Aids Treatment Drive Takes Off," *Africa Renewal*, April 2005, 20.

[16]"Aspen's upward slope," *The Economist*, October 6 2005, www.economist.com/business/displaystory.cfm?story_id=E1_QQJN RRQ; Aspen Holdings 2007 annual report, www.aspenpharma.com/ aspen_ar_2007/financial_highlights.htm.

[17]"Africa: LG Advances into Emerging Continent: Korean Companies Hope to Tap into Rising African Consumer Market," *Korea Times*, Thursday, November 9, 2006.

# Chapter 5

[1]Michael Wines, "Toiling in the Dark: Africa's Power Crisis," *New York Times*, July 29, 2007.

[2]Barry Bearak and Celia W. Dugger, "Power Failures Outrage South Africa," *New York Times*, January 31, 2008.

[3]"The Dark Ages," *The Economist*, January 31, 2008.

[4]"Western Union Awards Winners," *African Banker*, 1st Quarter 2008, 4.

[5]Michael Wines, "Toiling in the Dark: Africa's Power Crisis," *The New York Times*, July 29, 2007.

[6]www.kickstart.org/home/.

[7]Sam Olukoya, "Answering the Call of Nature in Lagos," BBC News, November 16, 2006.

[8]Priya Sahgal, "Toilet Training," *India Today International*, November 19, 2007, 42–43.

[9]Neil Ford, "Seeking Water Solutions for Africa," *African Business*, January 2008, 30–32.

[10]Amanda Leigh Haag, "Stove for the Developing World's Health," *New York Times*, January 22, 2008.

[11]Christopher Rhoads, "An Entrepreneur Has Quixotic Goals of Wiring Rwanda," *Wall Street Journal*, August 17, 2006, A-1.

[12]www.internetworldstats.com/stats1.htm, accessed February 7, 2008.

[13]Zachary Ochieng, "Race for Fibre Optic Cable Heats Up," *Africa Marketing*, July 31, 2007, www.bizcommunity.com/Article/410/144/16700.html.

[14]"High-Speed Internet for Africa," *Time*, August 20, 2007, 17.

[15]"African Nations Agree to $1 Billion Indian Satellite Project," Tripoli Post, www.tripolipost.com/articledetail.asp?c=2&i=1402.

[16]www.fgcwireless.com.

[17]www.bibalex.org.

[18]Alina M. Chircu and Vijay Mahajan, "Revisiting the Digital Divide: An Analysis of Mobile Technology Depth and Service Breadth in the BRIC Countries," June 21, 2007, McCombs Graduate School of Business, University of Texas at Austin.

[19]"Bleak Publishing Houses," *The Economist*, November 24, 2007, 54.

[20]"Africa's Green Revolution," *African Business*, December 2006, 12–16.

[21]"Impact of Biotechnology in Africa," Peter Rammutla, National African Farmer's Union.

[22]Celia Dugger, "In Africa, Prosperity from Seeds Falls Short," *New York Times*, October 10, 2007,

[23]Thandiwe Myeni, "Benefits of Biotechnology to Small Scale Farmers: Case Study Makhatini," Bio 2003 conference.

[24]"Local heroes," *The Economist*, February 3, 2007.

[25]Foreword for the Comprehensive Africa Agriculture Development Program (CAADP), NEPAD's blueprint for reviving the continent's agricultural sector.

# Chapter 6

[1]*2007 World Population Data Sheet*, Population Reference Bureau, 6, www.prb.org/pdf07/07WPDS_Eng.pdf.

[2]"World Population Prospects: Highlights," The United Nations, Department of Economic and Social Affairs, New York, 2007.

[3]George B.N. Ayittey, *Africa Unchained: The Blueprint for Africa's Future*, Palgrave MacMillan, 2005.

[4]Binyavanga Wainaina, "Nairobi: Inventing a City," *National Geographic*, September 2005, www7.nationalgeographic.com/ngm/0509/feature2/index.html.

[5]www.bizcommunity.com/Article/410/66/16325.html.

[6]www.bizcommunity.com/Article.aspx?c=74&l=410&i=17252&#contact.

[7]www.henry4gold.com/index.htm.

[8]Susan Taylor Martin, "Doll that has it all (almost)," *St. Petersburg Times*, May 18, 2005, http://wwwwww.sptimes.com/2005/05/18/Tbt/Doll_that_has_it_all_.shtml

[9]NPD Group, http://wwwwww.toyassociation.org/AM/Template.cfm?Section=Industry_Statistics&CONTENTID=3884&TEMPLATE=/CM/ContentDisplay.cfm

[10]http://wwwwww4.toysrus.com/our/intl/intlAfrica.cfm

[11]"A Not-So-Simple Plan to Keep African Girls in School," *New York Times*, November 12, 2007, A-11.

[12]www.nepad.org/2005/news/wmview.php?ArtID=36.

[13]Andrea Bohnstedt, "Top Marks for Classmate," *African Business*, January 2008, 46.

[14]Case Study: Bridging the Digital Divide in South Africa's Western Cape School System, www.ncomputing.com.

[15]www.cu.edu.eg/english/.

[16]http://ed.sjtu.edu.cn/rank/2007/ARWU2007TOP500list.htm.

[17]"Global MBA Rankings," *Financial Times*, http://rankings.ft.com/global-mba-rankings.

[18]"Deans Create First Africa-wide Association of African Business Schools," IFC press release, http://ifc.org/ifcext/bsn.nsf/AttachmentsByTitle/Association_Joint_Press_Release_Oct_05/$FILE/Association_Joint_Press_Release_Oct_05.pdf.

[19]Della Bradshaw, "A Study in African Ingenuity," *Financial Times*, January 13, 2008.

[20]Della Bradshaw, "African Schools in Search of New Ideas," *Financial Times*, February 19, 2007.

[21]Anthony Njagi, "PS Warns Illegal Colleges," *Daily Nation*, July 24, 2006, 6.

[22]David White, "Business Education: A University at Minimum Cost," *Financial Times*, July 12, 2004.

[23]Eileen Daspin and Ellen Gamerman, "The Million-Dollar Kid," *Wall Street Journal*, March 3, 2007.

[24]Allison Samuels, "Oprah Goes to School," *Newsweek*, January 8, 2007.

[25]www.ft.com/appeal2007.

[26]Celia W. Dugger, "Very Young Populations Contribute to Strife, Study Concludes," *New York Times*, April 4, 2007.

[27]Sam Knight, "Births of a Nation," *Financial Times*, February 29, 2008.

# Chapter 7

[1]A. O. Scott, "Ousmane Sembene, 84, Led Cinema's Advance in Africa," *New York Times*, June 11, 2007, A-1.

[2]"Nollywood Dreams," The Economist, July 27, 2006; "Nollywood Blazes a Trail in Africa," *Hindustan Times*, March 24, 2006, 16.

[3]www.bizcommunity.com/Article/196/17/16359.html.

[4]www.bizcommunity.com/Article/196/122/16251.html.

[5]"Precious Goes to Hollywood," *The Economist*, July 26, 2007, 47.

[6]Merissa Marr "Disney Rewrites Script To Win Fans in India," *Wall Street Journal*, June 11, 2007, A1.

[7]www.multichoice.co.za.

[8]www.worldspace.com.

[9]"New Kid on the Stock," *The Economist*, June 7, 2007.

[10]Ted Johnson, "Cost Conundrum: As Congloms Squeeze Movie Prod'n Costs, Primetime TV Budgets Start to Soar," *Variety*, October 29, 2006, www.variety.com/article/VR1117952819.html? categoryid=14&cs=1&query=cost+of+producing+television+episode.

[11]"Polygamy Beams," *The Economist*, November 19, 2005, 90.

[12]Thomas Crampton, "Wireless Technology Speeds Health Services in Rwanda," *New York Times*, March 5, 2007.

[13]Timothy Kasonde, "Interactive Mobile Phones for Zambian Farmers," Bizcommunity.com, June 2007, www.bizcommunity.com/ Article/410/78/15689.html.

[14]David Wessel, "Paper Chase: South Africa's Sun Targets New Class," *Wall Street Journal*, August 17, 2007, A-1.

[15]Lydia Polgreen, "Monrovia Journal; All the News That Fits: Liberia's Blackboard Headlines," *New York Times*, August 4, 2006.

[16]"Oprah Winfrey of Middle East Under Fire," *Egyptian Gazette*, September 18, 2006, 1.

[17]David White, "Hollywood's Flirtation with Africa," *Financial Times*, February 7, 2007.

# Chapter 8

[1]"Home Sweet Home, for Some," *The Economist*, August 11, 2005.

[2]Jason DeParle, "In a World on the Move, a Tiny Land Strains to Cope," *New York Times*, June 24, 2005, A-1.

[3]http://ipsnews.net/news.asp?idnews=34964.

[4]www.migrationinformation.org/datahub/countrydata/data.cfm.

[5]Renwick Mclean, "Spain Scrambles to Cope with Tide of African Migrants," *New York Times*, March 19, 2006.

[6]Carol Matlack and Joan Tarzian, "Say Hello to the Folks Back Home," *Business Week*, November 2006, 14.

[7]"Africa's Share of Remittances: $20 Billion and Counting," *African Banker*, 1st Quarter 2008, 14–15.

[8]Jason DeParle, "Western Union Empire Moves Migrant Cash Home," *New York Times*, November 22, 2007.

[9]Charlene Smith, "Beating Poverty through the Black Market," *Business in Africa*, May 2006, 59–61.

[10]www.africadiaspora.com/2005/events/ag/index.php.

[11]Charlene Smith, "Beating Poverty through the Black Market," *Business in Africa*, May 2006, 59–61.

[12]Richard Lapper, "The Tale of Globalisation's Exiles," *Financial Times*, August 27, 2007.

[13]William Wallis, "The Brotherhood," *Financial Times*, August 30, 2007.

[14]"Program Speeds Remittances with Cell Network" *Marketing News*, March 1, 2007, 29.

[15]www.waterhealth.com/worldwide-operations/ghana.php.

[16]"Africa Is Global Star Again," *African Business*, March 2007, 12.

[17]Vishakha Talreja and Moinak Mitra, "Incredible India Not Too Credible Among Tourists," *Economic Times*, September 27, 2007, 5.

[18]Trevor Ward, "International Hotel Chains Wake Up to African Potential," *African Business*, August/September 2007, 48–50.

[19]www.pataks.co.uk/story.html.

[20]Monica Davey, "In Bridge Collapse, Refugee Group Faces a New Ordeal," *New York Times*, August 8, 2007.

[21]www.maishafilmlab.com.

[22]Michael Backman, "UK Indians Taking Care of Business," *The Age*, March 8, 2006.

[23]William St. Clair, *The Grand Slave Emporium*, London: Profile Books, 2006, 3.

[24]http://abcnews.go.com/Business/WireStory?id=2857064&page=1.

[25]Caroline Brothers, "Immigrants Flock Proudly to Musee du Quai Branly," *New York Times*, August 21, 2006.

[26]Interview with authors, February 8, 2008.

# Conclusion

[1]www.highlandteacompany.com.

[2]Taressa Stovall, "High (land) Tea Come to Montclair," *Montclair Times*, January 18, 2006.

[3]http://rainwater.org/rainwater_press.html.

[4]*Parade* magazine, December 10, 2006, 24.

[5]Michael D. Conway, Srishti Gupta, and Kamiar Khajavi, "Addressing Africa's Health Workforce Crisis," *McKinsey Quarterly*, November 2007, 1–12.

[6]"Health Care in Africa: Of Markets and Medicines," *The Economist*, December 22, 2007, 121.

[7]"Malaria: Net Benefits," *The Economist*, January 31, 2008.

[8]Donald G. McNeil, "Child Mortality at Record Low; Further Drop Seen," *New York Times*, September 13, 2007.

[9]www.goldmansachs.com/iffim/.

[10]Jeffrey D. Sachs, "What a Little Fertilizer Can Do," *Time*, July 26, 2007, 54.

[11]http://abcnews.go.com/International/Politics/story?id=3399100.

[12]www.ashoka.org/node/3915.

[13]Sheridan Prasso, "Saving the World with a Cup of Yogurt," *Fortune*, May 5, 2007.

[14]http://other90.cooperhewitt.org.

[15]www.freeplayfoundation.org/.

[16]Christopher Palmeri, "Innovation Case Study: GE," *Business Week*, March 12, 2007, 24.

[17]By the end of its first year, the Red campaign had generated about $20 million for Africa, but retailers had collectively spent between $50 million and $100 million in marketing their products. Critics also pointed out there is a lack of transparency about profit from the campaign. (Ron Nixon, "Bottom Line for (Red)," *New York Times*, February 6, 2008.)

[18]William Easterly, *The White Man's Burden: Why the West's Efforts to Aid the Rest Have Done So Much Ill and So Little Good*, New York: Penguin Press, 2006, 4.

[19]Gregory Clark, *A Farewell to Alms: A Brief Economic History of the World*, Princeton, NJ: Princeton University Press, 2007.

[20]Michael Holman and Greg Mills, "The 2,000-Day Challenge: Planning an End to Aid in Africa," Brenthurst Discussion Papers, April 2006.

[21]Uzodinma Iweala, "Stop Trying to 'Save' Africa," *New York Times*, July 15, 2007, B07.

[22]Celia Dugger, "Rock Star Still Hasn't Found the African Aid He's Looking For," *New York Times*, May 15, 2007.

[23]"Helping Africa Help Itself," *The Economist*, July 2, 2005, 11.

[24]*The Trouble With Africa: Why Foreign Aid Isn't Working*, Robert Calderisi, ed., New York: Palgrave MacMillan, 2006.

[25]www.goodafrican.com/index.php.

[26]Andrew Rugasira, "The Economic Medicine That Kills," *Telegraph*, July 31, 2005, www.telegraph.co.uk/money/main.jhtml?xml=/money/2005/07/31/ccuganda31.xml&menuId=242&sSheet=/money/2005/07/31/ixcoms.html.

[27]Jason Pontin, "What Does Africa Need Most: Technology or Aid?" *New York Times*, June 17, 2007, http://select.nytimes.com/mem/tnt.html?tntget=2007/06/17/business/yourmoney/17stream.html&tntemail1=y&emc=tnt&pagewanted=print.

[28]Some individuals are bypassing governments and aid organizations to provide assistance to African communities. At least 30 organizations, such as Ambassadors for Children and the Nomad Foundation, offer opportunities for private citizens to use their vacation time in service projects in Africa, including projects in Niger, Malawi, Kenya, Morocco, Tanzania, and South Africa. These "volunteer vacations" offer service opportunities from less than a week to six months. Claire Spiegel, "In Niger, Using Vacation to Help the World's Poor," *New York Times*, August 20, 2006.

[29]National Brands Index, Q4 Report, 2005, 3.

[30]"10 Questions," *Time*, May 28, 2007, 6.

[31]Stephan Faris, "Starbucks vs. Ethiopia," Fortune, February 26, 2007; "Ending Dispute, Starbucks Is to Help Ethiopian Farmers," *New York Times*, November 29, 2007.

[32]Landon Thomas, Jr. "Emerging Marketing Produce New Giving," *International Herald Tribune*, December 14, 2007, 1.

[33]Jyoti Thottam, "A Reunion at the 'MIT of India'" *Time*, July 9, 2007, www.time.com/time/business/article/0,8599,1641232,00.html.

[34]Stephen Cohen, "No Longer a Large, Exotic Basket Case," *Financial Times*, August 14, 2007.

[35]www.weforum.org/en/events/ArchivedEvents/WorldEconomicForumonAfrica2007/index.htm.

[36]http://2008conference.avcanet.com/conference_Home.html.

[37]David Honigmann, "That Old Fighting Spirit," *Financial Times*, March 1, 2008.

# Acknowledgments

A book with this large a scope depends on the support and kindness of many people in sharing their knowledge and stories of successes and failures. Although it would be impossible to name everyone who contributed in some way to this project over its years of incubation and execution, and my apologies for any omissions, I would like to acknowledge as many people as possible.

I am thankful for the enthusiasm of the Coca-Cola Company in planning and developing this project, in particular the involvement of Alex Cummings in South Africa, Andrew Morrison and Andrew Bienkowski in London, as well as Vikas Tiku, Anne Sefu-Kobai, and Racquel White. I am thankful for the assistance of Maria Sidel, Zanele Sisilana, Angie Ho, and Tshidi Lebobe of Coca-Cola South Africa; Lanya Stanek of Coca-Cola Africa; Niyi Ayanlowo and Adeyanju Olomola of the Nigerian Bottling Company Plc; and Venkatesh Kini of Coca-Cola India. I also appreciated the insights of Alison Clark, Selina Masooane, and Sgidi Sibeko of Hope Worldwide; and Corne Theron, Boyce Lloyd, and Melanie Louw of ABI; from Coca-Cola Nigeria and Equatorial Africa, Irene Ubah, Anne Harte, Ruth Ode, Dayer Oluwla, and Emka Mba; from Coca-Cola East & Central Africa (Kenya), Maserame Mouyeme, Titus Mutiso, Suzan Mayienga, Suzan Mayienga, and Clarice Odhiambo; in Egypt, Simon Bartlett and Sherif Coutry (Fortune Promoseven); and in Morocco, Jamila Diani, Curt Ferguson, Adel El Fakir, Samia Bouchareb, as well as Souane Abdelrahmain and Abdelkrim El Boukhari of COBEGA Bottling.

Many people from Unilever contributed to this project, including Gail Klintworth, Ed Hall, Kim Daniel, Gavin Neath, Cliff Grantham, and Debby Lee of Unilever South Africa (Pty) Ltd.; Richard Morgan of Unilever's Africa, Middle East, and Turkey Group; and Gill Harrower formerly of the Unilever HIV/AIDS Resource Centre; in Nigeria, Fidelia Osime, Tim Rump, and Vera Ezomo; in Kenya, David Mureithi, Dominic Kimani, Richard Ponsford, Margaret Mwaura, and Hilda Maina; in Morocco, Ton Anbeek and Kenneth Bornauw;

and from Unilever South East Africa (Zimbabwe), Johnson Gapu, Vimbai Mkhosana, Edith Dewe, and Emilia Ndawana. I also am grateful for the assistance of Doug Baillie of Hindustan Lever.

I appreciate the early and continued involvement of Mathew Barwell of Diageo Africa, as well as his colleagues Norah Odwesso, Ivan Menezes, Bev Burnham, Gail Bradley, Reema Kapadia, Matthew Charlick, Ese Akpogheneta, and Janette Kuntscher; the staff of Guinness in Nigeria, including Archie Sadza, Cherry Eromosele, Charles Ogunwuyi, Francis Agbonlahor, Onyekachi Onubogu, Michael Onuoha, Doug Nicholls, and Ted Engelke; and in Kenya, Patricia Ithau, Gerald Mahinda, and Ken Kariuki of East African Breweries Limited.

Barclays Bank has been an invaluable partner, including the generous time of Dominic Bruynseels, Anurag Saxena, Jackie J. Wilken, and Janice Kemoli in Kenya; Stewart Lockie, Fatima El Ibrashi, Rasha Negm, and Maha Wafai in Egypt.

For their enthusiasm about the African market and *The 86% Solution*, thanks to the Novartis Emerging Growth Market (EGM) group—Jesus Acebillo, Hans Berger, Lorenzo Cazzoli, and Laura Utsat—and their many colleagues at Novartis, including Kevin Kerr, Stefan Stroppel, Christian Ripoche, Chris Ufomadu, Mburu Karanja, and Usegun Omalambe (Nigeria); as well as Dr. Klaus Leisinger and Marta Ros of the Novartis Foundation, and Noëlle Jude of Novartis Malaria Initiatives. In Egypt, thanks to Dr. Frederic Guerard, Dr. Ali Ghamrawy, Dr. Hussein El-Shishtawi, and Mounaz Attar, as well as Omneya Ismail of Thomas Cook Novartis. My thanks also to Ranjit Shahani of Novartis India for introducing me to colleagues in the EGM group.

Advertising agencies throughout Africa were very helpful in this project. From Saatchi & Saatchi, I am grateful to Eric Frank in Cape Town; in Nigeria, Udeme Ufot, Kemi Eubota, Ayo Elias, Friday Okuwe, Femi Eslio, and Biodun Adefila; in Kenya, Catherine Kinyany and Karen Gikunda of MCL Saatchi & Saatchi and Wael Hussein of Saatchi & Saatchi in Egypt. In South Africa, I also appreciated the insights of Nicole Wills of Stick; Lynn Madeley of Lowe Bull; Sharon Keith, Ed Hobson, and Sindiswa Mbude of brandhouse; and Craig Morris of RedRocket; in Nigeria, I am grateful for the assistance of Tolu Ogunkoya from mediaReach OMD Nigeria and dele dele-Olukoju from Richardson & Briggs; in Kenya, Sameer Ambegaonkar, Thomas Omanga, and Karen Ketibi from Lowe Scanad Kenya; Lolu Akinwunmi and Paschal Anyaso of Prima Garnet Ogilvy-Nigeria; and in Zimbabwe, Alice Bare of CM&A Ogilvy; and Mehdi Saqi from McCann in Morocco.

My sincere thanks to Ketan (and his wife Kanika) Patel, then of Innscor, for his knowledge and hospitality, as well as colleagues Peter Innsley, Leighton Shaw, and Suriya Narayanan; Vince Hogg of Innscor Distribution; Isaac Sibanda, Andrew Nzuwa, Georgiana Sitole, Isaac Sibanda, and Garikal Ntuli of Innscor Africa Ltd.; and Ian Dupreez and his family of Shearwater Adventures in Victoria Falls.

For their insights from private equity, I am grateful to Barbara James of the African Venture Capital Association; Jag Johal of CBA Capital Partners Limited; Runa Alam, formerly of Zephyr Management LP.; Sivendran Vettivetpillai and Shakir Merali of Aureos Capital; Jayesh Shah of the Sumaria Group; Piers Cumberlege of Cordiant; and Mahesh Kotecha and Sharon Ryan of SCIC.

In South Africa, I would like to thank Indian Consul General Suresh K. Goel for many contacts in South Africa, and Vijay Nakra of Mahindra South Africa; Ravikant, Atul Dhagat, and Rustom Nagporewalla of Tata Motors Ltd.; Ranjan Chakravarti of Ranbaxy (S.A.) Ltd., Dilnaz J. Gilder of Tata Group in India; and Niranjan Limaye, Deepak Gupta, and Sushant Mehta of ICICI Bank. I also appreciated the help of Luanne Grant of American Chamber of Commerce in South Africa; and the insights of Peter Pickering of Pioneer Hi-Bred RSA (Pty) Ltd., Worede Woldemariam of Pioneer-Ethiopia; Patrick Rogiers, Lehethi Thibethi, and Mala Suriah of 3M South Africa; Dave Botha of IBM South Africa; Thoko Mokgosi-Mwantembe and Claude Ibalanky of Hewlett-Packard South Africa (Pty) Ltd.; and Conrad Leigh and Bruce Cockburn of Leaf Wireless. Thanks to Mthuli Ncube, Geoff Bick, Frederick Ahwireng-Obeng, David Dickinson, and Charisse Drobis of Wits Business School; Steven M. Burgess of the University of Cape Town Graduate School of Business; Simon Maxwell of the Overseas Development Institute; and Peter Draper of the South African Institute of International Affairs. My

thanks, as well, to Steve Fitzgerald of CC Africa; Fred Swaniker of
the African Leadership Academy; Michael Farr of the South African
Breweries Limited; and my driver Josias Matlala from Imperial
Chauffer Drive, who was much more than a driver but served as
guide to the retail market and keen observer of South African life.

In Nigeria, I am very grateful to Bhudeb Mukherjee of Tower
Aluminum Nigeria Plc; from the High Commission of India in Abuja,
Nigeria, H. H. S. Viswanathan, high commissioner, Anil Trigunayat,
deputy high commissioner, and Awadh Kumar; Suresh Chellaram,
Premender Sethi, Dr. H. S. Batth, S. S. Kulkarni, and Bunmi Akin-
wale of Chellarams, Plc; Deepak Karcher from Far East Mercantile
Co. Ltd.; N. K. Somani and Ashutosh Bhargava from Dangote Sugar;
Joseph Chibueze from the *Financial Standard;* Sanjeev Tandon, Brig.
P. S. Gill (Rtd.), and Sanjeev Tandon of Multi-Links; Prakash
Keswani and Rajesh Syal from Park n Shop (Artee Group); and Dr.
Bosun Arilesere, M.D., of Epe General Hospital; Wole Ajao Adesoh
Johal and Christopher Patrick; M. Sidharthan of Pepsi/Seven Up
Nigeria and Pradipta Mitra of RMS International Group. I am grate-
ful for insights from Professor Pat Utomi of the Lagos Business
School, and the entrepreneurial knowledge of Peter Bamkole, Nneka
Okekearu, and colleagues at Enterprise Development Services of the
Pan-African University in Lagos.

In Kenya, my thanks to Titus Naikuni and Windrose Mungai of
Kenya Airways; Fatima Alimohamed from Bidco; Mark Gathuri from
the Nairobi Serena Hotel; Dr. Joseph Barrage Wanjui of the Univer-
sity of Nairobi; Manu Chandaria and Hirji Shah of Comcraft; Mwangi
Mathai, A. M. Kelkar, and R. S. Patil of Kirloskar Kenya Limited;
James Mathenge of Magadi Soda; Anna Othoro of Celtel Kenya Ltd.,
Catherine Ngahu of SBO Research; Samuel Gathama of Pioneer-
HiBred; Kaushik Shah of Mabati Rolling Mills Ltd.; Atul Shah and
Thiagarajan Ramamurthy of Nakumatt Holdings Inc.; Lawrence
Muye of Muthaiga Golf Club; Anil Ishani of Aga Khan Development
Network; Tim Carson of MicroKenya; Mohanjeet Brar of Game-
watchers Safaris in Kenya; Benjamin Mouton; and Joseph Kinyua and
Philip Wambugu of Intime Sightseers & Safaris. I also appreciate the
help of Adema Sangale, Tarek El Bardi, Greg Allgood, and Alvaro
Restrepo of Procter & Gamble, Southern & Eastern Africa.

In Zimbabwe, I am grateful to K. H. Patel of Barons Fashion, Natu Patel of Enbee Schoolwear, and Oliver Masawi of Imba Matombo.

In Egypt, I am grateful to many colleagues at the American University in Cairo for their insights, including David and Sherry Arnold, M. Maged Abaza, Sherif Kamel, Ahmed Tolba, Ahmed Taher, Ronald Fullerton, Nancy Martin, Rowaida Saad El Din, Sarah Tarek, and Ragia Mansour. Thanks to Mohanad Adly of Metro; A. S. Sundaresan of SCIB Paints; Suketa Mehta and Mahendra Patil of Kirloskar; Moataz Al-Alfi, E. K. Holding Co.; Amgad El Mofty, Borhan El Kilany, Karim Zein, and Tarek Tawfik of Americana Group; Michel Accad, formerly of Citigroup; Ian Gray, Khaled El-Khouly, Hazem Metwally, and Jasmeen El Bashary of Vodafone; A. Gopinathan, ambassador of India; Ram Narayana Boga and Iman Tolba of the State Bank of India; Chandra Srivastava of Indo Egyptian Fertilizer Company; Sameh Abhallah Aly of Khan El Khalib Restaurant; K. K. Baweja of the textile industry; Essam Mohsen El Hennawy of Al-Mansour Automotive; Amin El Masri of ASAP Film Production; Ihab Baligh Shoukry of Procter & Gamble; Sanjiv Malhotra of Oberoi Hotels and Resorts; Youssef El-Deeb of Takhayal Entertainment; Yasser El Sayyad of Multi Service for Trade; Ahmed Abdoun, Sara El Refaie, and Iman M. Tolba of Creative Lab and MarketingMix; K. N. Agarwal, Mona Abbas Morsi, and Mirette Medhat of Alexandria Carbon Black Co. S.A.E.; D. Banerjee and Jaideep Mazumdar of the Indian Embassy; and my drivers Yaser Afifi and Imad. I am also grateful to Rania Succor of McKinsey and Company for introducing me to several individuals in Egypt.

In Morocco, I am grateful to Ali Lakhdar of LGE; Hassan Joundy of Marriott; Abdesslam Sijelmassi of IlaiCom; Mohammed Iqbal El Kettani of the Association of Realtors in Morocco; Ghita Smyej and Aida Jbilou with Hewlett-Packard; Soraya Sebti of BMCE Bank; Hicham Said and Khalid Azbane from Azbane Cosmetics; Ali Kettani of Sigma; Farid Benchekroun of The Savola Group; Abderrafie Hamdi and Sanaa Ziati of Ministry for Moroccan Community Residing Abroad; Rabia El Alama and Carl Dawson of the American Chamber of Commerce; U.S. Ambassdor Thomas Riley and Indian Ambassador Prabhu Dayal. From Al Akhawayn University, I am thankful for the assistance of Driss Ouaouicha, Otmane Taoufiq, Moha Abdelkrim, Madjouline El Hossouni, Waha El Garah, Michel Lessure, L. Houssaine Chirich, Hassan Radoine, Aziza Boumahdi, and my drivers Houcine Ougchchou and Brahim Douche.

In Uganda, I am grateful to Rodney Schuster of Uganda Microfinance Limited; and Roni Madhvani of the Madhvani Group. In Ghana, thanks to Patrick Awuah of Ashesi University. In Ethiopia, I am grateful for the insights of CEO Girma Wake and the assistance of Guenet Berhe of Ethiopian Airlines, as well as industry leaders, including Tsegaye Abebe and Zewde Worku.

In Algeria, I am grateful to Slim Othmani of NCA-Rouiba, an amazing entrepreneur, and his assistant Nina Rouabhi and Tarik Chenikhar of On Time Travel for all the arrangements. I would also like to thank Bobby Salwan of Tata Motors and his wife, Rosy Sharma; Chafiq Hammadi of Bel-group; Fodil Korichi and Vincent Pinault of Numidis-Cevital; Ambassador Ashok K. Amrohi and his colleagues at the Indian Embassy; Michel Katlama of Henkel; Kamal Driss and Boutheina Beznine of Citigroup; Professor Bruno Ponson of ESAA; Francesc Goula of Fruital; Riad Fechkeur of Redmed; Khayam Turki of EIIC; Claude Joly of Danone; and, from the U.S. Embassy, Jeff Mazur, Rafik Mansour, Nabila Hales, and Kamel Achab.

In Senegal, I would like to thank Ambassdor Parbati Sen Vyas and Alok Jha of the Indian Embassy; Assobga Fanta Sidibe; Sonatel Mobile Sengal; Abhashek Singh Tata Motors/Senbus Industries; Fabrice Sawegnon and Steve Fayomi of Vodoo Communications; and my driver Ousman Cisse.

In Tunisia, my thanks to Mahmoud Triki, Maha Chaieb, Ihsen Jarraya, and Ramzi Hosni of the South Mediterranean University School of Business; Salah Jarraya and Sofia Souissi and Salah Jarraya of UTIC; Yahia Bayahi, Leila el Kebir, and Taieb Ghachem of TPR; Ambassador Basant Gupta of the Indian Embassy, Souheil Kallel and his colleagues at ASSAD; Monojeet Pal and his colleagues at the African Development Bank, as well as his wife, Divya Kapoor; Ferid Tanfous of ATB; Meriem Gaieb of Maille Club; Ahmed and Maher Bouchamaoui of Al Majd Holding;, François Lucas of Tunisie Telecom; Frederic Pecastaings of Groupe Mabrouk; Hassen Zargouni of

Sigma; Brahim Laroui of Coke; Habib Bouaziz, Selma Bouaziz, and colleagues at SNB; and Ambassador Robert Godec and Dorothy Shea of the U.S. Embassy, Aziz Mebarek of Tuninvest, and my driver, Fakhri Kholfaoui.

I am grateful for many key individuals who took the time to speak with me for this project, including Celtel founder Mo Ibrahim (and Robert Watkinson of Portland who introduced me to him, as well as Diana Jackson), and I am thankful to Her Majesty the Queen of Bhutan, Ashi Dorji Wangmo Wangchuck, and her assistant, Chime Paden Wangdi. I am thankful for the early enthusiasm and insights of Demba Ba, Vyjayanti Desai, and Praveen Kumar of The World Bank; Sherry Lee Abrahams of the Corporate Council on Africa, and Les de Villiers of Business Books International (author of *Africa 2007*). I also am grateful for the introductions of S. M. Gavai, consul general of India in Houston, Texas, and the help of Cecilia Kwak and David J. Olson of Population Services International, Chhavi Sharma of the Freeplay Foundation, Anne Marie Burgoyne of the Draper Richards Foundation, and Harish Kotecha of Austin, Texas. I am grateful to many organizations studying or reporting on Africa, including Robin Parker and Rod Baker of Bizcommunity.com and Carol Pineau of Africa Open for Business.

Thanks for insights on the diaspora and investment from Dr. Titi Banjoko of Africa Recruit, and Maude Meier of SC Johnson. Thanks also to Marcel Portman of the International Franchise Association; Jane McPherson and Lee Vala of Quiznos. I am thankful for the insights of Millie Naa Lamle Wulff of Stanford University, Lee V. Cassanelli of the University of Pennsylvania, and Al Greco and Hans Zell on African publishing. I am also thankful for the assistance of Martyn J. Davies of Emerging Market Focus, Richard Boulter of DFID, Jean Philippe Prosper and Jacqueline Omoke of the International Finance Corporation in Kenya, and James Viray of Texas Global.

I am grateful for the insights and support of colleagues around the globe, some of whom are acknowledged in their respective countries. This book would not have happened without the support and encouragement of many people at the University of Texas at Austin, including Dean George Gau, David Platt, Florence Atiase, Rob Meyer, Juliet Walker, Mark Regnerus, Susie Brown, Della Tyus,

David Wenger, Susannah Raulino, Eli Cox, Raj Raghunathan, Garret Sonnier, Frenkel Ther Hofstede, Josephine Mabry, Nan Watkins, and Dorothy Carner. Thanks also to MBA students Lookman Olusanya, Olamide Ogungbesan, and Pedro Silva for their contributions.

I would also like to thank my friend and colleague Jerry Wind, and Tim Moore and Martha Cooley of Wharton School Publishing, for their commitment to this project. I also am very grateful for the editorial expertise of Betsy Harris and Keith Cline, who made many improvements to the manuscript, and the help of Susann Sams and John Pierce of Wharton School Publishing.

A special thanks to Said Azbane, Gail Klintworth, Slim Othmani, Mahesh Kotecha, Farid Benchakroun, Robert Godec, Florence Atiase, Fatima Alimohamed, Janice Kemoli, Ihab Baligh, and many others who offered extensive and insightful comments on the manuscript.

And a very affectionate thanks to my children Ramin and Geeti for being volunteer research assistants and sharing various news and articles about Africa on a regular basis with me.

Last, but not least, my special thanks and gratitude for my friend and editor Robert Gunther, for believing in this book project. Despite his health, he not only traveled with me in some countries in Africa, but constantly challenged me to think differently. Robert, you are the best.

# INDEX